Making Money with Classified Ads

Melvin Powers
Mail Order Consultant

Melvin Powers
Wilshire Book Company

12015 Sherman Road, No. Hollywood, CA 91605

ISBN 0-87980-435-1
Library of Congress Catalog Card number 94-061030
Printed in the United States of America

Contents

Famous. 800 Phone Numbers . . . Do You Need Them? Your Product on TV? . . . It Could Happen! What Works . . . And What Doesn't.

Chapter One

Getting Started with Classified Ads

I started in mail order with less than $100 and made millions with classified ads. This book will teach you how you can do it, too. No matter who you are, or what your age or background. No matter where you are or what your reasons for wanting to make money in this fascinating business . . . you can do it! I'll hold your hand and guide you through the process, step-by-exciting step.

Over the past 40 years, I've published hundreds of self-improvement books and have sold millions of copies through the mail and in bookstores. Among my million bestsellers are such titles as *Psycho-Cybernetics* by Maxwell Maltz, M.D., *Think & Grow Rich* by Napoleon Hill, *The Magic of Thinking Big* by David Schwartz, Ph.D., *A New Guide to Rational Living* by Albert Ellis, Ph.D. and Robert H. Harper, Ph.D., and *Three Magic Words* by U.S. Andersen.

I have also sold a variety of mail order items, including everything from gadgets and health-related products to electronic equipment and automotive supplies. For decades, I have been a well-known mail order consultant to businesses, and for years taught mail order seminars in colleges and universities throughout the Los Angeles area. I've been called in to advise producers of television infomercials and produced and aired my own half-hour shows and two-minute spots. But my first love, selling books—especially through the mail—is still my favorite business interest.

This 16-Year Old with No Marketing Experience
Ran Successful Ads Right Away
So Can You!

Who is this teen whose mind was filled with curiosity and creative challenges when most of his peers were preoccupied with baseball? It was me. It all began with my enjoyment of reading magazines such as *Popular Science*. One day I saw a classified ad for a book called *How to Win at Chess*. That's exactly what I wanted to do, so I sent away for it. About a week later, the book arrived. Enclosed were circulars of other books for sale. I ordered several, including the hardcover edition of *Think & Grow Rich* by Napoleon Hill. The book had a profound effect on my thinking. After reading it, I believed that I could accomplish whatever I wanted to in life. Intrigued by the thought of someone on the other end of my book orders shaking my cash out of an envelope, I made what turned out to be a major life decision. I decided I would like to sell books through the mail.

I contacted the publishers of the books I had purchased and explained what I wanted to do. They agreed to sell me books at a 50% discount. Then I found the title, author, price, and publisher's name and address of other how-to books at the library in a reference book called *Subject Guide to Books in Print*. I chose the ones I was interested in selling and contacted each of the publishers and arranged for the same 50% discount.

Next, I wrote an ad similar to the one I had responded to when I ordered *How to Win at Chess* and I ran it in *Popular Science*. When I received my first order, I was so excited, you'd think I had won a lottery. As orders continued to come in, I was shaking checks, cash, and money orders from stacks of mail sent to me. It seemed like magic! And it was fun knowing my customers never suspected how young I was.

I ran ads in *Popular Mechanics*, *Field & Stream*, and numerous other magazines, selling books such as *Astrology Made Easy*, *How to Win at Bridge*, *Calligraphy Made Easy*, *How to Win at Chess*, *How to Win at Poker*, *How to Win at 21*, *How to Stop Smoking*, *Juggling Made Easy*, *Magic for All Ages*, *Stamp Collecting for Beginners*, *How to Win at the Races*, *Jokes for All Occasions*, *Handwriting Analysis Made Easy*, *Your Subconscious Power*, *How to Win at Pocket Billiards*, *Dog Training Made Easy*, and *Tennis Made Easy*.

At the beginning, some of the publishers drop shipped the books to my customers, so I didn't need to carry inventory. As my business grew, I ordered books to stock at home and did all the shipping myself. Knowing that the more ads I ran, the more money would come rolling in was like being able to go to the bank and take as much cash as I wanted from a never-ending supply! It wasn't long before I had a steady income of $1,000 a month.

Over the years, I wrote a series of books with the following titles and published them myself. They sold extremely well. *Hypnotism Revealed*, *Advanced Techniques of Hypnosis*, *Self-Hypnosis: Its Theory, Technique, and Application*, *A Practical Guide to Self-Hypnosis*, *A Practical Guide to Better Concentration*, *Dynamic Thinking*, *Mental Power Through Sleep Suggestion*, *How to Get Rich in Mail Order*, and *How to Self-Publish Your Book & Have the Fun & Excitement of Being a Bestselling Author*. I was also the ghostwriter of other very successful books that I published. Soon I began publishing other people's books, as well, and negotiating with publishers for the trade paperback rights to some of their hardcover books.

One such book was *Think & Grow Rich*. What a thrill it was to publish a book that had helped to shape my own personal and business philosophy! See pages 12 and 13 for my current list of books. As a publisher, I am still looking for unique books to publish. I'm especially interested in those that can be promoted effectively through mail order marketing.

I am basically still selling titles similar to those I started with, using many of the same techniques. Techniques that have stood the test of time. Techniques that have provided me with a lifetime of financial prosperity. Techniques that can do for you what they have done for me if you are motivated for success and do what it takes to achieve it. My practical, realistic, nuts-and-bolts approach to making money with classified ads will enable you to achieve whatever goals you set for yourself, selling whatever products you want.

Never Underestimate the Power of Classified Ads!

There are plenty of mail order businesses running mainly from classified ads. You'll see their ads in almost every magazine. Behind those few classified lines inviting you to send for a catalog or further information could easily stand a business doing millions of dollars a year in sales. What does that mean? That the ads are working. They are paying their way. Study those ads, send away for their literature and products, and become knowledgeable about their operations. And I'll help you make use of this information to get your own classified ad running.

Your Winning Mind Set

Success in any endeavor begins with having the right mind set. Your attitude must be that if others have become successful in mail order by starting with classified ads, you can too. Why not? There aren't any secrets and there are logical steps to take. But you must take them. That's something I can't do for you. It's your responsibility to do the research and assignments that I suggest. Simply reading this book as if it were a novel isn't going to do it. It's a must that you read and study the successful ad copy in this book. I want you to get the feel of ads that were, or are, pulling in inquiries and orders by the hundreds and thousands. And I'll be asking you to analyze the ads. Do it! And analyze other successful ads, too. Try to determine what makes them winners. Doing so will make you a winner.

I know from whence I speak. I once spent a year as a songwriter of country western songs. My partner was Tommy Boyce of Tommy Boyce & Bobby Hart, the famous team that wrote many of the songs recorded by the Monkees. Before we started our daily songwriting routine, Tommy and I listened to the top country songs of the week, analyzing why they were hits and we tried to duplicate in our own songs the elements we discovered. We also sang hit country songs for about 15 minutes before we started our writing. We wanted to immerse ourselves in the style, melody, and lyrics of winning songs.

It all helped make me an award-winning songwriter with hits on the charts and a producer of a successful album of music called *Willie Burgundy on the Midnight Train from Boston*, which I sold to MGM Records, Inc. for an advance of $15,000 plus royalties. I borrowed the song title idea from Gladys Knight who had a hit song at the time called "On the Midnight Train to Georgia." I share these accomplishments to demonstrate the importance of doing your homework. Analyzing and pondering elements that work and those that don't will help you develop the creativity necessary to become a successful mail order entrepreneur.

As a mail order lecturer, I observed that students who did their assignments eventually developed a profitable mail order business. Those who didn't do them, fell by the wayside. Giving up is easy. Staying with any endeavor takes fortitude. It takes time, energy, and thought to get started and running successfully. But success begets success. To get the ball rolling and keep it rolling, you'll need a game plan. Here's the one I recommend. I know it works. I'll elaborate on various points in subsequent chapters.

Steps to Success

STEP 1
Read and analyze all the classified ads in as many magazines and tabloids as you can.

STEP 2
Choose a category or categories of products that you would like to sell.

STEP 3
Look for ads selling similar products in consumer magazines and tabloids.

STEP 4
Buy some of the products and get your name on the companies' mailing lists. Code your name for each company.

STEP 5
Find the source of the products in trade publications. For a list of trade journals in your area of interest, see the *Standard Rate & Data Trade Publications*, a reference book which can be found at most large public or college libraries.

STEP 6
Print stationery and business cards.

STEP 7
Attend trade shows. You'll find locations and dates in the trade publications.

STEP 8
Ask manufacturers for black-and-white glossy photos or art work for specific products. Request their catalog. Discuss discounts. Establish credit if possible. If not, offer to pay cash with orders until credit is established.

STEP 9
Prepare all literature to be mailed out to inquiries in response to your first classified ad.

STEP 10
Write your first classified ad. Compare it to the competition. Run it under the same subhead as the competition in the same publication or in another appropriate one.

STEP 11
If selling directly off the ad, analyze your results after publication. If the ad is successful, run it again and place it in other appropriate publications. Be sure to key each ad. If it is not successful, consider running a two-step ad, asking readers to send for free information.

STEP 12
If you're running a two-step ad, send out literature promptly and save inquiries.

STEP 13
If the ad is successful, run it again and place it in other appropriate publications.

STEP 14
If you don't get enough inquiries to make the ad profitable, analyze the ad. If you get a lot of inquiries but not enough orders, analyze your literature. There's always a reason why things aren't working.

STEP 15
If the two-step technique is successful, rent mailing lists and start a direct mail campaign.

STEP 16
If the direct mail campaign is successful, consider running display ads incorporating key elements of your direct mail advertising copy.

STEP 17
If the display ads are successful, think about doing two-minute television spots and/or half-hour infomercials. Start watching and recording television direct-response commercials. Ask yourself if your product would sell on television. If so, start locally. Spend as little money as possible before expanding the television market. Keep careful

records of all expenditures and sales.

STEP 18
Set new goals for yourself.

STEP 19
You might want to consider selling on the Internet. You will be able to get orders from all over the world. See my Web site at www.mpowers.com.

STEP 20
Become intellectually curious about all forms of mail order. Study successful campaigns. Try to predict winning and losing ads in print, direct mail, and television. Visit your local public and college libraries and read all the books on mail order and direct mail advertising.

Questions and Answers to Help You Get Started

Question: Can I make money with classified ads?

Answer: Absolutely. It's one of the starting points for all types of mail order operations. And it's the least expensive way to begin your mail order business.

Question: How do I know my product is saleable?

Answer: If someone else is selling a similar product using classified ads, it means you can do it as well. They have done the research for you. Buy their product. Get on their mailing list.

Question: Why not start with display ads?

Answer: Display ads are more expensive than classified ads. Running classifieds should be the first step in your overall mail order plan. It is an outstanding learning experience that stimulates creativity, and it provides a solid foundation of tested advertising copy upon which to build a more aggressive, more expensive advertising campaign.

Question: What if my first ad doesn't make money. What's the answer?

Answer: There's always a reason for it. Either your ad needs improvement or the product can't be sold directly from a classified ad. If the ad is a two-step, either your literature isn't strong enough, the product is priced wrong, there isn't enough interest in it, or the public's interest in it has already peaked.

Question: *What's the best advice you can give me to help me get started making money in mail order?*

Answer: First, make your daydreams your goals and take a long range perspective in achieving them. Second, pay attention to your intuition, for it provides valuable information and will help you make the right decisions. And third, think of yourself as a mail order detective who has been assigned to find out how successful mail order campaigns work. Then use the information to reach your own mail order goals.

Question: *Can I run classified ads on the Internet and make money?*

Answer: Absolutely. Using the search engine Alta Vista, type: Free Classified Ads. You'll find plenty of places to advertise free of charge.

WILSHIRE SELF-IMPROVEMENT LIBRARY

ASTROLOGY

___ASTROLOGY—HOW TO CHART YOUR HOROSCOPE Max Heindel 7.00
___ASTROLOGY AND SEXUAL ANALYSIS Morris C. Goodman 10.00
___ASTROLOGY AND YOU Carroll Righter 5.00
___ASTROLOGY MADE EASY Astarte 7.00
___ASTROLOGY, ROMANCE, YOU AND THE STARS Anthony Norvell 10.00
___MY WORLD OF ASTROLOGY Sydney Omarr 10.00
___THOUGHT DIAL Sydney Omarr 7.00
___WHAT THE STARS REVEAL ABOUT THE MEN IN YOUR LIFE Thelma White 3.00

BRIDGE

___BRIDGE BIDDING MADE EASY Edwin B. Kantar 15.00
___BRIDGE CONVENTIONS Edwin B. Kantar 10.00
___COMPETITIVE BIDDING IN MODERN BRIDGE Edgar Kaplan 7.00
___DEFENSIVE BRIDGE PLAY COMPLETE Edwin B Kantar 20.00
___GAMESMAN BRIDGE—PLAY BETTER WITH KANTAR Edwin B. Kantar 7.00
___HOW TO IMPROVE YOUR BRIDGE Alfred Sheinwold 7.00
___IMPROVING YOUR BIDDING SKILLS Edwin B. Kantar 10.00
___INTRODUCTION TO DECLARER'S PLAY Edwin B. Kantar 10.00
___INTRODUCTION TO DEFENDER'S PLAY Edwin B. Kantar 10.00
___KANTAR FOR THE DEFENSE Edwin B. Kantar 10.00
___KANTAR FOR THE DEFENSE VOLUME 2 Edwin B. Kantar 10.00
___TEST YOUR BRIDGE PLAY Edwin B. Kantar 10.00
___VOLUME 2—TEST YOUR BRIDGE PLAY Edwin B. Kantar 10.00
___WINNING DECLARER PLAY Dorothy Hayden Truscott 10.00

BUSINESS, STUDY & REFERENCE

___BRAINSTORMING Charles Clark 10.00
___CONVERSATION MADE EASY Elliot Russell 5.00
___EXAM SECRET Dennis B. Jackson 7.00
___FIX-IT BOOK Arthur Symons 2.00
___HOW TO DEVELOP A BETTER SPEAKING VOICE M. Hellier 5.00
___HOW TO SAVE 50% ON GAS & CAR EXPENSES Ken Stansbie 5.00
___HOW TO SELF-PUBLISH YOUR BOOK & MAKE IT A BEST SELLER Melvin Powers 20.00
___INCREASE YOUR LEARNING POWER Geoffrey A. Dudley 5.00
___PRACTICAL GUIDE TO BETTER CONCENTRATION Melvin Powers 5.00
___PUBLIC SPEAKING MADE EASY Thomas Montalbo 10.00
___7 DAYS TO FASTER READING William S. Schaill 7.00
___SONGWRITER'S RHYMING DICTIONARY Jane Shaw Whitfield 15.00
___SPELLING MADE EASY Lester D. Basch & Dr. Milton Finkelstein 3.00
___STUDENT'S GUIDE TO BETTER GRADES J.A. Rickard 3.00
___YOUR WILL & WHAT TO DO ABOUT IT Attorney Samuel G. King 7.00

CALLIGRAPHY

___ADVANCED CALLIGRAPHY Katherine Jeffares 7.00
___CALLIGRAPHY—THE ART OF BEAUTIFUL WRITING Katherine Jeffares 7.00
___CALLIGRAPHY FOR FUN & PROFIT Anne Leptich & Jacque Evans 7.00
EXTRA SPACE HERE***

CHESS & CHECKERS

___BEGINNER'S GUIDE TO WINNING CHESS Fred Reinfeld 10.00
___CHESS IN TEN EASY LESSONS Larry Evans 10.00
___CHESS MADE EASY Milton L. Hanauer 5.00
___CHESS PROBLEMS FOR BEGINNERS Edited by Fred Reinfeld 7.00
___CHESS TACTICS FOR BEGINNERS Edited by Fred Reinfeld 10.00
___HOW TO WIN AT CHECKERS Fred Reinfeld 7.00
___1001 BRILLIANT WAYS TO CHECKMATE Fred Reinfeld 10.00
___1001 WINNING CHESS SACRIFICES & COMBINATIONS Fred Reinfeld 10.00

COOKERY & HERBS

___CULPEPER'S HERBAL REMEDIES Dr. Nicholas Culpeper 5.00
___FAST GOURMET COOKBOOK Poppy Cannon 2.50
___HEALING POWER OF HERBS May Bethel 5.00
___HEALING POWER OF NATURAL FOODS May Bethel 7.00
___HERBS FOR HEALTH—HOW TO GROW & USE THEM Louise Evans Doole 7.00
___HOME GARDEN COOKBOOK—DELICIOUS NATURAL FOOD RECIPES Ken Kraft 3.00
___MEATLESS MEAL GUIDE Tomi Ryan & James H. Ryan, M.D. 4.00
___VEGETABLE GARDENING FOR BEGINNERS Hugh Wilberg 2.00
___VEGETABLES FOR TODAY'S GARDENS R. Milton Carleton 2.00
___VEGETARIAN COOKERY Janet Walker 10.00
___VEGETARIAN COOKING MADE EASY & DELECTABLE Veronica Vezza 3.00

GAMBLING & POKER

___HOW TO WIN AT POKER Terence Reese & Anthony T. Watkins 10.00
___SCARNE ON DICE John Scarne 20.00
___WINNING AT CRAPS Dr. Lloyd T. Commins 10.00
___WINNING AT GIN Chester Wander & Cy Rice 10.00
___WINNING AT POKER—AN EXPERT'S GUIDE John Archer 10.00
___WINNING AT 21—AN EXPERT'S GUIDE John Archer 10.00
___WINNING POKER SYSTEMS Norman Zadeh 10.00

HEALTH

___BEE POLLEN Lynda Lyngheim & Jack Scagnetti 5.00
___COPING WITH ALZHEIMER'S Rose Oliver, Ph.D. & Francis Bock, Ph.D. 10.00
___HELP YOURSELF TO BETTER SIGHT Margaret Darst Corbett 10.00
___HOW YOU CAN STOP SMOKING PERMANENTLY Ernest Caldwell 5.00
___NATURE'S WAY TO NUTRITION & VIBRANT HEALTH Robert J. Scrutton 3.00
___NEW CARBOHYDRATE DIET COUNTER Patti Lopez-Pereira 2.00
___REFLEXOLOGY Dr. Maybelle Segal 7.00
___REFLEXOLOGY FOR GOOD HEALTH Anna Kaye & Don C. Matchan 10.00
___YOU CAN LEARN TO RELAX Dr. Samuel Gutwirth 5.00

HOBBIES

___BEACHCOMBING FOR BEGINNERS Norman Hickin 2.00
___BLACKSTONE'S MODERN CARD TRICKS Harry Blackstone 7.00
___BLACKSTONE'S SECRETS OF MAGIC Harry Blackstone 7.00
___COIN COLLECTING FOR BEGINNERS Burton Hobson & Fred Reinfeld 7.00
___ENTERTAINING WITH ESP Tony 'Doc' Shiels 2.00
___400 FASCINATING MAGIC TRICKS YOU CAN DO Howard Thurston 10.00
___HOW I TURN JUNK INTO FUN AND PROFIT Sari 3.00
___HOW TO WRITE A HIT SONG AND SELL IT Tommy Boyce 10.00
___MAGIC FOR ALL AGES Walter Gibson 10.00
___STAMP COLLECTING FOR BEGINNERS Burton Hobson 7.00

HORSE PLAYERS' WINNING GUIDES

___BETTING HORSES TO WIN Les Conklin 10.00
___ELIMINATE THE LOSERS Bob McKnight 5.00
___HOW TO PICK WINNING HORSES Bob McKnight 5.00
___HOW TO WIN AT THE RACES Sam (The Genius) Lewin 5.00
___HOW YOU CAN BEAT THE RACES Jack Kavanagh 5.00
___MAKING MONEY AT THE RACES David Barr 10.00
___PAYDAY AT THE RACES Les Conklin 7.00
___SMART HANDICAPPING MADE EASY William Bauman 5.00
___SUCCESS AT THE HARNESS RACES Barry Meadow 7.00

HUMOR

___HOW TO FLATTEN YOUR TUSH Coach Marge Reardon 2.00
___JOKE TELLER'S HANDBOOK Bob Orben 10.00
___JOKES FOR ALL OCCASIONS Al Schock 10.00
___2,000 NEW LAUGHS FOR SPEAKERS Bob Orben 7.00
___2,400 JOKES TO BRIGHTEN YOUR SPEECHES Robert Orben 10.00
___2,500 JOKES TO START'EM LAUGHING Bob Orben 10.00

HYPNOTISM

___HOW TO SOLVE YOUR SEX PROBLEMS WITH SELF-HYPNOSIS Frank Caprio, M.D. 5.00
___HOW YOU CAN BOWL BETTER USING SELF-HYPNOSIS Jack Heise 7.00
___HYPNOSIS AND SELF-HYPNOSIS Bernard Hollander, M.D. 7.00
___HYPNOTISM (Originally published 1893) Carl Sextus 5.00
___HYPNOTISM MADE EASY Dr. Ralph Winn 10.00
___HYPNOTISM MADE PRACTICAL Louis Orton 5.00
___HYPNOTISM REVEALED Melvin Powers 3.00
___MODERN HYPNOSIS Lesley Kuhn & Salvatore Russo, Ph.D. 5.00
___NEW CONCEPTS OF HYPNOSIS Bernard C. Gindes, M.D. 15.00
___NEW SELF-HYPNOSIS Paul Adams 10.00
___POST-HYPNOTIC INSTRUCTIONS—SUGGESTIONS FOR THERAPY Arnold Furst 10.00
___PRACTICAL GUIDE TO SELF-HYPNOSIS Melvin Powers 10.00
___PRACTICAL HYPNOTISM Philip Magonet, M.D. 3.00
___SECRETS OF HYPNOTISM S.J. Van Pelt, M.D. 5.00
___SELF-HYPNOSIS—A CONDITIONED-RESPONSE TECHNIQUE Laurence Sparks 7.00
___SELF-HYPNOSIS—ITS THEORY, TECHNIQUE & APPLICATION Melvin Powers 7.00
___THERAPY THROUGH HYPNOSIS Edited by Raphael H. Rhodes 5.00

JUDAICA

___SERVICE OF THE HEART Evelyn Garfiel, Ph.D. 10.00
___STORY OF ISRAEL IN COINS Jean & Maurice Gould 2.00
___STORY OF ISRAEL IN STAMPS Maxim & Gabriel Shamir 1.00
___TONGUE OF THE PROPHETS Robert St. John 10.00

JUST FOR WOMEN

___COSMOPOLITAN'S GUIDE TO MARVELOUS MEN Foreword by Helen Gurley Brown 3.00
___COSMOPOLITAN'S HANG-UP HANDBOOK Foreword by Helen Gurley Brown 4.00
___COSMOPOLITAN'S LOVE BOOK—A GUIDE TO ECSTASY IN BED 7.00
___COSMOPOLITAN'S NEW ETIQUETTE GUIDE Foreword by Helen Gurley Brown 4.00
___I AM A COMPLEAT WOMAN Doris Hagopian & Karen O'Connor Sweeney 3.00
___JUST FOR WOMEN—A GUIDE TO THE FEMALE BODY Richard E. Sand M.D. 5.00
___NEW APPROACHES TO SEX IN MARRIAGE John E. Eichenlaub, M.D. 3.00
___SEXUALLY ADEQUATE FEMALE Frank S. Caprio, M.D. 3.00
___SEXUALLY FULFILLED WOMAN Dr. Rachel Copelan 5.00

MARRIAGE, SEX & PARENTHOOD

____ABILITY TO LOVE Dr. Allan Fromme 7.00
____GUIDE TO SUCCESSFUL MARRIAGE Drs. Albert Ellis & Robert Harper 10.00
____HOW TO RAISE AN EMOTIONALLY HEALTHY, HAPPY CHILD Albert Ellis, Ph.D. 10.00
____PARENT SURVIVAL TRAINING Marvin Silverman, Ed.D. & David Lustig, Ph.D. 15.00
____SEX WITHOUT GUILT Albert Ellis, Ph.D. 7.00
____SEXUALLY ADEQUATE MALE Frank S. Caprio, M.D. 3.00
____STAYING IN LOVE Dr. Norton F. Kristy 7.00

MELVIN POWERS'S MAIL ORDER LIBRARY

____HOW TO GET RICH IN MAIL ORDER Melvin Powers 20.00
____HOW TO SELF-PUBLISH YOUR BOOK Melvin Powers 20.00
____HOW TO WRITE A GOOD ADVERTISEMENT Victor O. Schwab 20.00
____MAIL ORDER MADE EASY J. Frank Brumbaugh 20.00
____MAKING MONEY WITH CLASSIFIED ADS Melvin Powers 20.00

METAPHYSICS & NEW AGE

____CONCENTRATION—A GUIDE TO MENTAL MASTERY Mouni Sadhu 10.00
____EXTRA-TERRESTRIAL INTELLIGENCE—THE FIRST ENCOUNTER 6.00
____FORTUNE TELLING WITH CARDS P. Foli 10.00
____HOW TO INTERPRET DREAMS, OMENS & FORTUNE TELLING SIGNS Gettings 5.00
____HOW TO UNDERSTAND YOUR DREAMS Geoffrey A. Dudley 7.00
____MAGICIAN—HIS TRAINING AND WORK W.E. Butler 7.00
____MEDITATION Mouni Sadhu 10.00
____MODERN NUMEROLOGY Morris C. Goodman 10.00
____NUMEROLOGY—ITS FACTS AND SECRETS Ariel Yvon Taylor 5.00
____NUMEROLOGY MADE EASY W. Mykian 10.00
____PALMISTRY MADE EASY Fred Gettings 7.00
____PALMISTRY MADE PRACTICAL Elizabeth Daniels Squire 7.00
____PROPHECY IN OUR TIME Martin Ebon 2.50
____SUPERSTITION—ARE YOU SUPERSTITIOUS? Eric Maple 2.00
____TAROT OF THE BOHEMIANS Papus 10.00
____WAYS TO SELF-REALIZATION Mouni Sadhu 7.00
____WITCHCRAFT, MAGIC & OCCULTISM—A FASCINATING HISTORY W.B. Crow 10.00
____WITCHCRAFT—THE SIXTH SENSE Justine Glass 7.00

RECOVERY

____KNIGHT IN RUSTY ARMOR Robert Fisher 5.00
____KNIGHT IN RUSTY ARMOR (Hardcover edition) Robert Fisher 15.00
____KNIGHTS WITHOUT ARMOR (Hardcover edition) Aaron R. Kipnis, Ph.D. 10.00
____PRINCESS WHO BELIEVED IN FAIRY TALES Marcia Grad 10.00
____SECRET OF OVERCOMING VERBAL ABUSE Dr. Albert Ellis & Marcia Grad Powers 12.00

SELF-HELP & INSPIRATIONAL

____CHANGE YOUR VOICE, CHANGE YOUR LIFE Morton Cooper, Ph.D. 10.00
____CHARISMA—HOW TO GET "THAT SPECIAL MAGIC" Marcia Grad 10.00
____DAILY POWER FOR JOYFUL LIVING Dr. Donald Curtis 7.00
____DYNAMIC THINKING Melvin Powers 7.00
____GREATEST POWER IN THE UNIVERSE U.S. Andersen 7.00
____GROW RICH WHILE YOU SLEEP Ben Sweetland 10.00
____GROW RICH WITH YOUR MILLION DOLLAR MIND Brian Adams 10.00
____GROWTH THROUGH REASON Albert Ellis, Ph.D. 10.00
____GUIDE TO PERSONAL HAPPINESS Albert Ellis, Ph.D. & Irving Becker, Ed.D. 10.00
____GUIDE TO RATIONAL LIVING Albert Ellis, Ph.D. & R. Harper, Ph.D. 15.00
____HANDWRITING ANALYSIS MADE EASY John Marley 10.00
____HANDWRITING TELLS Nadya Olyanova 10.00
____HOW TO ATTRACT GOOD LUCK A.H.Z. Carr 10.00
____HOW TO DEVELOP A WINNING PERSONALITY Martin Panzer 10.00
____HOW TO DEVELOP AN EXCEPTIONAL MEMORY Young & Gibson 10.00
____HOW TO LIVE WITH A NEUROTIC Albert Ellis, Ph.D. 10.00
____HOW TO MAKE $100,000 A YEAR IN SALES Albert Winnikoff 15.00
____HOW TO SUCCEED Brian Adams 10.00
____I CAN Ben Sweetland 10.00
____I WILL Ben Sweetland 10.00
____KNIGHT IN RUSTY ARMOR Robert Fisher 5.00
____LAW OF SUCCESS Napoleon Hill (Two-Volume Set) 30.00
____MAGIC IN YOUR MIND U.S. Andersen 15.00
____MAGIC OF THINKING SUCCESS Dr. David J. Schwartz 10.00
____MAGIC POWER OF YOUR MIND Walter M. Germain 10.00
____NEVER UNDERESTIMATE THE SELLING POWER OF A WOMAN Dottie Walters 7.00
____PRINCESS WHO BELIEVED IN FAIRY TALES Marcia Grad 10.00
____PSYCHO-CYBERNETICS Maxwell Maltz, M.D. 10.00
____PSYCHOLOGY OF HANDWRITING Nadya Olyanova 7.00
____SALES CYBERNETICS Brian Adams 10.00
____SECRET OF OVERCOMING VERBAL ABUSE Dr. Albert Ellis & Marcia Grad Powers 12.00
____SECRET OF SECRETS U.S. Andersen 10.00
____SECRET POWER OF THE PYRAMIDS U.S. Andersen 7.00
____SELF-THERAPY FOR THE STUTTERER Malcolm Frazer 3.00
____STOP COMMITTING VOICE SUICIDE Morton Cooper, Ph.D. 10.00
____SUCCESS CYBERNETICS U.S. Andersen 10.00

____10 DAYS TO A GREAT NEW LIFE William E. Edwards 3.00
____THINK AND GROW RICH Napoleon Hill 12.00
____THINK LIKE A WINNER Walter Doyle Staples, Ph.D. 15.00
____THREE MAGIC WORDS U.S. Andersen 15.00
____TREASURY OF COMFORT Edited by Rabbi Sidney Greenberg 15.00
____TREASURY OF THE ART OF LIVING Edited by Rabbi Sidney Greenberg 10.00
____WHAT YOUR HANDWRITING REVEALS Albert E. Hughes 4.00
____WINNING WITH YOUR VOICE Morton Cooper, Ph.D. 10.00
____YOUR SUBCONSCIOUS POWER Charles M. Simmons 7.00

SPORTS

____BILLIARDS—POCKET ● CAROM ● THREE CUSHION Clive Cottingham, Jr. 10.00
____COMPLETE GUIDE TO FISHING Vlad Evanoff 2.00
____HOW TO IMPROVE YOUR RACQUETBALL Lubarsky, Kaufman & Scagnetti 5.00
____HOW TO WIN AT POCKET BILLIARDS Edward D. Knuchell 10.00
____JOY OF WALKING Jack Scagnetti 3.00
____RACQUETBALL FOR WOMEN Toni Hudson, Jack Scagnetti & Vince Rondone 3.00
____SECRET OF BOWLING STRIKES Dawson Taylor 5.00
____SOCCER—THE GAME & HOW TO PLAY IT Gary Rosenthal 7.00
____STARTING SOCCER Edward F Dolan, Jr. 5.00

TENNIS LOVERS' LIBRARY

____HOW TO BEAT BETTER TENNIS PLAYERS Loring Fiske 4.00
____PSYCH YOURSELF TO BETTER TENNIS Dr. Walter A. Luszki 2.00
____WEEKEND TENNIS—HOW TO HAVE FUN & WIN AT THE SAME TIME Bill Talbert 3.00

WILSHIRE PET LIBRARY

____HOW TO BRING UP YOUR PET DOG Kurt Unkelbach 2.00

WILSHIRE HORSE LOVERS' LIBRARY

____AMERICAN QUARTER HORSE IN PICTURES Margaret Cabel Self 5.00
____ART OF WESTERN RIDING Suzanne Norton Jones 10.00
____BASIC DRESSAGE Jean Froissard 5.00
____BEGINNER'S GUIDE TO HORSEBACK RIDING Sheila Wall 5.00
____BITS—THEIR HISTORY, USE AND MISUSE Louis Taylor 10.00
____BREAKING & TRAINING THE DRIVING HORSE Doris Ganton 10.00
____BREAKING YOUR HORSE'S BAD HABITS W. Dayton Sumner 10.00
____COMPLETE TRAINING OF HORSE AND RIDER Colonel Alois Podhajsky 15.00
____DISORDERS OF THE HORSE & WHAT TO DO ABOUT THEM E. Hanauer 5.00
____DRESSAGE—A STUDY OF THE FINER POINTS IN RIDING Henry Wynmalen 15.00
____DRIVE ON Doris Ganton 15.00
____DRIVING HORSES Sallie Walrond 7.00
____EQUITATION Jean Froissard 7.00
____FIRST AID FOR HORSES Dr. Charles H. Denning, Jr. 7.00
____FUN ON HORSEBACK Margaret Cabell Self 4.00
____HORSE OWNER'S CONCISE GUIDE Elsie V. Hanauer 5.00
____HORSE SELECTION & CARE FOR BEGINNERS George H. Conn 10.00
____HORSEBACK RIDING FOR BEGINNERS Louis Taylor 10.00
____HORSEBACK RIDING MADE EASY & FUN Sue Henderson Coen 10.00
____HORSES—THEIR SELECTION, CARE & HANDLING Margaret Cabell Self 5.00
____HOW TO CURE BEHAVIOR PROBLEMS IN HORSES Susan McBane 15.00
____HUNTER IN PICTURES Margaret Cabell Self 2.00
____ILLUSTRATED BOOK OF THE HORSE S. Sidney (8½" x 11") 10.00
____ILLUSTRATED HORSEBACK RIDING FOR BEGINNERS Jeanne Mellin 5.00
____KNOW ALL ABOUT HORSES Harry Disston 5.00
____LAME HORSE—CAUSES,SYMPTOMS & TREATMENT Dr. James R. Rooney 15.00
____POLICE HORSES Judith Campbell 2.00
____PRACTICAL GUIDE TO HORSESHOEING 5.00
____PRACTICAL HORSE PSYCHOLOGY Moyra Williams 10.00
____PROBLEM HORSES—CURING SERIOUS BEHAVIOR HABITS Summerhays 5.00
____REINSMAN OF THE WEST—BRIDLES & BITS Ed Connell 12.00
____RIDE WESTERN Louis Taylor 7.00
____SCHOOLING YOUR YOUNG HORSE George Wheatley 7.00
____STABLE MANAGEMENT FOR THE OWNER—GROOM George Wheatley 7.00
____UNDERSTANDING HORSES Garda Langley 15.00
____YOU AND YOUR PONY Pepper Mainwaring Healey (8½" x 11") 6.00
____YOUR PONY BOOK Hermann Wiederhold 2.00

Please add $2.00 shipping and handling for each book ordered.

Enclosed is my check ( ) money order ( ) for $_____

Name_____
(Please print)

Street_____

City_____ State_____ Zip_____

For our complete catalog, visit our Web site at www.mpowers.com

Help Yourself to Millions

Setting and meeting goals are the key lessons in Think and Grow Rich *by Napoleon Hill.*

Many people are skeptical about the value of self-help business books. They may not work for everyone, but they certainly work for some people. A self-made real estate developer who worried about paying a $200 debt 10 years ago is worth about $6 million today because of a self-help book.

Greg B. Randle, owner and president of home-based Monex Land Development in Los Angeles, California, lives in a million-dollar house he paid for in one year and drives a Mercedes Benz 560 that he owns free and clear.

But it wasn't always this way. Twelve years ago his wife, Debbie, worked full-time as a nurse while Greg sold life insurance. When they had their first child, their bills quickly mounted, and buying a washer and dryer became their biggest goal.

Then Greg's boss and mentor, life insurance salesman Bob Larsen, introduced him to the book *Think and Grow Rich* by Napoleon Hill. "The book teaches you to set goals," says Randle.

Following the book's advice, Randle focused on a few goals at a time, writing them down and telling people about them. He pulls out a poignant memento: the index card on which he listed his first goals—paying off the $200 debt and buying that washer and dryer. Randle had the card laminated long ago, and he keeps it as a reminder of how far he's come.

After reading *Think and Grow Rich*, he continued selling life insurance and began buying fixer-uppers in downtown Long Beach, which was then in the early stages of redevelopment. An ex-marine exhilarated by physical labor, he razed or refurbished and rented those early junkers, all the time focusing on the big goal he had set. Randle was going to become a real estate developer and a millionaire.

Today he is both. "I owe it all to the book," he says, "and Bob Larsen." And to his own determination, one might add.

Randle is building a $10 million condominium complex this year and is working diligently toward attaining his next goal, "50 at 50." The 40-year-old intends to be worth $50 million by the time he's 50.

Think and Grow Rich sells for $12.00 postpaid and is published by Wilshire Book Company, 12015 Sherman Road, North Hollywood, CA 91605.

Chapter Two

Everyone Loves to Read Classified Ads

There's a unique fascination with classified ads. People read them even when they aren't looking for anything in particular. I often read the Los Angeles Times business classified section hoping to find an interesting new challenge. I also read every ad in numerous magazines and tabloids, trying to catch a new trend or some interesting ad copy that might lend itself to my own ads. It's part of my never-ending research. I'm constantly answering ads, buying products, getting on mailing lists, coding my name and address—in fact doing exactly what I suggest you do.

View the assignments I give you as an exciting adventure with a gold mine at the end. All it takes to be able to scoop up as much gold as you want is the willingness to learn and try, and the motivation to keep on learning and trying until your goal is achieved. Remember, giving up and quitting is easy. Having the strength of character to continue on is what separates those who are successful from those who are not.

To make it in mail order, you need two things. One is knowledge of practical techniques that get results. The other is an entrepreneurial attitude. That means maintaining the belief that you'll be able to learn the mail order business and reach your goals. One of my favorite sayings is, "You are not only what you are today, but also what you choose to become tomorrow." Write it down and put it where you'll see it every day.

You may start out with a profitable ad right away, or you may not. But it doesn't much matter to your long range success, as ads that don't make it are a normal and necessary part of the mail order business. Not every one will be a winner. Building your business requires that you experiment with new items, ad copy, and publications. Setbacks are inevitable even for those of us already running profitable mail order businesses. But if you persevere, you will make money. And if you continue to persevere, you will make more and more money. When success comes—and it will—pat yourself on the back, stand tall, feel proud, and keep on learning, experimenting, and having fun. Now let's get started.

Your First Assignment

Go to your library, supermarket, convenience store, newsstand, and/or bookstore and read every classified ad in all the magazines and tabloids. I want you to get the feel of what is being advertised, of the various categories, of how many and what types of ads sell products directly off the ads and what percentage ask the reader to send for free information or further details. Notice how many have 800 numbers compared to the number that have regular phone numbers. To help you begin, I've reproduced classified sections from various popular magazines and tabloids. See pages 19 through 35.

It's also important in your research to note which magazines and tabloids contain few classified ads and which have many. What does that information tell you about the best places to run your ads? I would be cautious about running in publications with few ads and enthusiastic about running where there are many. An abundance of ads means that numerous advertisers are finding those particular publications profitable.

The following magazines and tabloids can be readily found: *National Enquirer, Star, Globe, Popular Science, Popular Mechanics, Entrepreneur, Success, Field & Stream, Writer's Market, Prevention, Working Woman, True Story, True Experience, Modern Romances,* and *True Confessions.*

Below are some interesting circulation figures for various publications. A high circulation means that you have a good chance of your ad being seen by more prospects. Here's a good tip. One of my best-pulling publications is Writer's Digest. It has a circulation of 250,000. I've been running in it every month for years. In fact, I now have two classified ads running. Your public library should have a copy. If not, call Joan Bambeck at (800) 234-0963. Ask her to send you a review copy and the advertising rate card. She has a wealth of experience. You'll find her extremely knowledgeable and helpful.

Quality Women's Group	5,758,000
National Enquirer	3,750,000
Star	3,200,000
Globe, Examiner, Sun	3,000,000
Popular Science	2,000,000
Popular Mechanics	1,600,000
Country Music	700,000
Firehouse Magazine	517,000
Entrepreneur	340,000
Spare Time	300,000
Writer's Digest	250,000

Publications such as *Popular Science* allow display ads in the classified section. They must be effective because the same ones keep running month after month. You might want to consider doing one sometime in the future. In the meantime, if you need help in running your classified ad, call Randi at (800) 445-2714. She'll give you excellent advice. Ask for a sample copy of *Popular Science* and an advertising rate card.

You'll need stationery. Start with 1,000 letterheads and business envelopes (size #10). Also order 1,000 business cards. Your local printer can show you various layouts. (Or if you have a computer with desktop publishing capabilities, you may want to create your own.) Ask for proofs of everything before giving your final OK to run. Things often look different in print than you expect them to. You might want to modify the layout and/or change the size of the text.

If you don't have a printer, you are welcome to try mine. I highly recommend him. He is Juan Luis Morales, Professional Print Shop, 10750 Burbank Blvd., North Hollywood, California 91601. Telephone (818) 506-8185. He does beautiful work. His service is excellent, his prices reasonable, he completes jobs when promised, and he takes a personal interest in all his customers.

Juan is running a very successful mail order stationery and printing business. As a matter of fact, I became acquainted with him through his direct mail advertising literature. In large type, his circular read: Need quality printing at reasonable rates? Excellent service. Call (818) 506-8185. His message was direct and to the point. He's been my printer ever since I first met him. The great part of his business is that his customers continually run out of stationery and advertising literature. Consumable products like Juan's are perfect mail order items.

Classified Advertising Rates

Many magazines and tabloids list the cost of weekly and/or monthly classified advertising rates at the beginning of the classified section. They usually give the cost per word and minimum number of words. For example, the cost per word might be $5.00 with a 10-word minimum. The least expensive ad would cost $50.00. A 15-word ad would cost $75.00.

If they don't offer this information, write or call. Request a sample copy of the publication, their advertising rate card, and media kit. The media kit contains their circulation number, a profile of their readers, and other pertinent information.

On pages 36 through 48 are copies of classified advertising rate cards from a variety of magazines and tabloids. If you think you might be interested in advertising in any particular publication, send away for a complimentary copy and the latest classified advertising rates.

To get classified advertising rates on over 200 publications, write or call National Mail Order Classified, Dept A-l, 2628 17th Street, Sarasota, Florida 34230. Telephone (941) 366-3003. If you need some help in determining where to run your ad, speak to Marilyn, a classified ad specialist. Ask what publications would be best for your offer. Report back to her with your results. She'll be able to make further suggestions based on your response.

I give my Internet address at the end of my classified ads. Readers go to my Web site, read my material, and send their order by mail, telephone, fax, or most often by e-mail. I am able to make sales without sending out literature. That means I save money on printing, postage, and labor. The system works like a charm. I get orders from all over the world, which have substantially increased my overall sales volume. Visit my Web site at http://www.mpowers.com.

You, too, can profit from the Internet. It's like a gold mine, waiting for you to pan for the gold. I urge you to become familiar with this exciting advertising tool. There are many places where you can run classified ads free or with a small expenditure, and returns can be big.

classified

businesses for sale

LASER TAG BUSINESS FOR SALE, includes everything you need and is transportable. 1 hour set-up, make $500 - $3,000 per day. Financing available. Call Phill: (510) 443-0442. P.S. Sales Agents needed.

advisory services

COMPLETE LEGAL SERVICES. Franchise and Business-Opp; State, National, International; FTC and other Disclosure Statements; State and Foreign registrations; related litigation; document review. Complete corporate, partnership and business services. Arnold Cohen, Attorney-at-Law, 2424 North Federal Highway, Boca Raton, FL 33431. 1-(407) 750-6706.

INVESTIGATE BEFORE YOU INVEST. Complete company background - history, sales, BBB. $49.95. 1-(914) 724-3086.

PARALYZED BY POOR CREDIT? Take control! Know your legal rights. Complete hassle-free solution to perfect credit. $9.97, SASE: Avant, P.O. Box 2951, Winter Park, FL 32790.

TAX HAVENS - Bank secretly, invest privately and keep ownership anonymous. Protect assets. Avoid capital gains, estate and other taxes. Establish international business corporations, simple trusts, overlying trusts. Bank accounts. Legal. Ethical. Free information. International Asset Strategies, Inc., 10 Paradise Drive, Laconia, NH 03246. (603) 528-1313; (800) 528-1313; Fax: (603) 528-4333.

agents wanted

SELL MANUAL ACCOUNTING SYSTEMS to small businesses. Earn $50 for every new system sold. Call Ed 1-(800) 445-1700 for information. We have over 40 years experience selling this product to small businesses.

DISPLACED EMPLOYEE? Earn your former salary now! F/T - P/T. Serious inquiries only! Free information packet. 1-(800) 365-7550, Extension 70226.

HOW ABOUT YOUR OWN RADIO STATION that airs nothing but your own commercial 24 hours a day, 7 days a week! Box 28307, Kenneth City, FL 33709.

NEW PRODUCT FOR DISTRIBUTION in U.S. market. Earn $1,000/day selling to retailers. Act now! This can't miss! $350 minimum investment. For details 1-(708) 672-3046 or write: J. Kulik Imports, 3423 Huntley Terrace, Crete, IL 60417.

NATIONAL BANK seeks agents to market no-fee secured MasterCard. (402) 597-6898.

books/publications

FREE 36-PAGE "Books For Your Business" catalog. 1-(800) 635-7654.

GET FREE PUBLICITY: Conduct a seminar. Start a newsletter. Stage an event - a demonstration, a party, whatever suits your business. These are just some of the guerrilla tactics that marketing guru Jay Conrad Levinson explains in his revolutionary book, "Guerrilla Marketing." It's packed with practical ideas on every aspect of marketing, all designed to deliver maximum impact on a modest budget. The completely revised new edition reveals exciting ways to exploit technological advances, the fastest-growing markets of the 90's, and much more. Available at bookstores or call 1-(800) 225-3362 to order. Monday - Friday 9 - 5 EST. $11.95 paperback.

999 LITTLE KNOWN SUCCESSFUL home businesses. $12.99. Heartland, Box 985, Windsor, CA 95492.

BUSINESS SUCCESS GUARANTEED. I've deposited $1,117,000 in 1993. Little start-up capital. Send $12.95: SBRV, 650 S.E. Paradise Point Road., Crystal River, FL 34429.

books/publications

DESIGN AND PLANT LANDSCAPING BUSINESS. Simplified, fully illustrated guidebook by retired professional gets you started. $29.95 postpaid. Thom, P.O. Box 1778, Janesville, WI 53547.

400 HOW-TO and self-improvement books covering almost every conceivable interest! Send for free illustrated circular. Serenity Sales, 10734-E Clancey, Downey, CA 90241.

FREE REPORT - Get rich - not ripped off! Discover today's hottest, most profitable small business and home business opportunities! Call: 1-(800) 889-5950, Extension 20.

RECYCLING BUSINESS - Start your own. Huge weekly profits. 1-(800) 377-7490 recording.

HOW TO RESEARCH BUSINESSES before venturing. Comprehensive booklet. $5.00. Guaranteed. O'Sullivan Publishing, 6050 Peachtree Parkway, Suite 340-212, Dept. 594E, Norcross, GA 30092.

1994 SMALL BUSINESS SUCCESS TIPS. Specify Canadian and/or U.S. trends and regulations. Send $7.95: At A Sales Pace, P.O. Box 484, Calgary, Alta. T2P 2J1.

TURN SPARE TIME INTO THOUSANDS with your home computer. SASE $1.00: Money Mill, Box 626, White House, TN 37188.

WHAT IS A TRADEMARK? $10. Professional Legal Assistors, 17216 Saticoy, #185, Van Nuys, CA 91406.

WRITING YOUR BUSINESS PLAN, small business guide $6.50. Financial Edge, P.O. Box 92574, Southlake, TX 76092.

business equipment

COMPUTER PORTRAIT MUG SYSTEM, equipment and supplies. Wholesale prices. 1-(800) 832-7410.

CARTS, KIOSKS, RMU's - stock or custom. B&W Woodcrafters, The Mall Street Cartmakers. 1-(215) 638-9672. Fax: 1-(215) 638-9679.

CONDOM/TAMPON VENDING: 10 machines and stock only $1,495. Secured territories available. 1-(800) 788-3456. Visa/MC.

INFLATABLE AMUSEMENT RIDES: Dinosaurs, Castles, Bungee Runs, Bouncy Boxing and more! 1-(800) JUMPING.

14 FAST PHARMACEUTICAL VENDING machines with product. Best offer. (817) 370-0206.

ALCOHOL BREATH ANALYZERS coin operated. Includes calibration unit. Used. (207) 873-6317.

business financing

LET THE GOVERNMENT FINANCE your small business. Grants/loans to $500,000. Free recorded message: 1-(707) 448-0270. (JB6)

WEALTHY INVESTORS seek business finance proposals. No front fee. 1-(615) 573-4655.

NEED MONEY FOR BUSINESS start-up, expansion, leveraged buyouts? Call: 1-(206) 932-7856.

BUSINESS FINANCING OR PURCHASERS available. Minimum transaction $500K. Information: 1-(703) 992-0505.

A BUSINESS PLAN AND EVALUATION. Simple as 1-2-3 guidebook! Mazzo, $19.95, bookstores. 1-(904) 794-4977.

MONEYFIND™ BOOKWARE™ - The fastest and easiest way to find money for your business. (Dealerships available.) 1-(800) 277-8484.

UNLIMITED CAPITAL AVAILABLE quickly, easily for all business/commercial needs. (800) 883-1535.

business financing

AMERICAN VENTURE CAPITAL EXCHANGE - Present your venture to investors nationwide. $150. 1-(800) 292-1993. Fax: (503) 221-9987. Modem: (503) 695-5701.

business opportunities

FREE! "JANITORIAL BUSINESS Moneymaking Secrets." Box 1087E, Valley Center, CA 92082.

MAILORDER MILLIONAIRE REVEALS moneymaking secrets! Free, exciting cassette. Melvin Powers, 12015 Sherman Road, North Hollywood, CA 91605E.

MAILORDER BOOKS, MANUALS, directories. 1,000% profit report. Select, Box 1140, Clearwater, FL 34617.

MAKE HOMEMADE BOOKLETS. Mine have earned $436,097. Money never stops. Free proof. Booklets, 507X Oak Drive, Friendswood, TX 77546.

NEW! GROW EXPENSIVE PLANTS. Sell for 2,000% profit. Free information. Growbiz, Box 306-J5, Seminary, MS 39479.

FREE MONEYMAKING MANUAL brings cash. Progress, Box 93248-EN, Los Angeles, CA 90093.

VENDING MACHINES/ROUTES. Free machine offer! All types available. MC/Visa. 1-(609) 384-0440.

$2,000 DAILY from your telephone answering machine. I've made over $1,000,000 using mine! 1-(303) 674-2219. Recorded details.

FREE DEALERSHIP - Sell mailing lists! Complete program free! 1-(305) 344-4113. PCW, Box 26418-EN54, Tamarac, FL 33320.

BIG MONEY REPAIRING auto windshields. Supplies and information. Rubbs Glass Patch, P.O. Box 243, Monticello, AR 71655. 1-(800) 242-2213.

MILLION DOLLAR HOME BUSINESS! Ideal for mail order. We supply everything. We drop-ship 3,500 best-selling products, priced far below wholesale. Immediate delivery. Free book, tape. SMC, 9401 DeSoto Avenue, Dept. 723-65, Chatsworth, CA 91311.

SELL GAMBLING BOOKS by mail! High profits - no investment! Sunnyside, Box 29-EN, Lynn, MA 01903.

IMPORT/EXPORT, business of the 90's. Start your own business. $8,500. 1-(800) 227-8417.

HOME IMPORT MAIL ORDER BUSINESS. Start without capital. Free report. Mellinger, Dept. C1396, Woodland Hills, CA 91367.

GET FREE CASH! Private money grants. Foundation giveaways. Loans. Millions available. Sources: Box 5529-T, Diamond Bar, CA 91765.

CABLE TV DESCRAMBLERS, CONVERTERS, accessories. Save money. Don't rent! Free catalog. Quantity discounts! 1-(800) 334-8475.

OWN YOUR OWN MAIL ORDER business selling books. TPCC, Box 4113, Torrance, CA 90510.

DRUG RAID SEIZURES: Buy dirt cheap! Cars, houses, boats, computers. Seizures, Box 51488-T, Ontario, CA 91761.

WE BUY newspaper clippings. $781.23 weekly. Send stamped envelope. Edwards, Box 467159EM, Atlanta, GA 30346.

CONSULTANTS, WRITERS, ACCOUNTANTS needed! Advise small businesses. Free information. 1-(800) 779-6093.

MAILORDER PROFITS. Sell books, tapes! Huge selection. Distributorship information. Mascor-Ent, Box 8308, Silver Spring, MD 20907.

VENDING MACHINE SECRETS REVEALED. Get all the facts. Newsletter tells all. 1-(800) 221-6066.

classified

classified

business opportunities

CONSUMER ELECTRONICS! Unlimited potential! The most exciting opportunity in networking history. Call now. 1-(617) 499-7921.

$100,000 GUARANTEED thru mail order network marketing! Unbelievable system! 1-(212) 560-7319, 24 hours.

"WE CREATE MILLIONAIRES"- Success Magazine. "Oxyfresh top ranked MLM" - Downline News. Call: 1-(800) 999-9551, Extension 389.

EARN $1,000 FEES EVERY DAY! New field of Business Arbitration. Free information pack. 1-(800) 866-8865 (24 hours).

GAVE IT ONE YEAR and it didn't work? Call: 1-(800) 887-7884.

CONSUMER ELECTRONICS - We send catalog to your network - you cash in! Free packet. 1-(503) 482-8486.

SECRET BANKING SYSTEM! Open bank accounts make thousands! Amazing recorded message reveals details. (815) 496-2684, Extension 37E.

SECRETS OF DOING ADVERTISING publications from home. Easy to follow start-up kit. Samples, agreements, layouts, sales presentations & 200-page manual for direct mail, dine-out books, community coupon programs. No franchise fees or royalties. Only $295. Money back guarantee. Free brochure. VF Associates: 1-(800) 925-4258.

PERFORM POWER LINE/VDT SURVEYS. Customers: homebuyers, health individuals. Meter, materials included. Call: 1-(800) 638-9121. Unique, profitable.

DISTRIBUTORS NEEDED - BIG PROFITS miniature satellite antennas for homes, R.V.'s, business. $1,800 refundable deposit required. 1-(800) 886-5008.

BIG MONEY fixing ugly houses. Small investment. Large profits. Part time or new career. Work at home. No layoffs. Free brochure. Fixer Jay, Box 491779EG3, Redding, CA 96049.

PROVEN MAILORDER PROFITS. Information reveals exciting plan. (919) 787-6644. Pencress-1, Box 6341, Raleigh, NC 27628-6341.

CONSULTANTS NEEDED - Outstanding professional growth seminars/resources. Free information. IEXCEL Associates (817) 754-3209.

MAJOR BREAKTHROUGH PRODUCT - Eat normally, lose weight. Distributors needed nationally PT/FT. Unsurpassed business opportunity. 1-(800) 525-7985, Extension 22AJM.

FREE 900#. Earn $10,000 per month. For details call: (210) 366-6715.

MAKE MONEY FROM HOME with your PC! Call Firefly Software Corp. for free details. 1-(800) 224-2778, Extension 25.

DISTRIBUTORS for personal emergency response system, dramatic lifeline to loved ones. Ground-floor MLM. Great compensation. 1-(800) 828-6602. Independent Distributor.

TURNKEY, COMPUTER PORTRAITS on cups, T-shirt, banners. Excellent opportunity. High profit. (813) 475-8791.

HOME-BASED BUSINESSES. Over 150 pages. Free information. Howe, 3319 Onyx, Rockford, IL 61102.

PRINT BROKING - Profits in the printing business. Little to no start-up costs. Booklet $4.00. 21st Century, Box 9625, Pittsburgh, PA 15226.

WAIT! DON'T GET RIPPED OFF by another moneymaking scam! Free information. Box 33E, Northampton, PA 18067.

LEARN SECRETS of salon shear sharpening. Sharpen in the salons. No overhead, low start up. (717) 784-6089.

business opportunities

BUNGEE BOUNCER! Jump into your own business! Become a distributor for the most exciting new exercise and recreation device on the market. Easy to sell; for family fun, exercise and entertaining. Make money from demonstrating product, as well as from equipment sales. Don't miss out on this opportunity. Prices start at $2,995. Phone: (800) 230-1939. Fax: (801) 752-1948.

EASY MONEY! 1,000's weekly. Start immediately. Send SASE and $5.00 for complete program. Aaron Cano, 1900 W. University, Suite #23, Edinburg, TX 78539.

MAKE BIG MONEY! Improve your lifestyle. Free details. PTP, Box 598, Smithville, TX 78957.

EARN MONEY in the marble polishing and refinishing business. Call: (407) 657-7878.

BE A HERO! Distributorships available with protected territory opportunity. Help millions of diabetics eliminate the need for a needle and syringe with "Freedom Jet - The Needle-Free Injection System." Will train the right individuals. $16K investment to market this space-aged equipment. Call now: (800) 662-2471.

START A TEMPORARY HELP AGENCY. Complete training guidance in light industrial and food service divisions of the fast growing temporary help industry. For free brochure, write: Temporary Help Consulting Services, Inc., Eight Park Plaza, Suite 318, Boston, MA 02116. Or call: (617) 859-7489.

BE YOUR OWN BOSS! Start prestigious, lucrative Kansas City barbeque business. 8 years' experience. Affordable options. No franchise. $2.00 SASE. Ozark/KC BBQ, Box 208, Independence, MO 64051.

CELLULAR PHONE RENTALS. $10,000+ per month. Low start-up. Free information 24 hours: 1-(800) 400-5630.

MILLIONAIRE'S WIDOW REVEALS husband's moneymaking secrets. Free manuscripts. Box 2355-E5, Redwood City, CA 94064.

DEALERS WANTED. Thousands of products. Dealerships, Box 218650-E, Houston, TX 77218.

WANT MONEY in the palm of your hand? Invaluable information. Free details. Shaw, 551 Innsbrook, Columbia, SC 29210.

ELECTRONIC MEDICAL CLAIMS SOFTWARE. Complete medical management software training and support by experienced claims processors. Marketing assistance provided. (800) 580-3669. 5915 N.W. 23, #220, Oklahoma City, OK 73127.

$3,600 MONTHLY using your cassette recorder! Free amazing report! Global, #280418ME, Dallas, TX 75228.

$720 DAILY sending fax ads with your home computer. (503) 440-6902.

YOURS $900+ WEEKLY! Unique home business. Free, guaranteed offer! LSASE today. American Resources, 30 Cornelia Street, #14, New York, NY 10014.

"INFORMATION IS THE NEW CURRENCY" - Bill Gates CEO, Microsoft. Huge profits brokering information. Take advantage of the information highway. Potential to rival Compuserve! Information $9.95. LSASE: Otis Online, 507-308D King Street, East Toronto, Ontario M5A 1M3.

HONEST EVALUATIONS of most nationally advertised business opportunities. Join the non-profit National Business Research Foundation and receive the Annual Index of Home Business Offers. $35 dues. 2020 Pennsylvania Avenue, Suite 400, Washington, DC 20006. (800) 264-1828.

START YOUR OWN BOOKKEEPING SERVICE with little or no money. Instructive guide $19.95. Bookkeeping Concepts, P.O. Box 809005-225, Dallas, TX 75380.

FREE NETWORK MARKETING Success Catalog plus Free MLM magazine. 1-(800) 786-5493.

business opportunities

EXTRA INCOME, WORK FROM HOME! Wholesale gift products. More information send SASE to: L. Mattioli, Dept. GWA, P.O. Box 1814, Lutz, FL 33549.

EXPLOSIVE HIGH PROFIT homebased business. Start-up under $300. Easy instructions. Send $19.95 to: Handlers, Box 1258, Smithtown, NY 11787.

CANADIAN EXPORTS ARE SOARING to record highs! Our Importing From Canada portfolio will provide all the details you need to start earning huge profits right away. Home-based importing business. No capital required. Free information. Curran International Group, 40 Endsleigh, Toronto, Canada M2J 3N6.

DISTRIBUTORS WANTED - Patented Instant CarKooler cools hot car interiors quickly, safely. Huge market. No competition. General Innovations, Dept. Ent, 6184A Old Franconia, Alexandria, VA 22310. (703) 719-0202.

$2,000/WEEK distributors/agents. Self-installed inexpensive Loudmouth home security systems. (702) 438-9487.

THIGH CREAM business opportunity is dream come true. Distributors needed. Call 1-(800) 975-0515 for instant success.

WORK AT HOME for 100+ companies nationwide. Send SASE for information. UHAE, 9582 Hamilton, #368, Huntington Beach, CA 92646.

I MAKE $1,000's MONTHLY desktop publishing part-time at home. So can you! I'll show you how! Free information. (610) 359-9558.

MYSTERY SHOPPING - Hundreds of businesses need you to evaluate their employees' performance. Fun! Profitable! Information $5.00. Herring Institute, 7380 Sandlake Road, Suite 519, Orlando, FL 32819.

IF YOU WANT TO EARN substantial dollars, like to sell, enjoy running your own business, this is a great opportunity. We require distributors to call on businesses for personalized greeting cards. You earn 50% commission and you control your time. This can work for you as it has for many others. Contact: G. Posner, Canadian Greetings, 965 Powell Avenue, Winnipeg, Canada R3H 0H4. 1-(800) 665-7441.

REPLICA SWISS WATCHES. Gift boxed. Guarantee. Variety. Quality. Wholesale. Full title 18 compliance. Brochure marketing. RST, 7831 Woodmont Avenue, Bethesda, MD 20814-3007. (301) 654-1101; (301) 907-7884 Fax.

COLLECT JUDICIAL JUDGMENTS. Earn $8,000/month. First time offered. Call: (602) 280-9930.

BIG INCOME in window cleaning. Free information. AWC, 27 Oakcreek, El Sobrante, CA 94803. (510) 222-7080.

HUGE PROFITS - "Intruder ID" home/business professional alarm system. Complete protection. Also takes a picture of intruder. Your cost $148 complete. Nothing else to buy. You sell $399. Very easy installation. Rostech, P.O. Box 2789, Plattsburgh, NY 12901. 1-(514) 522-2157.

MERCHANT ATM/BANKCARD SALES. $10,000 plus residuals monthly representing national bank. Huge untapped niche! (916) 721-6680.

YOU CAN MAKE MONEY with foreign investors. They have money to buy and invest in products, equipment, business ventures, real estate. One transaction can make you independent for the rest of your life. Top finders' fees paid. Free report. Global Exchange, 594ie1 Box 3574, Newport Beach, CA 92663. (714) 722-9260.

SELF-PUBLISHING OVER 1,000% profit! Free details on reproduction rights. Sunflower, 1810-EN1 West, Wichita, KS 67203.

PAYPHONES? DEBIT CARDS? Residual income from telecommunications? Check with the higher institute of earnings. 1-(800) 552-8742.

21

classified

business opportunities

MANUFACTURE PHOTO CUT OUTS. 2,000% profit! Fast. Easy. Inexpensive. (813) 593-0766.

MLM: DISCOVER THE INCOME to match your dreams. Free information: 1-(800) 456-9183.

MLM - Fat-burning coffee. Drink coffee, lose weight. Enhanced compensation plan. (800) 200-0888.

START YOUR OWN janitorial business. SMS, Inc., P.O. Box 70246, Ocala, FL 34470.

WOMEN - MEN - RETIREES - SINGLE PARENTS. Earn $200 per day doing touch-up painting for autodealers. Paint matches and covers damage like magic, leaves no brushmarks. No prior experience, flexible hours. Investment $450. Magic-Touch: 1-(800) 235-7313.

BODY WISE, International - MLM promotes health care, sports nutrition, weight loss products. Optimize physical and financial fitness. Call now! (202) 331-4448.

CHURCH MARKETING. $5,000 - $7,000 monthly working warm leads. $480 start-up. 1-(800) 659-3258 for free information.

DISTRIBUTORSHIP AVAILABLE revolutionary battery conditioner revives weak, dead batteries. Huge market, high profits, low start-up. M.P.I.: (214) 634-8224.

MAIL ORDER BUSINESS - Start from home under $400. No inventory. No selling. Unlimited income. (909) 424-5046. Amazing recorded message!

$3,000,000,000 WILL BE GENERATED this year by 900 numbers. Get your share now! Call Omni-Tel Corp: (800) 285-2224.

BULLETPROOF MLM! Stop getting shot down! 45% override protection. (404) 255-0014.

START YOUR OWN RESIDENTIAL commercial mortgage company. Comprehensive home study courses. Professional workshops available. Brokers welcome. Call or write: IFC, Inc., P.O. Box 1251E, Piedmont, SC 29673. (803) 295-3235. Brokers teaching brokers.

business services

DELAWARE INCORPORATIONS. Specialists in setting up Delaware corporations. General incorporations, airplane incorporations, boat incorporations (and documentations). Call or write for free kit. Delaware Registry, Ltd., P.O. Box 484-ENT, Wilmington, DE 19899. 1-(302) 652-6532; 1-(800) 321-CORP.

1-800 VOICEMAIL 16¢ minute. Low-cost long distance only 14.5¢ peak; 12.9¢ off-peak. Call: 1-(800) 743-5339.

OUR 800 SERVICE sets the standard. Efficient professional - message center, order taking, media response. Call today: 1-(800) CLUB-NOW (258-2669).

BUSINESS PLANS & FUNDING: Venture professionals help you write your own powerhouse, or we do it all. Acclaimed packages from $675. 1-(800) 346-2408.

NATIONWIDE DISCOUNTED LONG DISTANCE 13.9¢/minute - day, 11.9¢/minute - evening. Nationwide 800 service, 14¢/minute. 1-(800) 735-6542.

INCORPORATE IN TAX-FREE NEVADA: Brainstorm it with the pros! Call now, free, (800) 648-0966 to find out how a Nevada corporation can give you benefits like asset protection, maximum privacy, no state income tax. Even if already incorporated. Laughlin Associates, Inc., Carson City, NV 89706. Beats Delaware!

INCORPORATE YOUR BUSINESS - ANY STATE! Delaware incorporations instantly. Professional service, we invite comparison. CorpAmerica, Inc.: 1-(800) 622-6414; 1-(302) 736-5510. Fax: 1-(302) 736-5620. MC/Visa/Amex.

business services

INCORPORATE IN ANY STATE! No lawyer's fee. Instant Delaware incorporations. Call Inc. Plan (USA): 1-(800) 462-4633.

HEALTH CARE BILLING SOFTWARE for doctors, dentists, etc. $395. 1-(800) 547-7611.

INCORPORATE IN DELAWARE INSTANTLY, by phone or Fax, only $41, plus state filing fees. No attorney's fees required. Locate company headquarters in any state (or country). Free "Delaware Incorporations Handbook" (5th Edition) includes Subchapter S and Limited Liability Company (LLC) information. Registered Agent, telephone answering, mail services. Delaware Business Incorporators, Inc., Box 5722, Dept. E, Wilmington, DE 19808. Call toll free: 1-(800) 423-2993 or 1-(302) 996-5819 anytime. Fax: 1-(800) 423-0423 or 1-(302) 996-5818. Visa/MC/Amex.

INCORPORATE starting at $45 plus filing fees. Corporate Creations®: 1-(800) 780-8107.

BUSINESS PLANS PREPARED. Results-oriented publicity/advertising campaigns, product roll-outs. Trademark searches. More. Helping start-ups since 1978. Reasonable rates. John McCoy, 1442A Walnut Street, #306, Berkeley, CA 94709. 1-(510) 528-1110.

TRADEMARK SEARCHES $100. Application preparation $250. Attorney Jay Horowitz: 1-(301) 840-0509.

PRESTIGIOUS PENNSYLVANIA AVENUE, Washington, DC address! Mail/package receiving and forwarding, Fax, voice mail. 1-(202) 543-0850.

WE DESIGN AND PRINT gorgeous low-cost color brochures. 1-(708) 754-4858.

BUSINESS PLANS PREPARED by professional. Best prices available. Call: 1-(610) 353-9147.

CREDIT CARD PROCESSING. All types of businesses accepted. Call Pat at: 1-(305) 492-0315.

YOUR OWN CARD SERVICE VISA/MC merchant account. Large company wants to help even the smallest business. (916) 546-1274, Extension 150. Registered agent Humboldt Bank, Eureka, CA.

NATIONWIDE 800 ANSWERING SERVICE takes your company's orders, messages, seminar registrations, subscriptions, etc. (800) 235-6646.

INCORPORATE IN NEVADA: Tax savings, asset security. Free facts. 1-(800) 398-1077.

MLM SOFTWARE/COMPUTER SERVICES available for new or mature MLM companies. Call for free information package. Over 25-years' experience. Haven Systems, Inc.: (703) 471-6150.

NEED A MAILING ADDRESS, voice mail, branch office services? Call Addresses & Answers (Denver): (800) 536-4050. Fax: (303) 988-8609.

ACCEPT MAJOR CREDIT CARDS for your business. Home, mail and phone order business accepted. Call 1-(412) 375-9443 for information.

DEEPLY DISCOUNTED LONG DISTANCE. 12.9¢ anytime. 800 numbers 13.9¢ minute. 1-(800) 637-7534.

buy it wholesale

CABLE TV DESCRAMBLERS, CONVERTERS, accessories. Save money. Don't rent! Free catalog. Quantity discounts! 1-(800) 334-8475.

WHOLESALE SOURCES, USA, Asia. Lowest prices, all products. Unlimited, 8127-ET Maple, Fairchild, WA 99011.

WHOLESALE DIRECTORIES - Over 20,000 products, U.S. and overseas. GHB Pubs., Box 652, Hampstead, MD 21074-0652.

BUY BELOW WHOLESALE. Thousands of products. Factory direct, Asia, Europe, USA. Free information: TR Scott, 2501 22nd Avenue North, St. Petersburg, FL 33713.

buy it wholesale

LOWEST ORIENTAL factory prices. 10,000 products. Crestco, 668 Main, Wilmington, MA 01887.

WHOLESALE DIRECTORIES - Buy factory direct: USA, Asia, Taiwan. Stamp: Wholesale, Box 067, Highspire, PA 17034.

27,149 PRODUCTS, DIRECT - Taiwan, Philippines, Hong Kong! Small lots. Samples. Echo-E4, Shalimar, FL 32579-0739.

CLOSEOUT JEWELRY. 55¢ DOZEN. Catalog, 50¢. Roussels, 107-405 Dow, Arlington, MA 02174-7199.

PRICELESS INFORMATION! Product sources at lowest wholesale prices. Domestic, international suppliers. Free literature. JH, Inc., 94 Riverview, Neptune City, NJ 07753.

LOWEST FACTORY DIRECT wholesale prices. 15,293 products. Free report. GHE, 1508 James, Syracuse, NY 13203.

CLOSEOUTS, IRREGULARS, OVERRUNS branded footwear and apparel. Sold by the case. For resale only. Price list $1.00. Fontana + Fontana, Inc., P.O. Box 99, Indian Trail, NC 28079. (704) 882-1112.

TELEPHONE CALL SCREENERS and automatic fax/phone line-sharers $59. Sample $99 each to: DIMASY, P.O. Box 63110, 3002JC, Rotterdam, Holland. Europe Fax: +31-10-476 2806.

computers

100+ FREE CATALOGS - Don't pay top dollar, the newest list of computer/multimedia/electronics mail order catalogs with 800#s & descriptions. Send $4.00 to: Nuwave, 58 Fradkin Street, Wallington, NJ 07057.

computer/software

GREAT PROGRAM! We do documentation right! PAT Document Services: 1-(601) 477-3875.

MEDICAL BILLING/ELECTRONIC CLAIMS. Complete software under $500. Full training/support available. 1-(513) 772-5102; 1-(800) 825-2524. 24 hours.

computer/supplies

BUSINESS COMPUTERS, FAX/MODEMS. Buy direct and save. Information: (404) 473-4701.

education/instruction

INDEPENDENT STUDY MBA program emphasizing entrepreneurship and small business management. Or become a California attorney through our correspondence law program. Taft University: 1-(800) 882-4555.

CHADWICK UNIVERSITY - Earn BS/MS/MBA degree via guided home study. Programs in Business Administration, Environmental Studies, Computer Science. Military/work tuition reductions available! Free catalogue. 1-(800) 767-2423.

REAL ESTATE APPRAISER CAREERS. Home study. P.C.D.I., Atlanta, Georgia. Free literature. 1-(800) 362-7070, Dept. RF107.

FULLY APPROVED UNIVERSITY DEGREES! Economical home study for Bachelor's, Master's, Doctorate, fully approved by California State Superintendent of Public Instruction. Prestigious faculty counsels for independent study and life experience credits. Free information. Richard Crews, M.D. (Harvard), President, Columbia Pacific University, Dept. 3D45, 1415 Third Street, San Rafael, CA 94901. 1-(800) 552-5522 or 1-(415) 459-1650.

FREE VIDEO - External BA/BS, MS/MBA, PhD/Law. Accredited, financial aid. 1-(800) 677-2369. LaSalle University, Dept. #604, Slidell, LA 70459-2000.

classified

education/instruction

BECOME A PARALEGAL. Home study. P.C.D.I., Atlanta, Georgia. Free catalogue. 1-(800) 362-7070, Dept. LF107.

UNIVERSITY DEGREES WITHOUT CLASSES. Bachelor's, Master's, Doctorates. Accredited, economical, accelerated programs. Credit for prior accomplishments and work experience. Free brochure. Dr. John Bear, P.O. Box 826EP, Benicia, CA 94510. 1-(800) 835-8535.

LEARN PERSONAL COMPUTERS. Home study. P.C.D.I., Atlanta, Georgia. Free literature. 1-(800) 362-7070, Dept. KF107.

PARALEGAL GRADED CURRICULUM. Approved home study. Affordable. Since 1890. Free catalog 1-(800) 826-9228 or Blackstone School of Law, P.O. Box 871449, Dept. EN, Dallas, TX 75287.

BECOME A HOME INSPECTOR. Home study. Free literature. P.C.D.I., Atlanta, Georgia. 1-(800) 362-7070, Dept. PF107.

HOME STUDY Associate, Bachelor's, Master's, Doctoral degrees. Business Administration, Health Care, Human Resources, International Business, Paralegal, Law, Psychology, Technology Management. SCUPS Admissions, 202 Fashion-ET, Tustin, CA 92680. 1-(800) 477-2254.

STARTING YOUR OWN BUSINESS! This start-up guide reveals how. Step-by-step! Acquiring capital, planning, permits, taxes, regulations & so much more. Free details: Empire, P.O. Box 44306-ENT3, Cleveland, OH 44144.

BECOME A PROPERTY MANAGER. Home study - Rental/commercial property. P.C.D.I., Atlanta, Georgia. Free literature. 1-(800) 362-7070, Dept. MF107.

LEARN TO TYPE 50+ words a minute. Home study. Call: (713) 780-9389.

BE AN AUCTIONEER - Learn the lucrative career of auctioneering. Anything can be sold by the auction method of auctioneering. World Wide College of Auctioneering, Inc. Free catalog. (515) 423-5242 day or night. The finest auction educator since 1933.

BECOME A MEDICAL TRANSCRIPTIONIST. Home study. Free career literature. P.C.D.I., Atlanta, Georgia. 1-(800) 362-7070, Dept. YF107.

RETIRE, UPGRADE, TRAIN IN NEW CAREER. Life Skills Coach, Alcohol/Drug Counselor, Hypnotherapist, Cancer Outreach Consultant. Free career package. Above average income. 1-(800) 661-2099.

financial

FEDERAL LOANS for small businesses now available. 1-(800) 777-6342 for free details.

OVERDUE BILLS? Bad credit's no problem! Licensed/bonded. Applications to $50,000. Not loan company. TCAC, Dept. E, Box 26397, Birmingham, AL 35226, or 1-(800) 869-0607.

BORROW $500 - $40,000! On signature. No collateral. Action, Box 5499-T, Diamond Bar, CA 91765.

BORROW $100 - $100,000! FAST! No collateral. Personal, debt consolidation, business, auto, residential. 1-(800) 444-6599, 24 hours.

FREE MONEY POSSIBLY - Free contact definitely. Learn all about self-liquidating loans, arbitrage, roll-programs and other financial deals, etc. 2-hour video tape shows top government official and business leaders discussing various financial transactions. A must see for lay-people, investors, bankers, attorneys, accountants and brokers. As an additional bonus, I will divulge name of person to contact, which took me six long years to research and finally track down, with each paid order. Best investment you will ever make. Send $39.95 plus $4.00 shipping & handling to: R. Sherman, P.O. Box 1045, Clarkdale, AZ 86324. Phone inquiries welcome: 1-(602) 634-6797.

financial

UNLIMITED CAPITAL AVAILABLE any purpose - business, commercial expansion, mortgage, construction, development, receivables, start-up venture. Pisani, Box 605E, Pelham, NY 10803. Fax: 1-(914) 738-8653.

BORROW $100 - $100,000. Quickly, on signature/ secured immediately. Act now! 1-(404) 879-5514.

employment opportunities

EASY WORK! EXCELLENT PAY! Assemble products at home. Toll free: 1-(800) 467-5566, Extension 2440.

GET PAID FOR READING BOOKS! $100 per book. Send name, address to: Calco Publishing, Dept. C-607, 500 South Broad, Meriden, CT 06450.

EASY WORK! EXCELLENT INCOME! Assemble products at home. 1-(800) 377-6000, Extension 7270.

FIRMS NEED HOMEWORKERS! Send SASE to: RB International, Box 476, Brea, CA 92622.

STAY HOME MAKE $125 A DAY processing mail for local company. Work dropped off! Paid weekly. Send SASE to: Amerinet, 6929 JFK Blvd., Suite 20-336OP12, N. Little Rock, AR 72116.

HOME TYPISTS, PC users needed. $35,000 potential. Details. Call: 1-(805) 962-8000, Extension B-2311.

franchises

PUBLISH THE BINGO BUGLE. Nation's largest franchised monthly newspaper. High profit potential. Complete training. $1,500 - $4,000 investment. In Entrepreneur's Top 500 Franchises. Call: 1-(800) 447-1958.

FRANCHISE YOUR BUSINESS with the leading consulting firm in the country. McGrow Consulting: 1-(800) 358-8011.

NEW EXCITING FRANCHISE opportunities! Free information kit. Robert Ames Business Development: 1-(800) 796-3434.

PHILLY'S FAMOUS ITALIAN ICES. Mfg. & retail. 48 outrageous flavors. Starting at $49,995. Franchises nationwide. 1-(215) 634-8563. Be your own boss.

FRANCHISE YOUR BUSINESS $1,950; in two weeks! 25 years' experience. America's best franchise sales/marketing group. 1-(215) 236-5175.

EXCLUSIVE FRANCHISES available with National Property Registry. The national video inventory system. Write: NPR, Box 72376-E, Marietta, GA 30007-2376. Telephone: (404) 565-0565.

inventions

INVENTORS! Can you patent and profit from your idea? Call American Inventors Corp. for free information. Serving inventors since 1975. 1-(800) 338-5656.

INVENTORS - Don't be fooled. Call our Inventors Club: 1-(800) 466-1793.

INVENTORS: Utilize The Logical Process™ to protection and potential profits. Free advice. Your first step is important. APSI, Washington, DC: 1-(800) 458-0352.

INVENTIONS, IDEAS, NEW PRODUCTS! Presentation to industry. National exposition. 1-(800) 288-IDEA.

FREE INVENTION PACKAGE - Davison & Associates offers customized development, patenting and licensing. Proven results: 1-(800) 677-6382.

FREE protection forms and information kit. Affiliated Inventors Foundation: 1-(800) 525-5885.

inventions

INVENTORS' DIGEST. America's only Inventors' Magazine. $22/year. Satisfaction guaranteed. 1-(800) 838-8808.

ENTREPRENEURS: We represent people who want to patent and market their new product ideas. For your free information kit, call The Concept Network: 1-(800) 835-2246, Extension 197.

INVENT SOMETHING? ESI Inc. links unconnected individuals with decision-makers. Free brochure supplies help. 1-(800) 547-7885.

WORK DIRECTLY WITH REGISTERED PATENT Attorney/Graduate Engineer Michael Kroll. Patents, trademarks, copyrights. Thirty-three years engineering experience. Complimentary 148-page brochure. 1-(800) 367-7774.

FREE PATENT, DEVELOPMENT and marketing information, Richard Miller, Registered Patent Agent, 12 Parkside Drive, Suite E, Dix Hills, NY 11746-4879. 1-(516) 499-4343.

INVENTIONS AND IDEAS WANTED - MBA student seeks inventions/ideas for start-up company. I provide market analysis, business plan and financing. If interested in joint-venture or licensing of invention write to: Michael Lerner, 701 S.W. 62nd Blvd., I-53, Gainesville, FL 32607.

ELECTRONIC DESIGN SERVICE will turn your ideas into working reality. Analog, digital, electro-optical, data acquisition and packaging. Quick turn-around and competitive pricing. Opti-Sciences: (508) 851-5561.

INVENTORS: Best free self-help on developing ideas, patents, marketing. Call: 1-(800) 955-8888, Extension 860.

mailing lists

10-DAY HOTLINE. Freshest opportunity seekers. Immediate delivery. Mixed states. 250/$24; 500/$29; 1,000/$45. Free dealership information. Mascor Lists, Box 8308, Silver Spring, MD 20907. Visa/MC: 1-(800) 568-6127.

BUSINESS/CONSUMER LISTS! FRESH, responsive names. Select from 14,000,000 businesses, professionals, 100,000,000 consumers. Choose locally, nationally. Specialty lists, phones, computer disks available. Visa/MC/Amex. AccuData: 1-(800) 732-0463.

AMERICA'S BEST MLM/opportunity seekers' names. On label or disk. Free sample! Call/write: 1-(800) 628-7060. Venture-LE, Box 20336, Bullhead City, AZ 86439.

75,000 NEW NAMES MONTHLY. Opportunity seekers/multi-level enthusiasts/mail order buyers. 200/$24; 500/$35; 1,000/$50; 2,000/$70. Immediate shipment. MJG Lists, Box 3009-EM, Maple Glen, PA 19002-8009. Visa/MC: 1-(800) 880-8143.

NEW HOT OPPORTUNITY SEEKERS' NAMES! First order tripled free. Adhesive labels. 100/$8.00; 200/$12; 500/$19; 1,000/$29; 2,000/$45; 5,000/$89; 10,000/$159. Success Lists, P.O. Box 4106-E, Rocky Point, NY 11778. Visa/MC/COD. 1-(800) 382-6815.

FREE MAILING LISTS! Save thousands! Opportunity seekers and others. 10 sources for $25. E&S Enterprises, Box 1202, Mt. Pleasant, MI 48804.

HOTLINE OPPORTUNITY SEEKER names! Mailorder responsive! Adhesive labels. Send $1.00 plus SASE for details: Gilley's, P.O. Box 1471, Taylor, MI 48180.

FREE MAILING-LIST DEALERSHIP! Earn hundreds weekly. Free start-up kit. 1-(718) 645-4111.

marketing

PUT YOUR PRODUCT or 900# on nationwide TV. Millions of buyers. Turn key package. 1-(714) 752-0503.

classified

marketing

PROMOTE YOUR BUSINESS with The Business Card Alternative. For samples/ordering information, send $5.00 to: Legal Mark Graphics, 1403 Mosley, Dept. E, Irving, TX 75060.

WE PRINT AND MAIL your circulars or postcards. Free brochure. 1-(617) 683-0199, 24 hours.

VIDEO POWER INCREASES SALES! Producer, 15 years' Madison Avenue experience, will customize professional video for your company. (212) 228-4783.

AUDIO AND VIDEO DUPLICATION for education and seminar leaders. Baker Productions: 1-(800) 739-0388.

FREE LOCAL TELEVISION TIME - How to get it to promote your business. Free information. 312 Buena Vista, Santa Cruz, CA 95062.

FREE NATIONWIDE RADIO ADS. Per-inquiry broker seeks products. (209) 226-8559. 9AM - 2PM Pacific.

NATIONAL TELEVISION MARKETING - Sell your product or service on TV. Affordable, reputable, turn-key company. We offer several options. (800) 569-7326.

merchandise

CONTACT LENSES - All brands. Disposables $17. Huge savings. Information: (800) 521-3511.

moneymaking opportunities

PROVEN ROULETTE METHOD. 99.5% win factor. P.O. Box 26861, Austin, TX 78755. Call: 1-(512) 266-3112.

$1,500 WEEKLY MAILING OUR CIRCULARS! Begin now. Free packet! Mesa-M2, Box 4000, Cordova, TN 38018-4000.

FREE 900#'s - We're giving them away! Call for information: (914) 573-2067.

ACHIEVE FINANCIAL SUCCESS! Easy profitable business. $9.95 to: JG Associates, P.O. Box 86, Colts Neck, NJ 07722.

COIN TELEPHONES for business and vendors. Wholesale prices. For free information: 1-(800) 231-7539.

$4,000 WEEKLY with your telephone answering machine! Just pop in our free tapes! Never talk to anyone. Free packet. Mesa-DFM2, Box 4000, Cordova, TN 38018-4000.

HOME COMPUTER MONEY. 50+ ways to kiss the grind good bye. Only $1.00! Digatek, Suite 110, 2723 West Butler Drive, Phoenix, AZ 85051.

SERVICE COPIERS, fax, printers! Complete professional manual troubleshoots problems and illustrates repairs. Earn over $50/hour in growing market. Send $12.50 to: Martec, P.O. Box 654, Shasta Lake, CA 96019.

$2,500+ WEEKENDS scheduling flea markets from home! Rush $3.00: Ruffolo, East Coast Flea Markets, Box 147-E, Little Falls, NJ 07424.

AMAZING CASSETTE - How To Become a Millionaire in the 1990's. Send $9.95 + $2.00 S&H to: KMSABD, P.O. Box 2662, Orlando, FL 32802.

PROMOTE YOURSELF TO BOSS! Discover financial freedom! Proven quick, easy secrets for successful self-employment. $8.99, SASE: A. Garde, P.O. Box 181848, Casselberry, FL 32718-1848.

SLOT MACHINES: Win $80 hourly! Free details. Selex, Box 1578E, Rohnert Park, CA 94927.

TRUTH IN MONEY-MAKING! Amazingly candid manual, $3.00. Bonus: Three free commission dealerships. Mathews, Box 270750-ME1, Fort Collins, CO 80527-0750.

moneymaking opportunities

GOVERNMENT SEIZED cars, trucks, boats, computers, televisions. Surplus bargains galore! Your area. 1-(800) 601-2212, Extension SP7270.

$2K-5K/MONTH for 2 hours work per week. Are we nuts? You decide. Call: (602) 998-6008.

35-MONEYMAKING OPPORTUNITIES with reprint rights. $15 + $3.00 S/H: Heartland, Box 985, Windsor, CA 95492.

MLMers. Exciting new concept now forming. We help build your downline. Free pamphlet. 1-(800) 707-1579.

$500 WEEKLY AT HOME! Be a signwriter! Easy, inexpensive. Free details. Signs, Highlands P.O. Box 51025, Edmonton, Alberta, Canada T5W 5G3.

CASH IN BIG with the work at home explosion. Learn 250 realistic ways. Free details. M. Ebel Distributor, Box 1581E, Miller Place, NY 11764-8360.

BEGINNING MAILORDER? Over 1,000% profit, sell starting reports, series, reproduction rights. Free details. W.L.M. Marketing, 12104 Hillcrest Drive, Yelm, WA 98597. (206) 458-5799.

AMAZING PROFITS. With "Sand Art." Truly a gold mine. $1,500 one day sale, nets $1,250 profit. R.M. Sand Art Supply Center has the latest, from neon color sand to stretched bottles, teddy bears, and Sand Art Ice Cream Sundaes. Not a franchise. For catalog and expert guidance send $5.00, refundable with first order to: Rainbow Magic Co., 3265 "S" Street N.W., Washington, DC 20007.

CREME AWAY INCHES with TNT and eat cake and make dough. 1-(800) 394-0799. Preferred customer reference MC110089.

INCREASE YOUR INCOME, wipe out debt! Expert reveals secrets. Free details. Delta, 4195 Chino Parkway, #520A, Chino, CA 91709.

HOW TO MAKE $500 A DAY in your spare time! Free details and gift! (818) 821-4192.

CRAPS SYSTEM. 1,000-hour trail reveals $95 average hourly profit. Distributors needed. $20. H.D.I., Box 2367, Liverpool, NY 13089.

USED GRITTY CRITTER CART plus inventory. Bargain! Excellent opportunity! (609) 232-4569.

A MONEY MACHINE - Exciting new way to market the hottest products of the year. This will revolutionize the music and entertainment industry and create the rich and powerful of the 90's. It is easy and fun if you work hard. No up-front fees, our dealers take home huge sums of money. You won't believe it! We need distributors with a direct-to-the-home sales background who have guts, drive and determination. Territories are going fast. Call the President of Entertainment Industries, Inc.: (203) 878-9496.

FREE INSTRUCTION BOOKLET on how to make money 90-97% of the time in casinos playing blackjack and roulette. Send $3.00 for S&H to: Larj, Inc., 171 Rink Street, Unit 34, Peterborough, Ontario, Canada K9J 2J6.

professional services

TERMPAPER ASSISTANCE. 19,278 papers available! 272-page catalog, rush $2.00. Research, 11322 Idaho, #206ET, Los Angeles, CA 90025. Toll-free hotline: 1-(800) 351-0222 or 1-(310) 477-8226.

PROFESSIONAL ASSISTANCE locating venture capital sources, preparation of executive summaries and business plans. Additional services available. 1-(203) 261-2890.

telemarketing

TELECOMPUTERS WHOLESALE! $395+. New, used. Free NTN membership! 1-(916) 878-8800.

telemarketing

EARN MONEY running your autodialer! We buy & sell, leads & telecomputers. 1-(916) 395-7336.

tapes/videos

START-UP BUSINESS VIDEOS. Start off right with business plan, preparation tips and other how-to information. Many to choose from. Stepping Stone Productions: (703) 680-1663.

of interest to all

HOW TO GET FREE one hour of long distance calling a month and still save 10 - 30 percent on long distance charges. For details send $5.00 for shipping/handling: B.N.C., P.O. Box 8881, Green Bay, WI 54308-8881.

unusual items

VIDEO CLOSEOUTS! Exciting sampler $19.95; photolog $2.00: E.H.I., Box 2011-V, Chicago, IL 60690-2011.

venture capital

VENTURE CAPITAL COMPANY is seeking new projects. Call: 1-(619) 451-1001.

SELF-LIQUIDATING LOANS, offshore financing, grants, venture capital, factoring. 1-(602) 979-9177.

VENTURE CAPITAL SOURCES! P.O. Box 1361, Rancho Mirage, CA 92270. 1-(619) 324-0410.

classified order form

rates: $8.65 per word for one issue. $7.95 per word, per issue, for three or more issues. Minimum ad 10 words. All classified ads must be prepaid with order. Make checks payable to *Entrepreneur Magazine*.

circulation: *Entrepreneur Magazine's* average paid circulation is 385,000. Total readership exceeds 2.3 million per issue.

issuance & closing date: *Entrepreneur* is published monthly. The next available issue is August which closes, Wednesday, May 25th.

To place your classified ad, just complete the coupon below and mail it with your copy and payment to the Florida address shown below.

Please insert my ad _____ times, beginning with the August issue. Place my ad under the heading _____.

Enclosed is my check for $ _____.

Name _____

Address _____

City _____

State _____ Zip _____

Telephone No. _____

Mail to:

Entrepreneur.

Classified Department
P.O. Box 570, Clearwater, FL 34617
800-762-3555 • Fax: 813-442-2567

CLASSIFIED/READING NOTICES

READING NOTICES: Ad prices are calculated on a per word per issue basis. All contracts must be prepaid at the time of insertion. $4.60 per word for 1 issue (15 word minimum), $3.60 per word for 3, $2.90 per word for 6 or $2.50 per word for 12 consecutive issues. Street and number, city, state and zip code count as 4 words. Area code and phone number count as 2 words.

 PAYMENT BY Visa/Mastercard accepted with advertising orders of three or more consecutives issues.

A sample of any product and/or literature you plan to send must accompany your order. Literary Services and Editing/Revising advertisers must send a resume and a sample critique. Send ad with check or money order to: Joan Bambeck, WRITER'S DIGEST, 1507 Dana Avenue, Cincinnati, Ohio 45207. For additional information call 800/234-0963 or 513/531-2222. Fax: 513/531-1843. Closing date for the September 1994 issue is June 28, 1994.

BOOKS/PAMPHLETS

Book Sale! Write To Sell, $13.00 postpaid. Checks payable: Ruth Wucherer, 3370A S. 12th St., Milwaukee, WI 53215.

STUDIOS, PRODUCERS, DISTRIBUTORS, A-GENTS. Current addresses, phones, staff. Free brochure: Hollywood Creative Directory, 3000 Olympic, Santa Monica, CA 90404. 310/315-4815.

SECRETS OF MAKING BIG MONEY as freelance corporate writer. Free Information. W. Poole, PO Box 521694, Longwood, FL 32752.

WRITE CHILDREN'S BOOKS in spare time. Award winner SusanBeth Pfeffer shows how. $15.95 pstpd: Mine Brook Press, Dept. W, PO Box 517, New Hampton, NY 10958.

NEW WRITER'S MAGAZINE. Guidelines SASE. Sample $3.00. Subscriptions $14 year, $25 two. PO Box 5976, Sarasota, FL 34277.

END WRITER'S BLOCK! Use Source Cards to spark settings, characters, even plot ideas. Send $5 for 50 card sampler to Creative Spark, 3527 Oaklawn, Suite 667, Dallas, TX 75219.

THE WRITER'S EDGE, 8 pg. monthly newsletter, inspires creative excellence. $24.00, 12 issues (365 exercises, plus). Seasons Publications, PO Box 41, Round Rock, TX 78680-0041.

ABUNDANCE & PROSPERITY can be yours! Positive Penury News, bimonthly newsletter. Sample $2 or $18.95 (12 issues). Valerie Kennan, 115 West California #178, Pasadena, CA 91105.

TAP INTO YOUR CHILDHOOD! Ten surprising techniques to improve your writing. $6 (Check/M.O.) to SES, 173 Speedwell Ave. #127, Morristown, NJ 07960.

SHORT STORY WRITERS: Find out how to complete all your short stories with the SHORT STORY BLUEPRINT--an exclusive, six-step "workshop on paper" reprinted from WRITER'S DIGEST. Just $3. Send check or money order to Short Story Blueprint, 1507 Dana Ave., Cincinnati, OH 45207.

EXPERT WRITING INSTRUCTION from some of the world's leading writers, editors, and publishers. Writer's Digest Books will help you hone your writing skills as well as attain valuable marketing savvy -- no matter what your writing interests. For a FREE books catalog write to: Writer's Digest Books, Customer Service Dept., 1507 Dana Avenue, Cincinnati, OH 45207.

Interested in forming a writer's club in the U.S. or Canada? Learn how to find other writers, how to plan productive and stimulating meetings and how to get special discounts on books, etc. for the members. To receive your booklet "How To Start/Run A Writer's Club," send $1.00 to Lisa Turner, Writer's Digest Books, 1507 Dana Ave., Cincinnati, OH 45207.

Find out where the jobs and opportunites for writers are-with a newly revised booklet from Writer's Digest. **Jobs and Opportunities for Writers** lists the best markets for freelancers and part-time writers. You'll also learn how to break into these markets and what you can expect to be paid. Send check or money order for $3.95 to Writer's Digest, Dept. J0W 1507 Dana Avenue, Cincinnati, OH 45207. Ohio residents add 5.5% sales tax; outside U.S. send $4.95.

It's a damn good story. If you have any comments, write them on the back of a check.
-Erle Stanley Gardner, writing to an editor.

BUSINESS OPPORTUNITIES

MILLIONAIRE MAILORDER EXPERT reveals money-making secrets! FREE exciting hour cassette. Melvin Powers, 12015 Sherman Rd., Suite #7, No. Hollywood, CA 91605-3781.

GET PAID FOR READING BOOKS! $100 per book. Send name, address to Calco Publishing (Dept. C-552), 500 South Broad, Meriden, CT 06450.

Home Import Mail Order Business. Start without capital. Free Report. Mellinger, Dept. C2299, Woodland Hills, CA 91367.

AUTOGRAPHS, banners, political pins, leathers, baseball cards, sports memorabilia wanted. Highest prices paid. Stan Block, 128 Cynthia Rd., Newton MA 02159.

NO REJECTION SLIPS! Make homemade booklets. Mine have earned $645,057. Money never stops. FREE information. Booklets, 507F Oak Drive, Friendswood, TX 77546.

MAKE $85,000 A YEAR writing ads, brochures, promotional materials for local/national clients. Free details: Bob Bly, 174 Holland Ave., Dept. WDC, New Milford, NJ 07646.

$80,000 a year! Make big bucks now. Freelance for business & industries. Easy. Fun. Professional business writer shows how. $6.95: Brigada, 11365 Avant Lane, Dept. SE, Cincinnati, OH 45249.

MAKE MONEY WRITING GREETING CARDS. Send three $.29 stamps: GREETINGS, Box 521-W, Cleveland, OH 44107.

BECOME A PUBLISHED AUTHOR! Sell your book to major NY publishers. Free information: CTC, 22 E. Quackenbush, Dumont, NJ 07628.

FREELANCE READERS NEEDED! $30,000/Year Income Potential. Details: 619-491-1541 Ext. 77 24 Hrs.

CASH WITH YOUR CAMERA. Sell photographs fifteen or more times. Guaranteed details: SASE. PictureProfits , Box 102, WD794, Middle Island, NY 11953-0102.

FREE LITERATURE! Hundreds of money-making ideas for the nineties: JSA Publications, Box 919, North Arlington, NJ 07031.

FREELANCERS! Can your writing move people to action? There's big money in mail order! We supply catalogs, over 3500 products, full support. You supply talent & ambition--the profits are yours! FREE info. SMC, 9401 DeSoto Ave., Dept. 501-66, Chatsworth, CA 91311.

TURN WORDS INTO PROFIT. Easy. Honest. Effective. FREE information: New Leaf, 21 Union Street, Natick, Massachusetts 01760.

OPPORTUNITY KNOCKS! Enjoyable. Highly Profitable. No Investment. FREE information booklet: HMG, P.O. Box 254, Framingham, Massachusetts 01701.

RESIDUAL INCOME. Spare time profits add up quickly. Help save friends money, work from home. SASE: Lamar Self, P.O. Box 1257, Ft. Pierce, FL 34954-1257.

FORGET COMMUTING AND BOSSES! Profitable Home-Based Employment. FREE Details. LSASE: Pacific Rim, Dept. H, 30815 Overfall Dr., Westlake, CA 91362-4117.

CLASSIFIED/READING NOTICES

NICE SINGLES with Christian values wish to meet others. FREE Magazine. Send age, interests. Singles, Box 310-WD, Allardt, TN 38504.

BRITISH PENPALS ! Selections based on your interests, age, etc. Satisfaction Guaranteed! Free Details: Transatlantic Penfriends, Box 2176-WD, San Pedro, CA 90731.

BEAUTIFUL BRITISH LADIES & ELIGIBLE BRITISH GENTLEMEN seek friendship/romance with American ladies & gentlemen! All ages! Free details: English Rose Introduction Agency, (Dept W/D), Suite 2, 24 Cecil Square, Margate, Kent, England. Tel/Fax: 01144-843-290735.

THE WISHING WELL - 20TH ANNIVERSARY! - beautiful way for women loving women to meet. Confidential. Sample U.S. $5.00 (mailed discreetly). FREE information: PO Box 713090, Santee, CA 92072-3090. (619) 443-4818.

RUSSIA, SCANDINAVIA, FRANCE, USA, etc.: Professionals worldwide seek friendship, lasting relationships. Scanna, POB 4, W. Pittsford, NY 14534. 1-800-677-3170.

THE LETTER WRITER'S CLUB. Intriguing! Your protected correspondence creates/selects (rewarding) friendships! SASE: LWC, PO Box 770862, Woodside, NY 11377-0862.

RUSSIAN WOMEN DESIRE ROMANCE! Overseas, eager, sincere, and faithful! FREE 500 photo catalogue. Club Prima, 13164 Memorial Drive #240EL; Houston, TX 77079-7225 (713)973-1515 anytime.

RUSSIAN LADIES. Charming, Faithful, Educated. Sincerely seeking love and commitment with American men of all ages. Free Catalog. Anastasia, P.O. Box 906, Winchester, KY 40392-0906. 606-745-0776.

RUSSIAN LADIES, truly beautiful, educated, seek relationships. Free color photobrochure! Russia 179; P.O.B. 888851; Atlanta, GA 30356. (404) 458-0909.

ARTISTIC CONNECTIONS - linking single lovers of the arts across the nation. Write: WP, Box 116, Chatham, NJ 07928.

RUSSIA - ROMANIA - SCANDINAVIA - BRITAIN S. America, Etc. Single, professional men, women worldwide seek correspondence for friendship or romance. Scanna Int'l. POB 4-WD, Pittsford, NY 14534. (1-800-677-3170).

Writing is like walking in a deserted street. Out of the dust in the street you make a mud pie.
-John Le Carre

POETRY

* An asterisk denotes poetry competitions that may require the purchase of an anthology to ensure contest eligibility and/or publication of non-winning entries.

FEELINGS POETRY MAGAZINE PUBLISHES POEMS! Payment possible. Copy $5.50. SASE/Guidelines. P.O. Box 85, Easton, PA 18044-0085.

500 POEMS WANTED. International anthology. Unpublished writers welcome. No charges. Send poems. Editor, Box 3491, Knoxville, TN 37927.

STERLING HOUSE PUBLISHER (formerly Guyasuta) seeks poetry manuscripts. Send SASE for free brochure. 440 Friday Road, Pittsburgh, PA 15209. 412/821-6211.

YOUR ORIGINAL POETRY: Chapbooks, Frameable Prints. Monthly contest. SASE. Matt Hues, 4120-2 Frank, Tucson, AZ 85746.

HAIKU WRITERS' CLUB by mail/newsletter. Info - $2/SASE: HFB, PO Box 1026, Pendleton, OR 97801.

THE 23rd ANNUAL non-profit Mississippi Valley Poetry Contest is now open to poets of all ages everywhere, and with big cash prizes to winners. For rules, send self-addressed stamped envelope to Mississippi Valley Poetry Contest, PO Box 3188, Rock Island, IL 61204. Deadline: September 7, 1994.

PRINTING/TYPESETTING

POETRY CHAPBOOKS PUBLISHED. We specialize in printing highest quality Chapbooks. Surprisingly low prices. Details: Poetry Center Press, 3 Montevista Rd., Orinda, CA 94563.

PROFESSIONAL BOOK DESIGN & TYPESETTING Camera ready copy and free proof copy. Sonlight Press, P.O. Box 308, Presque Isle, ME 04769. 207/764-3470.

RESEARCH

FRUSTRATED? Let Research Etc. help. Historical/Political research; critique service fiction/nonfiction. SASE for references; rates. P.O. Box 133, Princeton, LA 71067-0133.

ALL SUBJECTS APA by experienced PhD. Comprehensive, Prompt, Confidential, Reasonable. 1-800-472-9994 Davie, FL. 24 hrs.

SCRIPTWRITING

Join FORUM - Screenwrite NOW! Send $.29 stamp for membership information or $4.00 for 60 page sample magazine to FORUM, PO Box 7WD, Baldwin, MD 21013.

SCREENWRITERS! Inside tips, MARKETS, advice from top agents, TV/movie writers, producers. Monthly. HOLLYWOOD SCRIPTWRITER, 1626 N. Wilcox, #385W, Hollywood, CA 90028. Sample $1.

Nationally known movie critic Susan Granger evaluates your screenplay's commercial potential, coaches your screen-writing. SASE Free information: 124 Cross Highway, Westport, CT 06880.

HOLLYWOOD SCRIPT DOCTOR 20 yrs. TV/Feature Film experience. Detailed analyses, specific development notes. Consultations on format, editing, inner workings of Entertainment Industry. 503/488-0491.

Introducing CREATIVE SCREENWRITING, the screenwriter's professional journal. Feature articles on Creative Approaches by Top TV/Movie screenwriters. LA/NY Markets. Software/Book Reviews. Send SASE/Free Details: 518 Ninth Street, NE, Suite 308D, Washington, DC 20002.

SCRIPTS - Thousands, Movie and Television. Learn what sells and WHY. Book City, 308 N. San Fernando Blvd., Dept. WD, Burbank, CA 91502. Catalog $2.50.

SELL YOUR SCREENPLAY WITHOUT AN AGENT! Insider Secrets - Contacts! Newsletter: HOLLYWOOD FILM MARKETPLACE, 20929-47 Ventura Boulevard, Suite 123N, Woodland Hills, CA 91364. Sample $1.

SCRIPT JUDGE offering critiques. Structure, dialogue and character analysis. SASE: Scripts, Suite 134wd, 662 Franklin Ave., Garden City, NY 11530.

SCREENPLAY CRITIQUES: Detailed analysis, constructive guidance by award-winning writer: Tracy Marks. 95 Bow St., Arlington, Mass. 02174. (617) 641-3371.

"THE SCREENWRITER'S RESOURCE GUIDE", a complete, informative directory of people, products, services involved in every area of screenwriting and related film endeavor. $8.95 + $2.75 S&H: SunWest Media, 4 S. San Francisco St. #221-WD, Flagstaff, AZ 86001.

SELL YOUR SCREENPLAYS. Over 300 Motion Picture Companies. 1994 addresses, phone #'s, & contacts. $7.50 to K. Foley, Box 32, Port Costa, CA 94569.

SELF-PUBLISHING

PUBLISH ANY BOOK! Reasonable, professionally attractive product. Newsletter, brochure, authors' accolades: PPC Books, Dept. WC794, 25 Sylvan Road South, Westport, CT 06880.

Full Service Book Production. 100 copies-$104.60. SASE to: CAL POB 298 WD, Thomaston, ME 04861 207/832-6665.

COSTS ARE LOW IN IDAHO! Editorial, design, production, distribution. Griffith Publishing: 800 359-9503. 3775 South Montana, Caldwell, Idaho 83605.

SUNSHINE PRESS PUBLICATIONS help writers publish quality books that sell. 6 Gardner Court, Longmont, CO 80501. (303)772-3556.

A SIMPLE GUIDE TO SELF-PUBLISHING. SASE or $7.20: Wise Owl Books, Box 621, Kirkland, WA 98083. 800/352-6657.

I type in one place, but I write all over the house.
-Toni Morrison

SONGWRITING

Note from WRITER'S DIGEST: Songwriting can be a rewarding experience, even though most songwriters don't sell enough songs to recoup their investment in subsidy song services. The fun and creative satisfaction of a professional song recording can easily be worth the cost.

FREE SONGWRITING SUCCESS BOOK! Complete professional songwriting help. Top Records, Box 23505-W, Nashville, TN 37202.

Award Winning Songwriter Co-Writing On Accepted Material, Send Best Lyrics Ramsey Kearney 602 Inverness Ave., Nashville, TN 37204

FREE SONGWRITING infopak! Write to : Platinum Studios, 6689 Orchard Lake Road, Suite 282, West Bloomfield, MI 48322.

ESTABLISHED NASHVILLE PUBLISHER looking for hit song material to present to recording artists. Guaranteed protection on material. Publisher, 400 Montigo Cove, Hermitage, TN 37076.

YOUR OWN SONG! Write just the words or words/music, we do the rest. Professional studio musicians. CD quality recording. Any style. $95-$150. Sample Available. Nashville Digital Demos: 1-800-484-8581 code #3631.

STATIONERY/SUPPLIES

WRITER'S HOME OFFICE SUPPLY CATALOG. Free Info/SASE. Transatlantic Arts, P.O. Box 6086-WD, Albuquerque, NM 87197. 505/898-2289.

SUBSIDY PUBLISHING

DO YOU HAVE A BOOK to publish? Contact established co-operative publisher with offices in USA, England and Scotland. Call 1-800-948-2786.

FAIRWAY PRESS - we care about your book (and its author). For free details and sample contracts, contact Niki C. Dunham, Fairway Press, 628 S. Main, Lima, OH 45804. (419)229-BOOK.

WRITERS WANTED

$25 PER SLOGAN- ORIGINAL, PROVOCATIVE, IRREVERENT, OUTRAGEOUSLY FUNNY BUTTONS (SASE) Ephemera, P.O. Box 490, Phoenix, Oregon 97535.

TRAVEL WRITERS WANTED by travel photographer with travel industry connections. Free travel/cruises. Jeff: 201-773-7966

COMIC WANTS JOKES. I'll send premise. SASE for guide! Steve DeLuca, 145 E. 15th St., 6M, New York, NY 10003.

SHORT STORY HORROR. Mail mss., SASE, Editor, Box 107, Newalla, OK 74857-8107. Pays Publication. (405) 386-4097.

SINGLE PARENTING ARTICLES. New pub. SASE guidelines. Hague Clinton Inc., P.O. Box 174, Cranford, NJ 07016.

CLASSIFIED ADVERTISEMENTS

Dorothy Nolan, Classified Manager

Rates: $11.65 per word. 10 word minimum.

Bold Face Type—$1.00 extra per word. (First word automatically set in Bold Face Type). Gray Background—Additional $54.00 per advertisement. Centered Headlines (5 words or less)—$60.00 per line. Our **NOVEMBER** issue closes on **SEPTEMBER 5TH**. (On sale date is **OCTOBER 15TH**). All advertising is payable in advance by check, money order or credit card. Advertisers wishing to charge their MasterCard, American Express or Visa accounts, please be sure to include number and expiration date. Send order and remittance payable to: Popular Mechanics, Classified Advertising, 224 West 57th Street, New York, NY 10019. Be sure to indicate classification under which advertisement is to appear. For additional advertising information call **1-212-649-3167** or FAX: **1-212-977-5415/1-212-586-5562**.

Advertisers using a P.O. Box number must furnish complete name and street address for our records. To avoid delay in the publication of your advertisement, please send samples and descriptive materials with your request if your advertisement does not state clearly what is being offered.

YES!!! We can take your order over the phone. For speedy placement of your advertisement contact Dorothy at 1-212-649-3167. Please have credit card information handy. Thank you.

PUBLISHER'S MART BOOKS & PUBLICATIONS

GAMBLING'S greatest moneymaking secret! Scientifically proved. Write Trailblazer, Box 7521, Dallas, TX 75209

HOME SECURITY The homeowner's security book! Comprehensive, how-to format. Learn to protect yourself. Only $19.97. Write: Dunn Loring Publishers, Box 143, Dunn Loring, VA 22027

OUTLAWS Sourcebook of forbidden devices/knowledge. Write: #365-X9, Penfield, NY 14526-0365

"ANARCHIST COOKBOOK" Available again! $25, delivered. Barricade Books, Box 1401-X, Secaucus, NJ 07096

"SHARPENERS REPORT" Monthly Newsletter. Valuable Tips—Sources—Buy/Sell Used Equipment. Free Brochure. Skog Company, Dept. PM9, P.O. Box 22187, Minneapolis, MN 55422

FREE BOOKLETS: Life, Death, Soul, Resurrection, Pollution Crisis, Hell, Judgment Day, Restitution. Bible Standard(PM), P.O. Box 67, Chester Springs, PA 19425.

MAKE More Money. Start Your Own Business Achieve Success. Smartcon, 6036 West Lawrence, Chicago, Illinois 60630

IMPROVE Your Writing Skills! Free Information: J. Blair, 148 Fenelon Drive, Don Mills, Ontario M3A 3K9 Canada.

DISCOVER THE INTERNET! Make International Contacts, Communicate By E-Mail, Download Public Software; Learn Popular Commands, Lots More. Send $6.95 For Guide. Rolmer Enterprises, Box 3548, Everett, WA 98203

"HOW TO PURCHASE YOUR FIRST PC" Informative Report. $5.95. Compu-Learn, Dept. 169, 7365 Main Street, Stratford, CT 06497

YOU CAN FIX Your **MICROWAVE OVEN!** Plus, VCR Know-How. Instructional Videotapes. **FREE** Brochure. Call/FAX 1-800-700-UFIX

TAKE THE PAIN OUT OF MATH. Best Self-Taught Math Text On The Market. $25.00 Includes P & H. Wyn-Jac Enterprises, 60 Canadice St., Shortsville, NY 14548

INFORMATION Letter - A guideline for those hard to find answers. $10.00. Dew Enterprizes, P.O. Box 4086, Fort Polk, LA 71459-1086

HOW-TO, Craft, Money Making Books. List $2.00. Publishing, 7174 Hoffman Rd., San Angelo, Texas 76905

PREVENT - Cure Colds Naturally $10. "E.Z." Publishing, Box 2132, Imperial Beach, CA 91932

PLANTS Poisonous To Pets Listing. Authoritative, Updated. $4.00 To: PETS, Rollins Publications, 2615 Waugh, Suite 244, Houston, TX 77006

CELLULAR: DOS disk full of sizzling info on reprogramming ESN/NAM on popular phones + theory, roaming, tumbling, part sources, etc. $15 cash, check, moneyorder. Zippy Computers, 2060 Emergy Ave. #202, LaHabra, CA 90631.

PROTECT YOUR FAMILY with Living Will and Will Planning Kits. $12.50 each/both $20.00. Gateway Marketing, P.O. Box 924, Travelers Rest, SC 29690.

FRANCHISES

OIL BUTLER INTERNATIONAL - Mobile on-site oil change franchise, total package under $6500.00, repeat customers, operate from home. 1599 Route 22W, Union, NJ 07083. (908) 687-3283.

CATALOGS

"SMALL ENGINE PARTS" catalog $1. Smith's, 513W Spring, Weatherford, TX 76086

73,560 Catalogs Listed, Described. Unlimited Sources! $7.95. Catalogs, Box 92452 N. Atlanta, Georgia 30314

"B"-WESTERNS & Serials On VHS! Rare! Not Available In Stores. Send S.A.S.E. For List. The Serial Fanatic, P.O. Box 173-PM, Boyertown, PA 19512

INTERESTED IN CLASSIFIED ADVERTISING?
READ POPULAR MECHANICS Latest Edition of **"TIPS ON HOW TO MAKE MONEY THROUGH CLASSIFIED ADVERTISING"**. This Informative 24-Page Booklet Will Show You The Do's And Don'ts of Classified Advertising And How You Can Make It Work For You. So Order Today. Only $1.00 Plus You'll Receive A $2.00 Coupon Refundable With Your First Order. Send To: **POPULAR MECHANICS CLASSIFIED, Dept. SG, 250 W. 55th Street, New York, NY 10019**

AUTOMOBILES

$225 DAILY "CHROME PLATING" Auto Parts, Motorcycles, inexpensive, easy. (Free) information. Chrome Finish, Box 2285, Waldorf, Maryland 20604

GOVERNMENT SEIZED Vehicles from $100. Fords. Mercedes. Corvettes. Chevys. Surplus. Buyers Guide. (1) 805-962-8000 Ext. S-20024.

VAPOR CARBURETOR TRIPLES MPG. Free information. H&A, R2E35P Bowling Green, MO 63334-9350

DRUG RAID SEIZURES: Buy Dirt Cheap! Cars, Trucks, Boats, Computers. Seizures, Box 51488-AT, Ontario, CA 91761

VEHICLES Under $200! Cars Auctioned By IRS, DEA, FBI Nationwide. Trucks, Boats, Motorhomes, Computers, And More! Call Toll Free! 1 (800) 436-6867 Ext. A-1922

TIRED of peeling bumper stickers? Express yourself without diminishing your cars' appearance. **STICKER STRUTTERS BUMPER STICKER HOLDER.** Durable, transparent, 12" long, clips to straight edge up to 3/8" thick. Can be easily moved or sticker changed. $9.95. CoonVentions, P.O. Box 2126, Alachua, Florida 32615-2126

"HOW TO BUY YOUR NEXT CAR" - Learn what the Pro's Know - Free Information, 12700 Hillcrest LB43, Dallas, Texas 75230. (214) 490-3356

ULTRA-SHIELD CAR POLISH with Teflon and Silicone Polymers. Free Information: Fichter Enterprise, 310 Brice, Hudson, IA 50643-2020

SECRETS TO AN IMMACULATE CAR!! Professional Detailer Tells All!!! Learn How To Get That Ultimate Stop And Stare Shine!! Just Send $6.00 To: Daryl Kreider, 897 Kreps Road, Lancaster, PA 17603.

AUTO SUPPLIES & EQUIPMENT

ALTERNATOR Generator Rebuilding Book. Details: HV Technologies, 7505 Barkentine, Las Vegas, NV 89128

MAKE Super Tire Cleaner For Pennies - $2.00. Recipe, Box 561, Social Circle, GA 30279

TRUCKS, PARTS & SUPPLIES

DUMP KITS AND COMPONENTS. Convert Your Pick-up/Flatbed Into A Dump Truck. No Welding Required. Reds Equipment, P.O. Box 555, Henrietta, Texas 76365, (817) 538-5601

GO-KARTS, MOTORCYCLES, & MOTORSCOOTERS

GO KARTS, Minibikes & ATV's. Assembled, Kits, Parts, Engines. Discount Prices, Large Selection. 88 Page Catalog $3.00. 216-357-5569. Kart World, Dept. C., 1488 Mentor Ave., Painesville, Ohio 44077

GO-KARTS All you'll need to know. 200 pages. $10. KMI, Box 101, Wheaton, IL 60189

KARTS, Minibike Plans $5.00 Each. Karts, 1020 Delprado Blvd., Suite 33, Cape Coral, Florida 33990

CONVERTING BUSES TO MOTOR HOMES

FREE INFORMATION -- Bill Lowman, 306M Riverbay, Tampa, FL 33619. 813-621-5296.

AVIATION, HANG GLIDING

BUILD/FLY Your own **BACKPACK POWERED PARACHUTE** for fun/profit. Takes off from level ground unassisted. Safe, Simple, Inexpensive. Detailed book with sources Now only $19.95. EASYUP, 617-M Anderson, Talent, OR 97540

HOMEBUILT AIRCRAFT - ILLUSTRATED SOURCEBOOK: New Second Edition. 300+ pages. Photos, Drawings, Specs for Every type aircraft plus hardware, accessories, etc. $20.00 plus $4.50 S/H (U.S.) to: Aerocrafter, 940 Adams #G(9) Benicia, CA 94510

AIRBOATS, Hovercraft, Airdrives, Propellers, Hulls, Engines, Plans, Accessories. Catalog $5.00. Arrowprop, Box 610M, Meeker, OK 74856

BOOMERANGS... HIGH-TECH DESIGNS!! Incredible Returns. Amazing Fun. **FREE CATALOG.** BoomerangMan, 1806-1 N 3rd, Monroe, LA 71201-4222

HOVERCRAFT

HOVERCRAFT Five New Designs, 8 to 120 Hp. Plansets, Kits, Videos. Information, $8 (Refundable). SEVTEC, P.O. Box 846, Monroe, WA 98272

FASTEST, CHEAPEST, QUIET HOVERCRAFTS Catalog $2.00. Box 281M, Cordova, IL 61242

CB'S, RADIO & HAM EQUIPMENT

SECRET SCANNER FREQUENCIES! FEDERAL AGENCIES, SURVEILLANCE, POLICE, MORE! FREE CATALOG! CRB, BOX 56, COMMACK, NY 11725

(Continued on next page)

Popular Mechanics

224 West 57th Street, New York, N.Y. 10019
Classified Advertising Dept. (212) 649-3167

FAX: (212) 977-5415
(212) 586-5562

DEADLINE FOR ADS: Copy and payment must be received by the 5th day of the 2nd preceding month for the issue in which the ad is to appear. See Head of Classified Section.

HOW TO COUNT WORDS: Name and address must be included in counting the number of words in your ad. Each initial or number used counts as 1 word: J.J. Smith, 224 West 57th Street, New York, New York 10019: 9 WORDS. Zip codes are not counted. Phone #: 2 WORDS, Symbols used as keys are charged per word. City or state count as 1 word each: New Brunswick, New Jersey: 2 WORDS. Abbreviations such as C.O.D., F.O.B., R.P.M., U.S.A., P.O., 5×7, 16mm are counted as 1 word. (P.O. Box 392 counted as 3 words) Webster's International Unabridged Dictionary will be used as our authority for spelling, compound words, hyphenations, abbreviations, etc. Send remittance payable and order to Popular Mechanics, Classified Department, 224 West 57th Street, New York, New York 10019. Please indicate Heading under which ad is to appear.

$11.65 per word—10 Word Minimum
BOLD FACE CAPS—$1.00 Per word (First Word: No charge for Bold Face)
$60.00—B/F CENTERED HEADLINE (5 Words or Less)
$54.00—Screening

Remittance of $ _____ is enclosed to cover _____ insertion(s) in the _____ issue(s). _____ Classification

NO CHARGE FOR CAPS	2	3	4	5	6	7
8	9	10-$116.50	11-$128.15	12-$139.80	13-$151.45	14-$163.10
15-$174.75	16-$186.40	17-$198.05	18-$209.70	19-$221.35	20-$233.00	21-$244.65
22-$256.30	23-$267.95	24-$279.60	25-$291.25	26-$302.90	27-$314.55	28-$326.20
29-$337.85	30-$349.50	31-$361.15	32-$372.80	33-$384.45	34-$396.10	35-$407.75
36-$419.40	37-$431.05	38-$442.70	39-$454.35	40-$466.00	41-$477.65	42-$489.30
43-$500.95	44-$512.60	45-$524.25	46-$535.90	47-$547.55	48-$559.20	49-$570.85

YOUR NAME _____   PHONE: _____
(PLEASE PRINT)
FIRM (NAME IN AD) _____
YOUR ADDRESS _____
CITY _____ STATE _____ ZIP _____
DATE: _____ YOUR SIGNATURE _____
(PLEASE PRINT OR TYPE COPY • FOR ADDITIONAL WORDS ATTACH SEPARATE SHEET)

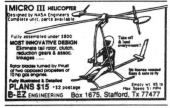

Classified Ads

Classified Rates And Information

To place a classified ad CALL TOLL FREE, 800-424-6746 (in Washington, DC call 463-5640) or write Nation's Business Classified, PO Box 1200, Washington, DC 20013. Closing date for advertising is five weeks preceding date of issue. Rates are based on frequency at a per line per insert cost as follows:

1x	3x	6x	12x	— frequency
$62	$55	$48	$34	— line rate
$870	$775	$675	$460	— per inch display

Ad minimums: solid set, 3 lines; display, 1 inch.

How To Reply To Box Numbers

Box (number in ad), Nation's Business Classified, PO Box 1200, Washington, DC 20013.

IF YOU NEED VIDEO TAPES DUPLICATED or FOREIGN TAPES CONVERTED, Call HIGH TECH PRODUCTIONS Toll Free 1-800-662-8336

SEIZED CARS, trucks, boats, 4wheelers, motorhomes, by FBI, IRS, DEA. Available your area now. Call (800) 436-4363 Ext. C-1389.

CORVETTES '53—'93...Over 100 in one location. Free catalog. Dealers Welcome! ProTeam, Box 606, Napolean, OH 43545. **419-592-5086** Fax: 419-592-4242. Corvettes Wanted.

STEEL BUILDINGS: From HERITAGE. delivered to your jobsite ready to bolt together. 5000 sizes, build it yourself and SAVE. Call with your builidng size. 1-800-643-5555. Heritage Building Systems, P.O. Box 470, N. Little Rock, AR 72115-0470.

Money Making Machine! Curbmate machine installs beautiful concrete lawn edging. Customers love this new product. Amazing profits from this simple cash business. 801-262-7509.

1-900# TELEPHONE Business Opportunities Earn up to $3500.00 per week, part time, from home. Minimal start-up fee. Call Now! 1-800-451-1383

HIGH PROFIT LIMO BUSINESS. Success Secrets Revealed! Start-up cost under $300. Work from home. No exp. or car necessary. Easy & simple. Free info. 800-954-2270 Dept. N.

SURPLUS BARGAINS GALORE!!! Government Siezed Cars, Trucks, Boats, Computers, TV's Your Area. 1-800-601-2212 Ext. SP6560.

Inc. 500 COMPANY Shows You How To Cash In Auditing Leases, Freight, Utility & Phone Bills For Overcharges, 4 Day Workshop, Airfare, 1 Year Support, more. $8900. FREE INFO 1-800-962-0177

LET THE GOVERNMENT FINANCE your small business. Grants/loans to $500,000. Free recorded message: 707-449-8600. (HS2)

MAIL ORDER INCOME! MONEY MAKING OPPORTUNITY. FREE DETAILS. PROCUREMENT, Box 163933-NB, Miami, FL 33116

DISTRIBUTORS NEEDED - BIG PROFITS. Miniature satellite antennas for Homes, RV's, Business. $1800 Refundable Deposit Required. 1-800-886-5008.

CAPITALIZE ON CRIME! Earn amazing profits on full line of crime prevention products that sell like crazy! Free wholesale catalog. 800-735-1797, POB 10154, #NB, Yakima, WA 98909.

MANUSCRIPTS WANTED, ALL TYPES Publisher with 70-year tradition. Free Examination, 'Guide to Publication'. Call toll free 1-800-695-9599

HOME IMPORT MAIL ORDER BUSINESS. Start without capital. FREE REPORT. Mellinger, Dept. C1553, Woodland Hills, California 91367

MAKE MONEY WITH FOREIGN INVESTORS. Top finder's fees paid. Dept. 194nb, THE GLOBAL EXCHANGE, 419 N. Newport Blvd., Ste. B, Newport Beach, CA 92663-4271. 714-722-9260.

FULL-TIME, PART-TIME, GREAT INCOME. MAIL ORDER, 22 OTHER PROGRAMS, 3500+ PRODUCTS FREE INFO: SMC, 9401 DESOTO AVENUE, DEPT. 825-61, CHATSWORTH, GA 91311

#1 MONEY MAKER Spare Time! No selling! No inventory! Publicly documented seven week $19,919 income! Free audio cassette and Report reveal everything. Real Money, 333-NB3 SW 5th Street, Grants Pass, OR 97526

INDONESIA—GREAT BRITAIN—NEW ZEALAND—MEXICO. Network marketing company opening internationally with herbal health drink. Your contact there can mean financial freedom for you. 1-800-828-4231.

Personalized Children's Books

COMPUTER BUSINESS SERVICES, INC. IS THE WORLD'S LARGEST RESOURCE FOR COMPUTER HOME BUSINESSES. CALL FOR FREE INFORMATION: 1-800-343-8014, EXT. 1164.

MAILORDER OPPORTUNITY! Start profitable home business in America's fastest growing industry. Nationally known authority will teach you. Write for free book, sample catalog, plus details. No obligation. Mail Order Associates, Dept. 70, Montvale, NJ 07645.

INCREASE SALES WITH 800 LINE AND CREDIT CARDS Our TeleRep™ 800 Sales Response Center answers 800 lines, sells products, stores/ships & then pays you via receipts from major credit cards. Call 800-638-2000, Canada call 800-678-4560. Over 20 years of successful selling for others!

THOUSANDS OF BUSINESSES 1994 Franchise Annual Directory describes 5,024 franchisors. Pros & cons. 374 new franchisors! 25th Anniversary Edition. 'When you buy a franchise, you buy risk-reduction.' $39.95 inclusive. Money Back Guarantee. INFO FRANCHISE NEWS, 728A Center St., Lewiston, NY 14092. VISA/MC. 716-754-4669.

WORKER'S COMP ALTERNATIVE

MID ATLANTIC CONSULTANTS, INC.

Introducing a Unique Alternative for Worker's Compensation for Large and Small Companies. Offices Coast to Coast.

Call for Free Information:
(214) 259-1022   FAX (214) 259-2214

LOWEST TELECONFERENCING RATE IN THE COUNTRY! JUST 5¢ Per Minute Per Port - Call Now & Reserve Your Next Teleconference Call. MLM'ers ONLY- EAGLE 212-758-3283

GET PAID NOW! The best kept secret for collecting past due accounts & bad checks. Call 1-800-569-4923 for a FREE RECORDED MESSAGE 24 Hours and FREE REPORT.

YOUR COMPANY LOGO IN BRASS Impressive wall logos of brass, chrome, or other cost effective finishes. Free estimates. METAL LOGOS, INC. 402-339-3264

SPORTS TICKETS

SUPER BOWL	FINAL 4
MASTERS	KY DERBY
500 RACE	WC SOCCER

PREFERRED TICKETS 800-925-2500

THE ECONOMIC & POLITICAL REVIEW-A bi-monthly news summary designed specifically for the busy executive. Send $3.00 for two copies to: the Economic & Political Review, P.O. Box 1189, Toms River, NJ 08754-1189.

BUSINESS PLANNING/APPRAISAL

Gain that competitive edge with true financial simulation/ valuation models: monthly, quarterly and 5-year annually.

Instant results with your Lotus 1-2-3, Quattro Pro, Excel (DOS/Windows and Macintosh).

$10,000 Value!	15,000+ sold.
Regularly $695.00	**Special $499.00**
Free Demo!	(Starter Kit: $299)

Call: (800) 777-4920; (714) 759-8987 FAX: (714) 720-1530 / 640-7233

ILAR SYSTEMS, INC.

331 Baywood Drive, Newport Beach, CA 92660, USA

Guaranteed Work! Excellent reliable income! Assemble easy products at home. Nation's most reputable program. For complete information call 1-800-377-6000 ext.6560.

$100,000+/year. Business Funding Consultants needed. Established network. Business/Medical accounts receivable, Commmercial Real Estate, Equipment Leasing. Huge finder's fees. Mr. Clark, Dept. NB, Two University Plaza, Suite 402, Hackensack, NJ 07601. 201-342-8500.

CARPET-VINYL-HARDWOOD-BRAIDED & CUSTOM RUGS-ORIENTALS. Mill-direct, Look No Further. Guar.Lowest Prices, Warranties. Free Quotes/samples 800-548-5815, Dalton, GA.

CARPET—Save up to 50% & more on major brands. We also manufacture our own beautiful styles. For information & samples, call 1-800-848-7747, Ext. 45. Dalton, Georgia.

WHO'S WHO IN WASHINGTON AND HOW TO REACH THEM

FEDERAL SOAPBOX

Powerful Lobbying Software

SOAPBOX SOFTWARE 1-800-989-7627

BECOME A HOME INSPECTOR APPROVED HOME STUDY. FREE Literature. P.C.D.I., Atlanta, Georgia. 800-362-7070, Dept. PA637.

33

BUMPER SNICKERS   BY BUNNY HOEST

"Options? Sure it's got options. Take it or leave it."

NATIONAL ENQUIRER

34

CLASSIFIED ORDER FORM

FROM THE EDITORS OF SUCCESS MAGAZINE

WORKING at HOME

☑ **CHECK ONE OF THE FOLLOWING**

☐ Please insert my ad in *both* the *WORKING at HOME winter issue* and the regular *January* issue of *Success Magazine* at the **special discounted rate** of $16.10 per word for regular classified or $1,095 per column inch for display, please include artwork. Enclosed is my check for $_____. For credit card orders, complete authorization below. My classified ad is to appear under the heading_____ .

☐ Please insert my ad in only the *WORKING at HOME winter issue* at the rate of $8.90 per word for regular classified or $595 per column inch, please include artwork. Enclosed is my check for $_____ . For credit card orders, complete authorization below. My classified ad is to appear under the heading _____.

☐ Please insert my ad in only the *January* issue of *Success Magazine* at the rate of $9.85 per word for regular classified or $675 per column inch, please include artwork. Enclosed is my check for $_____ . Credit card orders complete authorization below. My classified ad is to appear under the heading _____ .

CLASSIFIED HEADINGS

Advertising Services	Capital Available	Investments	Real Estate
Advisory Services	Computers/Hardware	Legal Services	Self Improvement
Agents Wanted	Computers/Software	Mailing Lists	Seminars
Books/Publications	Education/Instruction	Marketing	Tapes/Videos
Business Equipment	Employment Opportunities	Merchandise	Telemarketing
Business Financing	Financial Services	Miscellaneous	Toner Cartridges
Businesses For Sale	Franchises	Network Marketing	Travel
Business Opportunities	Internet	Printing	Venture Capital
Business Services	Inventions	Professional Services	

Name _____

Address _____

City_____ State _____ Zip _____

Telephone Number _____ Fax _____

Authorization for credit card orders (*Visa or MasterCard only*) complete the following:

Account Number _____ Expiration Date_____

Charge my account _____ to cover the payment of my classified ad below.

Signature_____

No advertising agency commission given on credit card orders.

COPY FOR REGULAR CLASSIFIED ADVERTISEMENT (Please type or print copy. 10-word minimum.)

_____

_____

_____

_____

_____

_____

_____

_____

WORKING at HOME, Classified Department, P.O. Box 570, Clearwater, Florida 33757-0570
Overnight Delivery: 1510 Barry Street, Suite D, Clearwater, Florida 33756
National 800-762-3555 • International 813-449-1775 • Fax 813-442-2567 • E-Mail RPIads@aol.com

WORKING at HOME

Attention Classified Advertisers...

A HOT NEW MAGAZINE THAT TARGETS THE PROFOUND CHANGE IN THE WORKPLACE

WHERE MILLIONS OF AMERICANS ARE RETURNING HOME!

WORKING at HOME opens the door for the reader to a whole new world - the Entrepreneurial Life. Rather than leaving their homes to go into the workplace, as many as 47 million entrepreneurs, salespeople, consultants, telecommuters and professionals are choosing to mesh home, family and work. They are finding greater independence, satisfaction and in many cases, more wealth than they have ever known. WORKING at HOME magazine represents an historic turning point. For the first time since the beginning of the Industrial Revolution, the movement of workers is back to the home.

WORKING at HOME, the business magazine for the next century, was test marketed last winter and was a smash hit on the newsstand. Now, after intensive research and preparation, WORKING at HOME will be launched as a quarterly publication with 300,000 paid circulation beginning in September.

SPECIAL COMBINATION ADVERTISING OFFER

Buy both the winter issue of WORKING at HOME (which goes on sale January 6th) and the January issue of *Success Magazine* at these special low combination rates: regular classified $16.10 per word, minimum ad ten words or classified display at $1,095 per column inch. The rates for WORKING at HOME by itself are: regular classified $8.90 per word and classified display $595 per column inch. By taking advantage of this special combination ad buy, you save 15%!

Seize this dynamic marketing opportunity. Mail or fax your classified ad order today. We need both your copy and payment no later than October 25th. For your convenience we have enclosed an order form for your copy. For display ads, please include your camera ready artwork.

Sincerely,

Ann Marie Johnson,
Classified Ad Manager

AMJ:rp

WORKING at HOME, Classified Department, P.O. Box 570, Clearwater, Florida 33757-0570
Overnight Delivery: 1510 Barry Street, Suite D, Clearwater, Florida 33756
National 800-762-3555 • International 813-449-1775 • Fax 813-442-2567 • E-Mail RPIads@aol.com

ADVERTISE IN THE
CLASSIFIED
SECTION OF WRITER'S DIGEST

* Our readers are the world's largest audience of freelance writers. And they have an inexhaustible need for your products and services.

* An astounding 94% have made purchases via the mail (71% books, 44% clothing, 42% records/tapes, 22% computer software).

* 42% have attended writing seminars, and 80% have a permanent place set up for writing.

These active writers are interested in every aspect of the writing life. They're not only dedicated to perfecting their craft, they're also hungry for any writing-related news, information, or opportunity.

To reserve space for our **CLASSIFIED SECTION**, just mail the form below or call Joan Wright at 800-234-0963.

Classified Display
THE WRITER'S MART—Small display ads (cuts, headlines, illustrations, rules, etc.) of 1-3 inches in depth and 2 1/4 inches wide. If needed, we'll typeset your ad for an additional one-time charge of $15 per inch.

1x	3x	6x	12x
$255	$210	$200	$180

Reading Notices (Non-Commissionable)—15 word minimum. All reading notices must be prepaid. Box number is $20 per month. Street number, street, city, state and zip code count as four words. Area code and phone number count as two words. Per word/per issue:

1x*	3x*	6x*	12x*
$5.45	$4.20	$3.35	$2.85

* During a contract year of 12 consecutive issues.

A sample of any product and/or literature you plan to send must accompany your order.
☐ Payment enclosed ☐ Visa ☐ MasterCard

Card # _____ Exp. Date _____

Signature _____ Amount $ _____

☐ Reading Notice: _____ Words
☐ Classified Display: _____ Inches
Issues_____
Classification _____
Copy _____
_____
_____
_____
_____
_____
_____
Name _____
Address _____
(Include a street address for our records if you are using a box number in your ad.)
City _____ State _____ Zip_____
Phone (   ) _____
(Where you can be reached during regular business hours.)
Authorizing Signature _____

TV GUIDE

CLASSIFIED MART ORDER FORM

Reach More Than 20 Million Responsive Readers With Your Ad In The

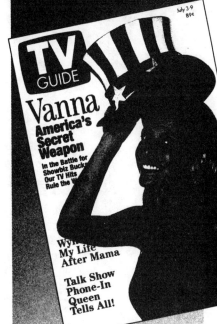

MAIL TO   TV GUIDE CLASSIFIED MART
100 East Ohio Street, Suite 632
Chicago, IL 60611

TEL 312-337-3090
800-424-3090
FAX 312-337-5633

ISSUE DATES ❑ Please run my _____ word ad _____ times beginning with the next available issue.
❑ Please run my _____ word ad "till forbid" beginning with the next available issue.

CLOSING DATES The **Classified Mart** appearing in the first issue of each month closes on the 5th of the month prior to issue date. The **Classified Mart** appearing in the third issue of each month closes on the 19th of the month prior to issue date.

RATES $39.95/word (15 word minimum)
5% frequency discount for scheduling 3 or more consecutive issues

CLASSIFICATIONS (Check appropriate box)
❑ Antiques & Collectibles
❑ Astrology
❑ Beauty/Fashion
❑ Books/Periodicals
❑ Business Opportunities
❑ Computers/Software
❑ Contact Lenses/Glasses
❑ Education/Instruction
❑ Entertainment/Memorabilia
❑ Financial Services
❑ Health/Fitness
❑ Home/Gardening
❑ Inventions
❑ Newsletters
❑ Real Estate
❑ Recipes/Cookbooks
❑ Self-Improvement
❑ Sports/Hobbies
❑ Talent/Modeling
❑ Travel/Vacations
❑ Other_____

PAYMENT Enclosed is my ❑ check or ❑ money order for $ _____
Please charge my ❑ VISA ❑ MasterCard
Card No._____ Exp. Date _____ / _____
Signature _____

NAME *(Not for publication)* _____
COMPANY _____
ADDRESS _____
CITY/STATE/ZIP _____
PHONE/FAX _____

PLEASE PRINT YOUR AD. MINIMUM 15 WORDS.
USE SEPARATE SHEET IF NECESSARY.

1	2	3	4	5
6	7	8	9	10
11	12	13	14	15
16	17	18	19	20
21	22	23	24	25
26	27	28	29	30
31	32	33	34	35

CLASSIFIED HEADINGS

Please choose one of the headings below and indicate on your order. If you don't request a heading, The NATIONAL ENQUIRER will place your ad under the classification which we consider will be most convenient to the reader, thereby bringing in more business for you. No special headings permitted.

Arts & Crafts
Astrology
Automotive
Books & Booklets
Business Opportunities
Buy Wholesale
Catalogs
Children's Items
Coins & Medals
Collectors Items
Computers/Software
Contests & Sweepstakes
Education & Instruction
Employment Information
Fashion Accessories
Financial Loans & Insurance
Food & Beverage
Games & Toys
Garden, Plants
Gifts
Government Surplus
Health & Beauty
Home Care
Home Decoration
Home Entertainment
Household Items
Inventions
Investigations
Jewelry & Gold
Legal Services
Mailing Lists
Make It Yourself
Merchandise For Sale
Miscellaneous
Moneymaking Opportunities
Musical
Of Interest To All
Of Interest To Men
Of Interest To Women
Personal
Pets & Supplies
Real Estate
Recipes
Religious
Safety
Self Improvement
Sports & Outdoors
Stamps
Tapes/Video
Travel
Unusual Items
Vacation
Work At Home

CIRCULATION & COVERAGE

A. Rate Base: 3,750,000 copies weekly.
B. Publisher estimates total readership per issue approaches 20 million.
C. Member: Audit Bureau of Circulations.
D. Coverage: National – All states plus Provinces of Canada.

ISSUANCE

Published weekly, every Tuesday. On sale one week before cover date.

CLOSING DATE

Closing date is six weeks prior to issue date. No classified ad may be cancelled or changed after the closing date.

ADVERTISING COPY GUIDELINES

A. No blind box numbered ads accepted.
B. The following types of advertising are not acceptable:
   1. Fake I.D.s, diplomas or certificates
   2. Medical "cure" ads
   3. Drug advertising
   4. Sexually-oriented advertising
   5. Pen Pal advertising
   6. Inflated/definite earnings claims encouraging unrealistic expectations
   7. Envelope stuffing.
C. We reserve the right to reject or cancel any advertising, for any reason at any time.
D. Advertiser must submit sample of that being offered.
E. California and New York laws require all mail order advertisers in those states carry a legal street address in all ads.

COPY & CONTRACT POLICIES

See reverse side.

Send all copy, correspondence and payments to:

NATIONAL ENQUIRER

Classified Department
P.O. Box 10178, Clearwater, Florida 34617
National (800) 223-6226 ☐ Local (813) 443-7667
FAX (813) 445-9380

COMMISSION & CASH DISCOUNTS

A. Commission to advertising agencies: 15%.
B. No 2% cash discount permitted.

BILLING & CREDIT

A. Classified ads may be prepaid with check or money order payable to NATIONAL ENQUIRER, or charged to your MasterCard or VISA.
B. Canadian ads must be paid in U.S. funds.
C. There is a $20 charge for returned checks.

SPECIAL FREQUENCY DISCOUNT

Run your ad five (5) consecutive weeks, the sixth week is FREE. To earn this discount your ads must be placed and prepaid at the same time.

OPTIONAL HEADLINES

You can start your ad with one or more of these special headlines. The maximum number of characters and spaces allowed per line is listed for each size. When ordering, please clearly state the type number for each choice of headline.

Type Number	Type Styles Available	Characters and Spaces per Line	Cost per Line
18C	CASH AWARD	10	$140
18L	Money Secrets!	13	$140
14C	BILLS PRESSING?	14	$105
14L	Success–Easy Way	15	$105
10C	CLIP NEWSPAPER ITEMS	19	$72
10L	You Can Play Piano By Ear	23	$72

Count each letter, space and punctuation mark as one character. You can order one or more headlines.

In addition to your choice of headline(s), count each word of your ad to determine the correct cost. See sample below.

SAMPLE AD FORMAT

ATTENTION
NATIONAL ENQUIRER

The largest circulation of any paper in America. There is no better place for your ad. Write: P.O. Box 10178, Clearwater, FL 34617. Or call: 1-800-223-6226

18C Headline......................................	$140.00
10C Headline......................................	72.00
26 words x $8.75 per word	227.50
One-time Total	$439.50

40

Classified Headings

Please choose one of the headings below and indicate on your order. If you don't request a heading, your ad will be placed under the classification which we consider will be most convenient to the reader, thereby brining in more business for you. No special headings permitted.

Agents Wanted
Arts & Crafts
Astrology
Automotive
Books/Publications
Business - Home Based
Business Opportunities
Buy-It-Wholesale
Children's Items
Collectibles
Computers/Software
Contests/Sweepstakes
Education/Instruction
Employment
Fashion

Financial
Games & Toys
Gardening
Gifts
Government Supplies
Health & Beauty
Help Wanted
Home Decoration
Inventions
Legal Services
Make-It-Yourself
Mailing Lists
Merchandise
Miscellaneous
Moneymaking Opportunities

Music
Of Interest To All
Of Interest To Men
Of Interest To Women
Pets/Pet Supplies
Real Estate
Recipes
Religion
Safety
Self Improvement
Stamps & Coins
Tapes/Videos
Travel
Unusual Items

Billing & Credit

A. Classified ads may be prepaid with check or money order payable to STAR or charged to your MasterCard or VISA.
B. Canadian ads must be paid in U.S. funds.
C. There is a $20 charge for returned checks.

Commission & Cash Discounts

A. Commission to advertising agencies: 15%.
B. No 2% cash discount permitted.

Copy & Contract Policies

See reverse side.

Special Display Ads

All ads are set uniformly, with no artwork or logos permitted. All advertising copy is set in powerful bold-face. Here are samples and printing specifications for all five display advertising units. There is the right size ad for every budget.

LOSE WEIGHT SAFELY, EASILY!

Remarkable new plan can help you lose weight and keep it off! This sensible diet contains all the vitamins and nutrients your body needs, naturally from the foods you eat. Contains delicious foods from all four food groups. This diet was recommended by a physician to help reduce and maintain an ideal body weight. Low salt and sodium, low cholesterol, low fat, high protein and vitamins. Lose weight safely, slowly and correctly. Write today for free information. It could make your life happier, longer and fuller. Write to: Nutritional Diet Plan, 91190 North Main Street, P.O. Box 51510, Your Town, FL 33516. For informational, 12-page, illustrated booklet, sent to your home today, call: (100) 555-1234.

— 2 INCH AD —

HEADLINE
Two lines set in 8½ pt. extra-bold face caps. You can get up to 16 characters and spaces on each line.

BODY COPY
Maximum of 18 lines set in 6 pt. upper and lower case. You can get an average of 35 characters and spaces per line.

BONUS OFFER

Your STAR CLASSIFIED can be published and highlighted in WEEKLY WORLD NEWS for just a little more.

You receive these advantages with just one order, using STAR/WEEKLY WORLD NEWS combo rates below.

• Over 640,000 additional circulation
• Highest circulation combination available anywhere
• Eye-catching grey background for your ad in WEEKLY WORLD NEWS
• Extra selling power at very low cost

BONUS RATE

WORD ADS	1 Time	4 Times or more*
Minimum: Ten (10) words		
Cost per word, per issue	$8.45	$8.15

SPECIAL DISPLAY ADS	1 Time	4 Times or more*
One-half inch (1/2") ad	$445	$420
Three-quarter inch (3/4") ad	560	525
One inch (1")	730	675
One and one-half (1½") ad	1,060	1,005
Two inch (2") ad	1,355	1,295

*In order to earn the four-time rate, your ad must be placed and prepaid for four (4) or more issues at the same time. If ad is canceled credit will be based on the 1 time rate.

GUIDELINES

A. Your ad in WEEKLY WORLD NEWS will reach the public during the same week(s) as in STAR.
B. No ad changes are allowed for WEEKLY WORLD NEWS, including identification key.
C. WEEKLY WORLD NEWS classifieds section is available only through the STAR BONUS OFFER.
D. STAR reserves the right to terminate or change this bonus offer without prior notice.

BE A WINNER

Be in STAR CLASSIFIEDS, then take advantage of this BONUS OFFER. This is the best and most inexpensive way to reach an extra 640,000 subscribers weekly.

Advertising Copy Guidelines

A. No blind box numbered ads accepted.
B. The following types of advertising are not acceptable:
1. Fake I.D.s, diplomas or certificates
2. Medical "cure ads" ads
3. Drug advertising
4. Sexually-oriented advertising
5. Pen Pal advertising
6. Inflated/definite earnings claims encouraging unrealistic expectations
7. Envelope stuffing
C. We reserve the right to reject or cancel any advertising, for any reason at any time.
D. Advertiser must submit sample of that being offered.
E. California and New York laws require all mail order advertisers carry a legal street address in all ads.

— 1/2 INCH AD —

HEADLINE
Two lines set in 8½ pt. extra-bold face caps. You can get up to 16 characters and spaces on each line.

BODY COPY
Maximum of 12 lines set in 6 pt. upper and lower case. You can get an average of 35 characters and spaces per line.

OLD-FASHIONED SOUTHERN COOKING

Make mouth-watering, southern dishes with this new, "Southern Recipes" cookbook. Truly traditional recipes such as dumplings, fried chicken, sawmill gravy, pork chops and cornbread. This new book is complete with helpful tips to insure a perfect dish, every time. 365-pages set in easy-to-read type with full-color illustrations. Handy index for quick reference. Money-back guarantee. Send $5.95 to: Southern Recipes, P.O. Box 1234, Southern City, GA 12345.

— 1 INCH AD —

HEADLINE
One line set in 8½ pt. extra-bold face caps. You can get up to 16 characters and spaces on that line.

BODY COPY
Maximum of 9 lines set in 6 pt. upper and lower case. You can get an average of 35 characters and spaces per line.

INVENTORS

Can you profit from your idea? Call us today regarding the marketing of your invention, or write for your free information package. Over a decade of service. Russell Johns Associates, Ltd. P.O. Box 1510, Clearwater, FL 34617. (813) 443-7666. (Not an answering service). A fee based marketing company, offices nationwide.

— 1/4 INCH AD —

VISA/MASTERCARD

Star Classified ads can now be ordered by FAX using your credit card. Send us ad copy, cost, card number, expiration date and your signature. Direct to: Star Classified (813) 445-9380 (24 hours).

HEADLINE
One line set in 8½ pt. extra-bold face caps. You can get up to 16 characters and spaces on that line.

BODY COPY
Maximum of 6 lines set in 6 pt. upper and lower case. You can get an average of 35 characters and spaces per line.

— 1/2 INCH AD —

GIFT BASKETS

Choose from wide variety for any occasion. Will send direct. Send for free catalog. SASE: Gifts By Mail, 1 First, Joy, NY 12345.

HEADLINE
One line set in 8½ pt. extra-bold face caps. You can get up to 16 characters and spaces on that line.

BODY COPY
Maximum of 4 lines set in 6 pt. upper and lower case. You can get an average of 35 characters and spaces per line.

Send all copy and payments to:

Classified Department
P.O. Box 1510, Clearwater, Florida 34617
Telephones: National (800) 223-8558 □ Local (813) 443-7666
FAX (813) 445-9380

STAR is represented exclusively by Russell Johns Associates, Ltd. for classified advertising.

41

A-Z Classified & Display Rates

ALL PAGES IN THIS FOLIO ARE NUMBERED

This sheet, below and on the back, contains an alphabetical list of publications we represent, classified and display rates & page numbers.

DIFFERENT READERSHIPS

Page numbers for publications appealing to different readerships are listed below and in the A - Z listings.

EASY TO ORDER

Handy order blanks are included

SIMPLE TO FIGURE OUT THE COST OF YOUR CLASSIFIED

Astrology 34	Electronics 40	National Shopper 42
Black Publications 22, 32	Home Business 33	Sophisticated (Sex Oriented) 43-50
Classified & Display	Jackpots 25, 30, 35-38, 48	Sports 28, 39
Condensed Listings A-1-A-5	Lottery & Casino 34	Tabloids 22-24
Crafts 12, 18	Men's 26-28, 37, 39, 50	Teens 29-31
Display Information 52	Music 29-31	Useful Information 50-52
		Women's 12-22, 32, 37

A

Adult Cinema Review $1.50 word—Display $75. inch (43, 46)

All American Craft Group $13.95 word—Display $575. inch (12)

American Astrology $2.75** word—Display $130.** inch (34)

American Tabloid Group $6.25 word—$325. inch (24)

American Woman $3.00 word—$125. inch (15)

B

Bad Boys Group $4.50 word—Display $300. inch (45)

Beauties of Wrestling $2.50 word — Display $150. inch (28)

Best of Genesis $2.75 word — Display $150. inch (49)

Best Teen Group $9.50 word—Display $495. inch (29)

Best Women's Group $9.50 word—Display $525. inch (11)

Big Jackpot $57.25* word—Display $3,230. inch (35-36)

Big 2—Women's Mags—$3.00 word—$150. inch (16)

Blac Tress $1.75 word—Display $60. inch (32)

Black Belt $3.50 word—Display $175. inch (39)

Black Hair Care $1.75 word—Display $60. inch (32)

Budget Jackpot $36.00 word—Display $1,850. inch (38)

Buf $2.50 word — Display $125. inch (47)

Business Group $3.50 word—Display $150. inch (33)

C

Cappers $2.20 word—Display $129.50 inch (5, 6)

Casino Review $2.75 word—Display $150. inch (34)

Complete Black Group $7.25 word—Display $325. inch (32)

Complete Sophisticated Group $36.50 word—Display $1,900. inch (44)

Complete Woman $3.00 word—Display $125. inch (14)

Condensed Listings (A-1-A-5)

Contemporary Group $2.50 word—Display $125. inch (47)

Country Chatter $7.00 word—Display $375. inch (22)

Country Song Roundup $1.50 word—Display $80. inch **(40)**

Craft Works $2.50 word—Display $100. inch (12)

Creative Wood Works & Crafts $2.50 word—Display $100. inch (12)

Crochet Fantasy $2.50 word—Display $100. inch (12)

D - E

Ebony Group $5.95 word—Display $295. inch (22)

Electronics Now $3.10 word (40)

Erotic X - Film Guide $3.00 word—Display $145. inch **(47)**

Expert's Choice — 3 packages (9)

F

Family Group $7.50 word—Display $415. inch (19)

Fantasy Group $4.95 word — Display $250. inch (47)

Fashion Knitting $2.50 word—Display $100. inch (12)

Fill 'Em Up Special $1.50 word—Display $50. inch (41)

Film Threat $3.95 word—Display $250. inch (40)

Fly $1.50 word — Display $80. inch (29)

Forty Plus $3.00 word — Display $145. inch (43, 46)

G

Gem $2.50 word—Display $125. inch (43)

Genesis $6.25 word — Display $325. inch (49)

Gent $3.00 word—Display $150. inch (43, 46)

Glamour Title $1.50 word—Display $50. inch (19)

"Good News" Tabloid Group $9.50 word—Display $525. inch (23)

Grit $2.20 word—Display $129.50 inch (7-8)

NATIONAL MAIL ORDER CLASSIFIED

P.O. BOX 5 — SARASOTA, FL 34230

Telephone 941-366-3003

GENERAL OFFICES AT 2628 17th STREET

FAX # 941-951-2672

A-Z Classified & Display Rates

H - I

Hadassah Magazine $6.95 word—Display $350. inch (21)
Hairdo Ideas $1.75 word—Display $60. inch (16)
Hit Parader $2.50 word—Display $100. inch (30)
Hockey Illustrated $1.75 word — Display $60. inch (26)
Home Business Connection $5.00 word — Display $225. inch (33)
Home Business Journal $3.50 word — Display $175. inch (33)
Home Business Magazine $3.25 word — Display $150. inch (33)
Homemaker Group $7.50 word—Display $375. inch (21)
Iron Horse $2.50 word—Display $125. inch (50)

J - K

Jackpot Two $2.95 word—Display $150. inch (48)
Karate Kung-fu $2.00 word—Display $100. inch (39)

L

Ladies' Talk $6.00 word—Display $295. inch (21)
Lady's Circle Patchwork Quilts $2.50 word—Display $125. inch (12, 18)
Little Jackpot $16.50 word—Display $800. inch (25)
Livewire $1.95 word—Display $85. inch (30)
Lottery & Casino News $2.75 word—Display $150. inch (34)
Low Cost Women's Package $4.00 word—Display $200. inch (13)

M

MA Training $2.00 word—Display $100. inch (39)
Martial Arts Group $5.95 word—Display $295. inch (39)
Men's Jackpot $23.25* word—Display $1.425. inch (37)
Men's Special $1.50 word—Display $50. inch (27)
Men-Women Combination $10.95 word—Display $495. inch (25)
Metal Maniacs $2.50 word—Display $100. inch (31)
Modern Screen's Country Music $2.00 word — Display $100. inch (31)
Money Maker Group $7.00 word—Display $325. inch (13)

N

National Beauty Group $4.50 word—Display $150. inch (17)
National Biker Group $3.75 word—Display $195. inch (50)
National Black Group $2.75 word—Display $150. inch (32)
National Shopper $1.25 word—Display $50. inch (42)
National Tabloid Group $10.25* word—Display $725. inch (23)
National Women's Group $15.00 word—Display $750. inch (18)
New Ideas for Hair Styling $1.75 word—Display $60. inch (19)
New Rave $4.00 word—Display $200. inch (44)
New Writer's Magazine $1.75 word—Display $60. inch (41)
Nugget $2.25 word—Display $125. inch (43, 46)

O

Oui Magazine $7.95 word—Display $395. inch (49)
Outlaw Biker $1.75 word—Display $95. inch (46, 50)

P - Q - R

PaintWorks $2.50 word—Display $100. inch (12)

Popular Electronics $1.75 word—(40)
Portfolio $2.00 word—Display $125. inch (45, 46)
Postman's Selection $11.25 word—Display $950. inch (11)
Profitmaker Group $2.50 word—Display $80. inch (41)
Psychic Advisor $2.50 word — Display $125. inch (34)
Rappages $2.50 word—Display $125. inch (29)
Rapport $1.75 word—Display $75. inch (26)
Real Crime $2.00 word — Display $75. inch (27)
Real Men's Group $5.25 word—Display $350. inch (27)
Real Vibrations Group $12.50 word—Display $600. inch (45)
Religious Group $2.25 word—Display $125. inch (18)
Romance Group $6.75 word—Display $325. inch (21)

S

Set 'N Style $1.75 word — Display $60. inch (16)
Sophisticated Four $4.95 word—Display $225. inch (44)
Sophisticated Money Saver $15.95 word—Display $895. inch (46)
Sophisticated Special $1.50 word (48)
Sophisticated Test Jackpot $11.95 word—Display $595. inch (48)
Sports Special $1.75 word—Display $50. inch (26)
Stag $3.75 word—Display $195. inch (43)
Sterling Women's Display Group — Display $199. inch (A-2)
Sugah $2.00 word—Display $125. inch (45)
Super Special ''15'' $14.75 word (25)
Super-Super Women's Group $13.75 word—Display $695. inch (20)
Super Tabloid Group $26.25* word—Display $2,490. inch (24)
Swank $5.25 word—Display $275. inch (49)
Swank Special $2.75 word—Display $150. inch (48)

T

Teen Jackpot $19.95 word—Display $825. inch (30)
Teen Network $5.95 word — Display $300. inch (29)
Teen Throb Group $8.95 word—Display $395. inch (31)
Test-A-Tabloid $7.00 word—Display $350. inch (23)
Times Group $2.50 word—Display $75. inch (11)
Today's Woman Group $7.50 word—Display $295. inch (17)
Top Tabloid Group $41.25* word—Display $3,630. inch (22)
Top Quality Sophisticated Group $12.25 word—Display $650. inch (46)
Traditional Quilter $2.50 word—Display $100. inch (12)
Treasure Seekers $2.95 word—Display $150. inch (27)
Turn-on Group $8.50 word—Display $400. inch (43)
Tutti Frutti Teen Group $2.00 word — Display $100. inch (31)

U - V - W

UFO Universe $1.75 word—Display $90. inch (26)
Velvet $5.95 word—Display $275. inch (44, 46)
Women's Jackpot $20.50 word—Display $1,110. inch (37)
Women's Nine $10.95 word—Display $495. inch (20)
Women's Special $1.50 word—Display $50. inch (16)
Wonderful World of Women $3.25 word—Display $130. inch (19)
Wrestling All Stars $3.95 word—Display $195. inch (28)
Wrestling Group $6.95 word—Display $295. inch (28)
Wrestling World $1.75 word—Display $50. inch (28)

X - Y - Z

Yesterday's Magazette $1.75 word—Display $60. inch (41)

*Psychic/Astrology & Occult advertising add $1.00 per word.
**900 Numbers — ½ page Minimum.

NATIONAL MAIL ORDER CLASSIFIED
P.O. BOX 5 — SARASOTA, FL 34230

Please Read Carefully Before Placing Your Advertisement!

RATES — $11.65 per word insertion payable in advance. Words to appear in all **BOLD FACE** capital letters — $1.00 per word additional, except first word of ad which is set uniformly in **BOLD FACE** capital letters at no charge. Minimum charge for each insertion of 10 words or less is $116.50. BOLD CENTERED HEADLINE — $60.00. Screening — $54.00. Contract rates are not available. 15% Commission to Recognized Advertising Agencies. Orders accepted at these rates for not more than three issues in advance of last issue closed; for subsequent issues at rates prevailing. Rate and conditions subject to change without notice.

HOW TO COUNT WORDS — Name and address must be included in counting the number of words in your ad. Each initial or number used in your advertisement counts as one word: D. A. NOLAN, 224 West 57th Street, New York, N.Y. 10019, NINE WORDS. Real zone numbers and zip codes are not counted. Phone numbers count as two words. Symbols used as keys are charged for. City and state counts as one word each; New Brunswick, New Jersey is two words. Abbreviations such as C.O.D., F.O.B., R.P.M., M.P.H., H.P., U.S.A., P.O., A.C., 5 × 7, 16mm are counted as one word (P.O. Box 392 counted as 3 words). Webster's International Unabridged Dictionary will be used as our authority for spelling, compound words, hyphenations, abbreviations, capitals, etc. Please make checks payable to POPULAR MECHANICS.

POSITION — Ad will be placed only under headings listed below. Special headings permitted only if you run your ad in three subsequent issues and payment for all three paid in advance. When no heading is requested we will use our own judgment in classifying an ad.

CLOSING DATES — Classified advertising forms close the 5th of the second month preceding date of publication. (September issues closes July 5th.)
Orders cannot be cancelled or changed after the 5th of the second month preceding date of publication. (September issue classified ad cannot be changed or cancelled after July 5th.)

STYLE — All advertisements are set uniformly. The first word in every ad will be set in **BOLD FACE** capital letters at no charge. All other words may be set in **BOLD FACE** capital letters at additional charge. (See Rates.) No cuts permitted.

TERMS — We reserve the right to request any advertiser to submit literature and/or merchandise prior to acceptance of advertisement. We also reserve the right to refuse advertisements we consider objectionable.

Advertisements directing replies in care of our office not accepted. Position requests not accepted.

Advance proofs of classified ads are not submitted. No deduction will be allowed for any error in key number or for any error due to illegibly written copy. Accuracy in receiving ads over the telephone cannot be guaranteed. Popular Mechanics is responsible for only the first incorrect insertion. The advertiser and its agency, if there be one, each represents that it is fully authorized and licensed to use (i) the names and/or the potraits or pictures of persons, living or dead, or of things, (ii) any trademarks, copyrighted or otherwise private material and (iii) any testimonials, contained in any advertisement submitted by or on behalf of the advertiser and published in Popular Mechanics, and that such advertisement is neither libelous, an invasion of privacy or otherwise unlawful as to any third party.

As part of the consideration and to induce Popular Mechanics to publish such advertisement, the advertiser and its agency, if there be one, each agrees to indemnify and save harmless The Hearst Corporation, publisher of Popular Mechanics, against all loss, liability, damage and expense of whatsoever nature arising out of copying, printing or publishing of such advertisement.

All orders are accepted subject to acts of God, fires, strikes, accidents or other occurences beyond publisher's control which prevent publisher from partially or completely producing, publishing or distributing Popular Mechanics.

ALPHABETICAL LIST OF CLASSIFIED HEADINGS

Advertising Agencies, Adv. Services,
  Mailing Lists
Agents Wanted
Air Conditioning
Animals, Birds
Antiques, Relics, Etc.
Arts, Crafts, Supplies
Astronomy
Athletic Equipment/Bodybuilding
  Courses
Auctions
Automobiles
Automotive Supplies & Equipment
Aviation, Hang Gliding
Balding
Bankruptcy
Batteries, Alternators
Bicycles, Supplies
Binoculars, Telescopes, Microscopes
Boats, Outboards, Trailers & Kits
Books, etc. (see Publishers Mart)
Burglar Alarms & Home Protection
Business Opportunities
Business Services
Buy It Wholesale
CB's, Radio & Ham Equipment
Cable TV Equipment
Cameras & Equipment
Campers Trailers, Kits, Plans
Camping & Equipment
Cartooning, Commercial Arts, Sign
  Painting
Christmas Gift Shopping (Oct., Nov., Dec.
  issue only)
Clocks, Watches, Old Gold, Jewelry
Coins, Tokens, Currency
Computers & Software
Contests
Contact Lenses

Decals, Emblems, Patches
Divorce
Dogs, Pets
Do-It-Yourself
Domes
Drinking Water Purifiers
Education & Instructions
Electrical Supplies
Electric Vehicles
Electronics
Employment Information
Energy Saving
Engines, Motors
Export-Import
Eyeglasses
Fiberglass
Financial
Fishing, Tackle, Lures
Flags
Flowers, Plants & Nursery Supplies
Foreclosures
Formulas, Plans, Etc.
Gardening & Lawn Care
Gift Shopping
Gold
Government Surplus
Greenhouses
Gummed Labels
Guns, Decoys, Hunting
Hairpieces For Men
Health, Vitamins
Hearing Aids
Heating, Fuel Savers
Help Wanted
Herbs
Hobbies & Collections
Home Building & Remodeling
Home Craftsman
For The Home

House Plans
Hovercraft
Hydroponics
Inventions Wanted
For Inventors
Jewelry, Stones, Minerals
Knives, Cutlery, Etc.
Loans By Mail
Machinery, Tools & Supplies
Magic Tricks, Jokes, Ventriloquism
Magnets
Mailorder Opportunities
Miscellaneous
Mobile Homes
Models, Models Supplies
Moneymaking Opportunities
Motorcycles, Motorscooters, Supplies
Music Instruction & Instruments
New Products
Of Interest To All
Of Interest to Men
Office Supplies & Equipment
Outdoor Equipment
Personal
Photo & Photo Supplies
Plans, Blueprints, Projects
Plastics
Plays, Songs, Manuscripts
Plumbing
Printing Supplies, Printing
Profitable Occupations
Publishers Mart—
  Books & Publications
  Catalogs
  Magazines
Rabbits, Chinchillas, Fur Bearing Animals
Real Estate

Recipes, Cooking, etc.
Recreational Vehicles
Recycling
Remailing Service
Repairs & Servicing
Reproduction Molds
Robots, Robotics
Rubber Stamps
Salesmen — Distributors
Satellite-TV
Schools
Science & Chemistry
Self-Improvement
Shop Equipment
Silver
Solar & Alternate Energy
Space & Astronauts
Special Services
Sporting Goods & Equipment
Stamp Collecting
Stereo, Cassette, Tapes, Etc.
Swimming Pools
Telephone & Service
Tobacco
Tools For Sale
Toys, Games, Kites, Puzzles, Novelties
Trailer Parts
Travel & Resorts
Treasure Finders
Trucks, Parts & Supplies
TV, Video & Video Equipment
Wanted Miscellaneous
Wearing Apparel
Welding, Soldering, Plating
Winemaking, Beermaking
Women's Interests
Wood, Woodworking
Work Clothing

Popular Mechanics is a Publication of Hearst Magazines,
a Division of The Hearst Corporation.

DOROTHY NOLAN, *Classified Manager*
224 West 57th Street, New York, N.Y. 10019
(212) 649-3167 FAX (212) 586-5562

44

Kipen Publishing Corporation

SPARE TIME

The Magazine of Money Making Opportunities

5810 West Oklahoma Avenue, Milwaukee, Wisconsin 53219-4384
Phone: (414) 543-8110   Fax: (414) 543- 9767

Your classified ad in SPARE TIME can reach 1,000 eager opportunity seekers for less than the cost of just <u>one</u> stamp!

Dear Advertiser,

It would cost you 29¢ in postage to mail your classified ad to just one opportunity seeker. But for as little as $80 (our minimum), we'll include your 15-word ad in all 300,000 copies of our next issue. Which averages out to just 27¢ for every 1,000 opportunity seekers! Want a longer ad? It's just $5.30 per word additional.

Look through the classifieds in several issues of SPARE TIME, and you'll keep seeing the same names again and again. That's because so many advertisers are on a "till forbid" basis – repeating their successful ads in issue after issue after issue!

You can place your ad under any of the following headings (please specify):

- ADDITIONAL INCOME
- ADVERTISING SERVICES
- AGENTS WANTED
- AUTOMOTIVE
- BARGAINS & CLOSEOUTS
- BOOKS & MANUALS
- BUSINESS OPPORTUNITIES
- BUY IT WHOLESALE
- EDUCATIONAL
- FINANCIAL

- FOR ADVERTISERS
- HELP WANTED
- INVENTIONS
- JEWELRY
- LOANS BY MAIL
- MAILING LISTS
- MISCELLANEOUS
- MONEY MAKING OPPORTUNITIES
- MUSIC

- OF INTEREST TO ALL
- OF INTEREST TO WOMEN
- PERSONAL
- PLASTICS
- PRINTING
- REAL ESTATE
- SALESPEOPLE WANTED
- SERVICES OFFERED
- VENTURE CAPITAL

THE CLOSING DATE IS 45 DAYS PRECEDING THE ISSUE DATE.

So go ahead – send us the copy for your ad, along with your check or money order...*now!*

Cordially,

Dennis Wilk

Dennis Wilk, *Publisher*

P.S. Interested in display ads? Just look for our rate card. A one-inch ad is only $220.00! Why not run a comparison test: classified *vs.* display!

SPARE TIME is published in JANUARY · FEBRUARY · MARCH · APRIL · MAY/JUNE · AUGUST · SEPTEMBER · OCTOBER · NOVEMBER/DECEMBER

COUNTRY MUSIC CLASSIFIEDS GET RESULTS!

Country Music Magazine is booming!It is the hottest music magazine published today. In the past year alone, circulation has grown a whopping 47% ... from 475,000 to 700,000 paid copies per issue! *Country Music* is not only the best read, but it is by far, the largest publication in its field. Now with more than 3 million avid, highly responsive mail order buyers reading every issue, there is just no better marketplace for your classified ad.

Join the winner. *Country Music Classifieds* will be a profitable new source of business leads for you. The enclosed rate sheet will give you complete advertising information and has an order form for your copy. For your payment convenience, we now accept Visa or MasterCard.

If you have any questions, just call us at 1-800-762-3555.

Sincerely,

Russ Palmer

Russell E. Palmer
Classified Ad Manager

REP:sr
Enclosure

Country Music, Classified Department, P.O. Box 570, Clearwater, Florida 34617-0570
National 1-800-762-3555 • International 813-449-1775 • Fax 813-442-2567

New Title —

UNcommon Marketing Techniques

by Jeffrey Dobkin © 1998 5¹/₂" x 8¹/₂" • 270 Pages of Lean,
How-To Marketing Information. Over 33 of Dobkin's best, most
requested articles - includes all the articles shown here and more!

Chapters:

Increase Your Ad Response 10 Times
Here's how, step by step.

The One Evening Marketing Plan
*Write your marketing plan in an evening?
Then complete the execution of your entire PR
plan the very next day? Here's specifically how.*

The 15 Page Marketing Plan
*If you can write 15 pages, this, without question,
is the plan to implement.*

How To Buy a Great Mailing List!
*A step-by-step procedure for figuring out, finding,
and buying the best mailing list at the right price.*

Real Estate Action Marketing Plan
Want to see an actual 10-page promotional plan?

How To Find a Product to Market
*Still stuck for products? Here's how to go about finding
them in an easy and logical fashion.*

How To Find the Markets for Your Invention
*There are some great and easy-to-use reference tools to
make the marketing function easy. Here's a selection of
marketing directories found in most libraries, and how
to use them.*

Getting Your Press Release into Print
*The press release selection process is simple, fast, brutal,
and very unforgiving of mistakes or poor work. Here's how
to create a release that is effective, and get it published.*

A Simple Rule for Creating Winning Headlines - The 100 to 1 Rule
*How to write attention-getting, reader-capturing headlines,
envelope teaser copy, slogans, signage, and more. Specific
techniques and recommendations.*

Best Campaign I Ever Wrote
*They call it Multiple Exposure Marketing. Here's an
actual series of letters—ready to send to your own clients.*

Self-Help for Self-Publishers
Thinking of writing a book? Don't—until you read these tips.

The BIGGEST Mistake Every Firm Makes in Marketing, and What You Can Do to Correct It in Your Firm, for $1.92
*Find out what the mistake is. Do you really make it?
Can you really correct it for $1.92?*

Questions People Ask Me the Most About Direct Marketing
*Everyone asks the same questions: What is marketing?
What's the best response percentage to receive from a
mailing? Does long copy work better than short copy?
Should you use teaser copy on your envelope?*

This Lawnmower Makes Cutting the Grass So Fast and Easy, I Bought It for My Wife
*A specific nine-step procedure to increase your direct
marketing response.*

*The World's
Most Practical Book
On Marketing!*

How To Write a Small Classified Ad
*Follow a few simple rules, triple your response,
make a whole lot of money.*

How To Create Your Own Great Ad, Or Get One You Like from an Agency, the First Time. *Yes!*

How To Write an Effective Direct Mail Letter
*An in-depth article showing step-by-step how to
write compelling copy for the most important part
of your direct mail package.*

The Art of a Direct Mail Letter
*Part two of creating an effective direct mail letter:
the design. Explicit instructions and examples.*

How To Create a Winning Direct Mail Package
*You have ten seconds to initiate success. How to
make your mail draw maximum response.*

The 13 Fastest and Best Ways to Get Business Right Now! *Yep.*

The 10 Worst Mistakes in Direct Mail
*Learn from my experience! Don't worry, there are still
plenty of mistakes left for you to make on your own!*

Magazine Publishers Hate Me!
*Exactly how to buy magazine space at a discount—
20%, 40%, up to 80% off!*

The Most Valuable Letter You Can Write
*This simple letter is the most powerful motivator in getting
you new business. How to make it really pay off.*

Plus - Plenty More! 33 Articles Altogether!

48

Chapter Three

How to Find a Money-Making Product

Let's begin this chapter by examining some of the reasons people buy through the mail. One of the leading consumer magazines ran a survey of its readership. When asked, "Why do you purchase items by mail?" the response included the following, with the most frequent answers heading the list:

Access to items not easily found elsewhere
Convenience
Variety
Service
Fun
Price
Quality
Unique gifts

It's not surprising that the number one reason people shop by mail is that they can find items that are not readily available in retail stores. Mail order catalogs provide by far the largest selection of goods anywhere, and you can see them all in one place—your own home. The convenience of shopping in the comfort of home rather than traveling, parking, and searching for needed items is very appealing to busy people whose time and energy are at a premium. That's why convenience is the second most important reason why people shop by mail. Ordering is as easy as making a phone call or checking off an item on an order form and dropping it in the mail. And shopping by mail is particularly helpful for people who are ill, have handicaps, are elderly, or for whatever reason find it difficult to shop in the stores.

The good service representative of mail order houses is in sharp contrast to the poor service we have come to anticipate receiving when shopping in retail stores. I frequently shop at one particular department store in Los Angles called Nordstroms. Why? Because the personnel have been trained to give A-1 service, and I don't want the hassle and frustration that unfortunately has become more and more commonplace in retail shopping. Now let's get down to the business of finding product for you to sell to these ready future customers.

How to Start the Wheels of Creativity Turning

Your second assignment is to pour through magazines in various categories to see what is being advertised in both the classified and display sections, and determine which types of products are of interest to you. If there is no classified section in a particular publication, notice the size of the smallest display ad. Are one-inch ads being used to do the work of classified ads?

If a variety of magazines aren't readily available to you, go to the library and ask the reference librarian for one or more of the following books: *Bacon's Publicity Checker, Gale Directory of Publications and Broadcast Media, Literary Market Place, Ulrich's International Periodicals Directory, Standard Periodical Directory,* and *Standard Rate & Data/Consumer Publications.* Scan the categories to find one that particularly interests you. Then get the names and addresses of the magazines listed that specialize in that category and send away for a copy. They are all free directly from the publisher if you write on your business stationery requesting a sample copy, an advertising rate card, and a media kit. To whet your appetite, I've included a partial list of consumer magazines in various categories at the end of this chapter.

Another good way to get ideas about what you might like to sell is to order a copy of *The Best Catalogs in the World.* It's a beautiful, full-color, fully-illustrated catalog that describes hundreds of mail order operations, some in categories you probably never knew existed. When you receive the catalog, look through it to find a category of products that interests you. Then request catalogs from various companies that are selling those products. To get a copy of *The Best Catalogs in the World* send $3.00 to: Publisher Inquiry Services, 951 Broken Sound Parkway NW, Building 190, PO Box 5057, Boca Raton, Florida 33431-0857. See page 62.

You can also find a list of thousands of mail order companies under numerous categories in reference books at your library. Two of the best are *The Directory of Mail Order Catalogs* published by Grey House Publishing, Inc. and *The National Directory of Catalogs* published by Oxbridge Communications, Inc. Follow the same procedure of sending for catalogs that contain the types of products you think you would like to sell. This process helps the wheels of creativity to start turning.

Check Out Your Future Competition

Once you zero in on a category and have the consumer magazines that specialize in your area of interest, send for information, catalogs, and actual products advertised in them. Be on the look-out for one great product to use as a lead item. That means it's the one you will initially offer for sale—the strong product that will attract new customers. Also search for related items that the same customers might want to buy. (More about this later.)

Key all your mail by using a different distinguishing code number or letter with each request and order you send out. For example, you might add Suite 1 to your address to one advertiser, Suite 2 to another, etc. Or you can give yourself a different middle initial on each, such as John A. Smith, John B. Smith. The point is, you want to be able to track what each advertiser is doing with your name—how many times he is renting it and to whom. This information will prove valuable later.

The best way to organize the literature is to keep a separate 9" x 12" envelope or file for each key. Save all literature and subsequent mail sent to you in the envelope or file marked with the corresponding key.

As the literature comes in, read it thoroughly. It's a great education and you never know when you can incorporate some aspect of the advertising copy, literature design, program ideas, or offers into your own mail order solicitations.

Finding the Source of Products

OK, you've determined the category of products you want to sell and seen what other mail order companies in that field are doing. What's next? You are going to track down the sources of the same or similar products. Don't worry, it's easy. You simply look in the appropriate trade publications, a list of which can be found in library references books. The best is the *Standard Rate & Data/Trade Publications*. It gives information on 3,500 trade and technical publications in the United States, arranged in many categories.

On your business stationery, request a complimentary copy of the trade publications you want, and again, remember to request an advertising rate card, and media kit. Also inquire whether or not the publication has a trade annual or directory of products and services (which contain thousands of manufacturers) and ask the cost. Some are free.

One of the best sources of products is the monthly publication *Retailers Forum: A Wholesale Merchandise Guide*. Every issue contains over 200 jam-packed pages, and there's a monthly update of all types of forthcoming trade shows. I suggest that you get a sample issue. See page 61.

In the trade magazines, you'll find manufacturers' advertisements. Send for information on products that you may want to sell. There will also be lists of trade shows and their dates and locations. Attend some shows if you possibly can. It is important to your business and it'll be fun.

See pages 63 through 65. You'll find information about 11 Hong Kong product magazines to which you can subscribe. I personally get *Hong Kong Enterprise* every month. There are approximately 900 pages of products. If interested in any of the magazines, write for a sample copy on your business stationery. Write to: Hong Kong Trade Development Council, Suite 3800, 38 Floor, Office Tower, Convention Plaza, 1 Harbour Road, Wanchai, Hong Kong.

One of the most popular places for trade shows is the Las Vegas Convention Center. Get on the mailing list by writing to: Las Vegas Convention Center, 3150 Paradise Road, Las Vegas, Nevada 89109. Also write to convention centers near your home and get on their mailing lists for both consumer and trade shows. Then go, go, go! Have a good time, and Uncle Sam will help you pay for it. It's a legitimate business expense that your accountant can advise you on. You'll see lots of products and you'll make important contacts. Be sure to take plenty of business cards and wear comfortable walking shoes. (You'll thank me someday for the tip about the shoes.)

Get on the mailing list of the ASD/AMD National Trade Shows, 2525 Ocean Park Blvd., Santa Monica, CA 90405-5201. Call toll free from anywhere in the United States (800) 421-4511. From Los Angeles (310) 396-6006. (English and Spanish)

They have several tremendous trade shows every year in Las Vegas and elsewhere. There are over 5,000 booths selling such items as art, boutique items, clocks, collectibles, cookware, cosmetics, housewares, dolls, fashion accessories, food products, giftware, handbags, handicrafts, health & beauty aids, hosiery, jewelry, kitchenware, Latin American imports, leather goods & accessories, lingerie, posters, premiums & incentives, rugs, sunglasses, T-shirts, toys, undergarments, video tapes, wallets, watches, and western items.

There are special sections selling the following items: automotive parts & accessories, boots, buckles, camping equipment, computer parts & supplies, computer software, closeouts, cutlery, consumer electronics, fishing tackle & accessories, government surplus, knives, martial arts & karate supplies, military equipment & supplies, outdoor products, safety products, sporting goods, tools, and vintage clothing.

I think of trade shows as a treasure hunt. There's a pot of gold waiting for you somewhere in those aisles of widgets and gadgets and things. Looking for the gem that's going to get your business up and going can be an exhilarating experience. And being surrounded by the end product of scores of people's creative efforts is testimony to the fact that it can be done. An idea can blossom into a thriving business. It's done all the time by people no smarter than you.

When talking to manufacturers at trade shows and when writing to companies in whose products you are interested, ask if they can supply advertising literature, line drawings, black-and-white glossy photos of products, and advertising copy. Also be sure to ask if they will drop ship products. (Fulfill your orders from their warehouse.) If not, find out the quantity of their minimum purchase. Don't be bashful about letting them know you're just beginning your career as a mail order entrepreneur. Most manufacturers will be cooperative and full of valuable information and suggestions that will help you get started. Remember, it's to their benefit. When you successfully sell their products, they make money, too.

Give Them What They Want

Keep in mind when conducting your search that a product has the best chance of success if it appeals to one or more of the following basic human desires:

1. Good health: Feel better, have more energy, live longer.

2. Abundance of money: Earn extra cash, enjoy a grand lifestyle, gain financial security and the freedom to live as you want.

3. Attractive appearance: Look younger, thinner, more prosperous.

4. Attract other people: Find friends, lovers, feel comfortable and converse easily in social and business situations.

5. Increased leisure time: Spend less time working and more time playing.

6. Success: Be self-confident, fulfilled, prosperous, admired.

7. Sex appeal: Be alluring, exciting to others, noticed, accepted, appreciated. (This is one of the most powerful desires and is used both blatantly and subtly to sell a wide variety of products.)

8. Business opportunities: Change your career. Learn new skills. Be your own boss. Enjoy your work. Make more money.

9. Recognition: Feel special, be noticed, appreciated, respected.

10. Food satisfaction: Enjoy tastier foods. Try interesting, new products.

11. Ultimate comfort: Luxuriate in the best, most satisfying things available.

Items that fulfill a strong need, solve a particular problem, or make people's lives more enjoyable generally do well. It is also vitally important that you be enthusiastic about the products you market. Your enthusiasm will be reflected in your advertising copy and your conversations with customers, and it will do wonders for your determination to succeed.

The Backbone of Your Business

Customers who buy one product are often interested in other similar ones. If they're happy with the initial product they receive from a particular company, they often order additional items from them. These repeat sales, known as the back end, are critical to the success of mail order ventures. In fact, back-end profits are the backbone of most mail order businesses. I say most because there are occasional exceptions—mail order entrepreneurs who sell single, unrelated products and still succeed.

Back-end sales are a very important part of my book business. Customers frequently buy almost all the books I publish in a particular category. How does it happen? Included in all outgoing Wilshire book orders is a catalog of all my books. The customer sees additional titles in his category of interest and invariably orders some of them.

Most people who buy one of my horse books, for example, order others. Many eventually purchase all of the 50 titles I offer. The reorder rate is similar for customers who order from my collection of gambling books. See pages 12 and 13. Readers of my books on playing bridge also purchase one after another, often until they have them all. I am fortunate to have Edwin B. Kantar, one of the highest-ranking bridge players in the world, as one of my authors. His full-time profession is playing and teaching bridge in countries around the world and on cruise ships. Readers of his books tell me they're delighted with the quality of information and that it has helped them enormously to become better players. They develop quite a healthy appetite for bridge books.

Customers of self-help, inspirational books buy many of them, not only for themselves, but for family members, friends, and business acquaintances. Once they get enthusiastic about a book, they want to share it with the world.

As an avid reader of books, I, too, buy every one I can find on subjects that interest me. At one time, I probably had one of the world's largest collection of books on self-improvement, positive thinking, and motivation. Doing all that reading developed my sense of what elements make a top-selling self-help book and guided me in choosing profitable ones to publish. In fact, I was so excited by *Psycho-Cybernetics* when I first published it, that for 15 years I taught courses in it to thousands of students. Teaching kept my spirits high, and I felt good about sharing invaluable information that literally changed many people's lives. The students loved the classes and bought lots of my other motivational books. I'm convinced that my enthusiasm for the category helps make it my best selling one.

So, in addition to the one great product you have found—your lead item—you will need some follow-up products to offer your customers when the initial sale is made. For example, let's say you have decided to sell a package of special hybrid seed that grows the largest, reddest, most delectable-looking tomatoes on the face of the earth. Your classified ad pulls lots of inquiries. Your follow-up literature makes your potential customers' mouths water just thinking of those tomatoes. (The literature may have been supplied by the manufacturers. If not, you can write your own by reading books on writing advertising at the library. My favorite is *How to Write a Good Advertisement* by Victor O. Schwab.)

Orders pour in. You've read *Making Money with Classified Ads* by yours truly and you've done your homework. You're ready with special hybrid seed for scrumptious radishes, carrots, and cucumbers. You have enticing literature on them, which you enclose with the initial order for tomato seed. Happy with their tomato seed and with your easy, expert instructions for planting them and harvesting an abundance of enviable tomatoes, some of your customers order other seed right away. Others are so delighted with their crop that they later order seed for radishes, carrots, and cucumbers. And voila! You have the beginnings of a great mail order business. Bird seed is also an excellent item to sell. Seeds are lightweight, there's no breakage, and reorders are high.

As your customer base grows, you add trowels, gardening gloves and soil treatments, miraculous fruit and vegetable nutrients, etc. Now you can afford to make up a snazzy color catalog that will boost sales even more. You are on your way! Great scenario, isn't it? Well, it's much more than fiction. It can happen to you just as it has to thousands of other mail order entrepreneurs.

It happened to Harris Seeds. They put out an 82-page colored catalog of vegetables and seeds. They include a section called "Tips & Tricks for Successful Home Gardening." That's an intriguing title for those interested in gardening. The company mails out a million catalogs a year and does not use an 800 number. Isn't that interesting? To find out more about running a perfectly run mail order business and possibly to order their products, write or call: Harris Seeds, 60 Saginaw Drive, Rochester, New York 14623-3132. Telephone (716) 442-0410.

Your Business is Going Great . . . Now What?

When your ads and follow-up literature are pulling in orders and you have successfully increased the number of publications you advertise in, it's time to rent other advertisers' names and do a mailing. How can you find the best ones? By choosing lists of people who have demonstrated by previous purchases that they are interested in the type of items you are offering, and by testing, testing, testing!

I'm constantly testing new mailing lists. One day soon, you will be, too. Now I'm going to share one of the Melvin Powers's mail order rules that can save you a lot of money: Walk before you run. When you rent names, order the minimum number only. Some companies won't rent fewer than 3- to 5-thousand. When that's the case, I order their minimum but use only 1,000 or fewer for my first mailing. That's how I test the list for profitability before spending money on literature and postage for the additional thousands of people on the list. If my mailing is successful, I double the number of names I mail to the next time. If that's successful, I keep on doubling the names with each successive mailing. That's exactly how I recommend you do it.

How to Get Thousands of Extra Dollars
Into Your Pocket . . . Effortlessly

One of the extra sources of income enjoyed by people in the mail order business is the renting out of customers' names to other companies. They pay a fee per thousand to use a mailing list one time. I rent my names for $100 per thousand. I have steady customers who purchase the new names I get every month. I also have arrangements that provide for me to be paid a commission on all orders generated by my names.

As you build your customer list, you, too, will be able to rent out your names. When you have a minimum of 10,000 (and you will, probably sooner than you think) contact a list broker, who you can find in the yellow pages and in reference books at the library, and ask if he would like to handle your names.

Partial Consumer Magazine List

A complete consumer magazine list is available in reference books at the library.

ANIMAL
   Western Horseman
   Dog Fancy
   Cat Fancy
   Bird Talk
   Horse Illustrated
   Horse & Rider
   Wildbird

Aquarium Fish
Equus
Practical Horseman

AUDIO/STEREO
Car Audio & Electronics
Stereo Review
Audio/Video Interiors
Audio

AUTOMOBILE
Hot Rod
Car & Driver
Truckin'
Road & Track
Motor Trend
Road & Track
Four Wheeler
Popular Hot Rodding
Hemming's Motor News

AVIATION
Flying
Private Pilot

BOATING
Boating
Wooden Boat
Sail

BUSINESS
Barron's
Money
Entrepreneur
Smart Money
Inc.
Black Enterprise
Your Money

COMPUTERS
Computer Shopper

PC Magazine
PC World
Byte
PC Computing
Windows Magazine
PC Sources
MacWorld

CYCLE

Easy Riders
Mountain Bike Action
Cycle World
Motorcyclist
Dirt Bike
Motorcross Action
In The Wind
Dirt Rider

FITNESS & HEALTH

Prevention
Muscle & Fitness
Fitness Magazine
Flex
Vegetarian Times

GUNS

Guns & Ammo
Shooting Times
Guns

HOBBIES/CRAFTS/MECHANICS

Beckett Baseball Cards
Country Sampler
Popular Mechanics
Popular Science
Crafts 'n Things
Model Railroader
Family Handyman
Workbasket
Trains
Sew News

HUNTING & FISHING
: *The In-Fisherman*
Game & Fish
Field & Stream
Bowhunter

MEN'S GENERAL
: *Penthouse*
Playboy
Men's Health
Men's Fitness
EM (Ebony Man)

NEWS
: *National Enquirer*
Star
Globe
National Examiner
Weekly World News
Sun

OUTDOORS/GENERAL
: *Outdoor Life*
Backpacker
Sports Afield

PHOTOGRAPHY
: *Popular Photography*
Petersen's Photographic
American Photo
Shutterbug

ROMANCE
: *True Story Plus*
True Story

SPORTS
: *Golf Digest*
Sport
Golf
Bicycling

Runner's World
Golf Illustrated
Sports Afield
Skin Diver
Tennis
Ski
Triathlete
Climbing
Bowling Digest

TEEN

YM
Seventeen
'Teen
Sassy
Sixteen Magazine

WOMEN'S GENERAL

Woman's Day
Family Circle
Cosmopolitan
Woman's World
New Woman
Self
Shape
Parent's
Working Woman

Melvin Powers
Wilshire Book Company

12015 Sherman Road
No. Hollywood, CA 91605-3781

Phone: (818) 765-8579
Fax: (818) 765-2922
E-mail: mpowers@mpowers.com
Web site: www.mpowers.com

RETAILERS FORUM
A Wholesale Buyers' Guide

Every successful mail order entrepreneur invests time in finding products to sell. We think of that search as an exciting treasure hunt with a pot of gold at the end—because that's exactly what it is. Be diligent in looking for your first product. It is the one that will launch your new business and finding it can be a most exhilarating experience.

One of the best monthly magazines in which to find descriptions of products from Taiwan, Hong Kong, Singapore, Korea, and China is the United States published *Retailers Forum*. It's an encyclopedic source that will stimulate you to find a money-making product with which to begin your mail order business.

The pages are filled with illustrations of excellent mail order products and with names and addresses of hundreds of sources in the United States where you can buy merchandise at the lowest prices possible. Send for a copy or subscribe today.

When you receive your copy of *Retailers Forum*, mark each of the merchandising companies located near you. Visit them, introducing yourself (you'll be establishing valuable contacts) and exploring their products. In addition, write to the non-local companies that carry items in your field of interest or call their toll free 800 numbers. Ask every company to place your name on its mailing list so you will receive announcements of new products. It's a good way to find out about unique items before they are advertised to the general public.

Print business cards with your name, address, and telephone number to leave with your contacts and to hand out at trade shows. If you do not have a company name, print Mail Order Entrepreneur under your own name. Not only will you present a good business image to others, but every time you look at your card, you'll be programming yourself for success.

Follow these suggestions and you'll be proceeding in a logical, business-like manner that will eventually spell success for you.

To start your mail order career, invest $7.00 for a sample copy of *Retailers Forum* or send $30.00 for a full year's subscription (Canada—$60.00 in United States funds). Make your check payable to Melvin Powers and send to:

Melvin Powers, 12015 Sherman Road, No. Hollywood, California 91605

62

WHY SHOULD YOU *subscribe* TO THE TDC PUBLICATIONS ?

Be certain to get every single issue of the product publications of your choice. You miss an issue and who knows what new products and suppliers will slip by into your competitor's hands.

Keeping abreast of the latest products. It is the key to beating the competition. At the TDC, we publish thousands and thousands of pages, chock-a-block full of products, products, and more products — just about everything under the sun in your specific product category.

Subscribe now and get the right publications on your desk before your competitors.

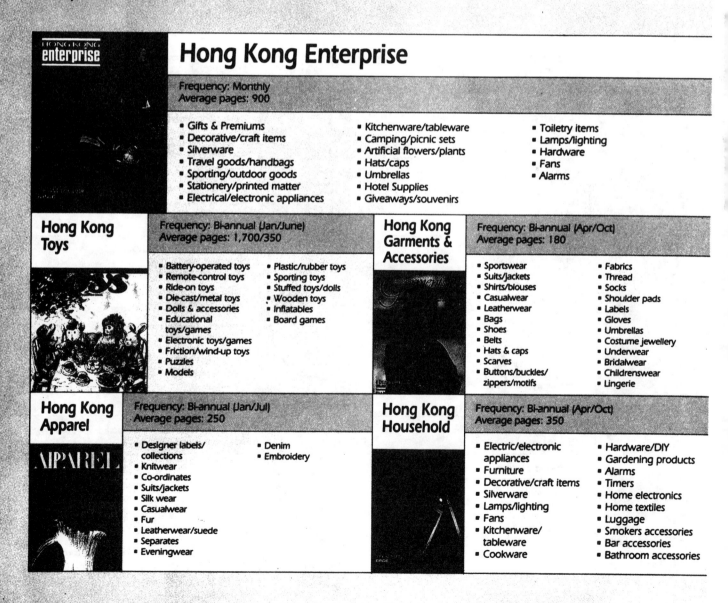

Hong Kong Enterprise

Frequency: Monthly
Average pages: 900

- Gifts & Premiums
- Decorative/craft items
- Silverware
- Travel goods/handbags
- Sporting/outdoor goods
- Stationery/printed matter
- Electrical/electronic appliances
- Kitchenware/tableware
- Camping/picnic sets
- Artificial flowers/plants
- Hats/caps
- Umbrellas
- Hotel Supplies
- Giveaways/souvenirs
- Toiletry items
- Lamps/lighting
- Hardware
- Fans
- Alarms

Hong Kong Toys

Frequency: Bi-annual (Jan/June)
Average pages: 1,700/350

- Battery-operated toys
- Remote-control toys
- Ride-on toys
- Die-cast/metal toys
- Dolls & accessories
- Educational toys/games
- Electronic toys/games
- Friction/wind-up toys
- Puzzles
- Models
- Plastic/rubber toys
- Sporting toys
- Stuffed toys/dolls
- Wooden toys
- Inflatables
- Board games

Hong Kong Garments & Accessories

Frequency: Bi-annual (Apr/Oct)
Average pages: 180

- Sportswear
- Suits/jackets
- Shirts/blouses
- Casualwear
- Leatherwear
- Bags
- Shoes
- Belts
- Hats & caps
- Scarves
- Buttons/buckles/zippers/motifs
- Fabrics
- Thread
- Socks
- Shoulder pads
- Labels
- Gloves
- Umbrellas
- Costume jewellery
- Underwear
- Bridalwear
- Childrenswear
- Lingerie

Hong Kong Apparel

Frequency: Bi-annual (Jan/Jul)
Average pages: 250

- Designer labels/collections
- Knitwear
- Co-ordinates
- Suits/jackets
- Silk wear
- Casualwear
- Fur
- Leatherwear/suede
- Separates
- Eveningwear
- Denim
- Embroidery

Hong Kong Household

Frequency: Bi-annual (Apr/Oct)
Average pages: 350

- Electric/electronic appliances
- Furniture
- Decorative/craft items
- Silverware
- Lamps/lighting
- Fans
- Kitchenware/tableware
- Cookware
- Hardware/DIY
- Gardening products
- Alarms
- Timers
- Home electronics
- Home textiles
- Luggage
- Smokers accessories
- Bar accessories
- Bathroom accessories

SUBSCRIPTION RATES

Publication		Subscription Rates (US$)		
		Airmail		Seamail
		Zone 1	Zone 2	
HK Enterprise	12 consecutive issues	300	400	180
	6 issues (altenate months) per year	180	240	100
	3 issues/per year ★	80	100	———
HK Toys	2 issues	70	80	40
HK Electronics	4 issues	80	100	
HK Jewellery	2 issues	30	40	
HK Watches & Clocks	2 issues	30	40	
HK Household	2 issues	30	40	
HK Gifts & Premium	2 issues	30	40	
HK Apparel	2 issues	30	40	
HK Garments & Accessories	2 issues	30	40	
HK Leather Goods & Bags	2 issues	30	40	
HK Optical	1 issue	20	20	

Zone 1 - Asia (as far west as Afghanistan)
Zone 2 - Americas, Europe, Middle East, Africa, Oceania, Australia & New Zealand

All TDC product publications are printed and despatched from Hong Kong.

AIRMAIL
approximately 10-15 days and
SEAMAIL
approximately 6-8 weeks.

★ Random combinations of the
JAN/MAY/SEPT, FEB/JUNE/OCT, MAR/JULY/NOV & APR/AUG/DEC issues

Hong Kong Electronics

Frequency: Quarterly(Jan/Apr/Jul/Oct)
Average pages: 300

- Computers
- Computer parts/ accessories/ peripherals
- Electronic appliances
- Electronic watches/ timers
- Electronic toys/games
- Translators
- Diaries
- Calculators
- TVs
- Radios
- Radio/cassettes
- Portables
- Karaokes
- Consumer electronics
- Electronic parts/ components
- Telephones
- Fax machines

Hong Kong Watches & Clocks

Frequency: Bi-annual (Apr/Sep)
Average pages: 250

- Mechanical watches
- Electronic/quartz watches
- Premium watches
- Jewellery watches
- Children's watches
- Dress watches
- Sports watches
- Diving watches
- Timers
- Electronic/electrical clocks
- Desktop clocks
- Wall clocks
- Cases
- Dials/crowns/hands movements
- Watchbands/straps

Hong Kong Gifts & Premiums

Frequency: Bi-annual (Apr/Oct)
Average pages: 300

- Consumer electronics
- Watches/clocks
- Toys/games
- Decorative/craft items
- Ceramics/crystal/ glassware
- Travel goods/handbags
- Silverware/metalware
- Sporting/outdoor goods
- Stationery/printed matter/ gift packaging
- Camping/picnic sets
- Hats/caps
- Umbrellas
- Hotel items
- Smoker accessories
- Giveaways/souvenirs/ novelties
- Bar accessories
- Soap/toiletries

Hong Kong Optical

Frequency: Annual (Nov)
Average pages: 150

- Spectacles
- Sunglasses
- Goggles
- Lenses
- Mountings
- Accessories
- Optometric instruments
- Glass cases
- Promotional items
- Glass holders

Hong Kong Jewellery

Frequency: Bi-annual (Mar/Sep)
Average pages: 250

- Diamond jewellery
- Gem-set jewellery
- Gold jewellery
- Platinum jewellery
- Silver jewellery
- Antique jewellery
- Jade
- Pearls
- Jewellery watches/clocks
- Engravings
- Silverware
- Gemstones
- Precious stones
- Semi-precious stones
- Objèts d'art
- Costume jewellery
- Designer collections

Hong Kong Leather Goods & Bags

Frequency: Bi-annual (Apr/Oct)
Average pages: 200

LEATHERWARE
- Belts
- Hats & caps
- Gloves
- Shoes
- Slippers
- Handbags
- Suitcases/travelling bags
- Wallets/purses
- Briefcases
- Executive desk sets

BAGS
- Shopping bags
- Luggage
- Handbags
- Travelling bags
- Wallets/purses
- Sport bags
- Promotional bags
- Cosmetic bags
- Packsacks
- Ice bags

To : Hong Kong Trade Development Council (**Attn** : Subscription Section)

YES. I wish to subscribe the following TDC publications :-

▪ For speedy and accurate computer processing, complete this form clearly. Please print, type or attach your business card.

Mail to: Hong Kong Trade Development Council
Suite 3800, 38 Floor, Office Tower
Convention Plaza, 1 Harbour Road,
Wanchai, Hong Kong

Company Name _____

Address _____

Country _____ Zip/Post Code _____

Name of Recipient _____
(Mr./Mrs./Miss)   Family Name   Given Name

Position _____ Department _____

Tel _____ Fax _____
        Country Code + Area Code + Number   Country Code + Area Code + Number

Please tick your choices in the appropriate boxes on the right ‖‖‖➡

Publication		Subscription Rates (US$)			Subscription Choice (Please tick)	
		Airmail		Seamail	Airmail	Seamail
		Zone 1	Zone 2			
HK Enterprise	12 consecutive issues	300	400	180		
	6 alternate issues per year	180	240	100		
	3 issues/per year	80	100	———		———
HK Toys	2 issues	70	80	40		
HK Electronics	4 issues	80	100			
HK Jewellery	2 issues	30	40			
HK Watches & Clocks	2 issues	30	40			
HK Household	2 issues	30	40			
HK Gifts & Premiums	2 issues	30	40			
HK Apparel	2 issues	30	40			
HK Garments & Accessories	2 issues	30	40			
HK Leather Goods & Bags	2 issues	30	40			
HK Optical	1 issue	20	20			

▪ Please allow 4 weeks for processing.

Payment

☐ I enclose bank draft/cheque for US$ _____ made payable to Hong Kong Trade Development Council

☐ I wish to pay by credit card. (Please SIGN BELOW and send by air-mail/courier the original form to HKTDC for processing. Fax copies will not be accepted.)

☐ ■   ☐ VISA   ☐ MasterCard

Name of Cardholder _____

Card No. _____   Expiry Date _____

Total Amount US$ _____ Date _____ Signature _____

Melvin Powers' Mail Order Library

HOW TO WRITE A GOOD ADVERTISEMENT

by Victor O. Schwab

256 Pages...$22.00 postpaid

MELVIN POWERS' TEN-HOUR MAIL ORDER SEMINAR ON CASSETTE TAPES

Here is an opportunity for those of you unable to attend my mail order seminar to hear me discuss many aspects of running a successful part-time or full-time business. In the privacy of your home, office, or car, you'll hear the same seminar that thousands of entrepreneurs all over the country have attended. The ten hours of audio tape instruction will answer many of the questions you have wanted to ask. It will teach you how to successfully become your own boss.

After listening to the tape program, you will better understand mail order fundamentals and procedures, and will have an overall plan that will help you start making money right away in your own mail order business. The tape program is sold on a one-year, money-back guarantee. It must be of tangible help in teaching you how to make money in mail order, or I'll refund your money—no questions asked.

Here's how to gain maximum benefit from the tapes: (1) Listen to the material several times to fully comprehend the practical suggestions and information; (2) Put into practice the specific elements to be incorporated in your mail order plan; (3) Run your first classified or display ad; (4) Do a test mailng to one thousand or as many as three thousand people who would logically be interested in your product; (5) Evaluate the results; (6) Call or write to me to discuss your mail order plan and receive my suggestions for increasing your chances to attain success.

Send for Melvin Powers' Mail Order Seminar on Cassette Tapes. $65.00 postpaid.

Send your order to:
Melvin Powers
12015 Sherman Road
No. Hollywood, California 91605

Chapter Four

Write Classified Ads
That Make Money

Congratulations! You have found a product you're excited about, planned for back-end sales, and you're ready to start making money with your first classified ad. But, alas, you've never written one before, except possibly to sell your car. That's OK. This chapter will teach you how to write great ads. Now, let's get started by sharpening your skill to distinguish between strong and weak advertising copy. Read the following three ads.

LOSE WEIGHT! Secrets of sticking to your diet revealed in physician's book, *Mind Over Platter*. Guaranteed results or money back. $7.00 postpaid

STOP SMOKING! New method guarantees results or your money back. $7.00 postpaid

ACNE? ARTHRITIS? Headaches? Painful feet? Cellulite? Fatigue? Treatment secrets revealed. Special reports only $1.00 each

MAKE EXTRA MONEY in your spare time. Free details

FREE, INTERESTING, illustrated, self-improvement book catalog. Write: Melvin Powers, 12015 Sherman Road, Suite 711, North Hollywood, California 91605

Do any of these ads interest you personally? Might they interest you if you had extra pounds to lose, wanted to quit smoking, had one of the medical problems mentioned, wanted to make extra money, or were interested in self-improvement? Would they motivate you to send for the information or products? A basic test you can use to determine whether or not ad copy is effective is to ask yourself these two questions: Would the first few words of the ad grab your attention if you were interested in the product or service being advertised? And would the body of the ad motivate you to send for the information or product?

Read Ad Copy Written by the Pros

The best way to learn how to write money-making classified ads is to study how the professionals do it. Study classified ad copy in magazines and newspapers, asking yourself the two basic test questions above. Buy the *National Enquirer*, the *Star*, or the *Globe* at the checkout counter of your grocery store and study their classified ads. These weeklies are key publications for certain types of mail order sales. Their circulation is in the millions, people read and respond to the classified section, their rates are reasonable, and the closing dates for classifieds are relatively short.

It would also be helpful to read books on writing advertising copy. There are many available at the library. As mentioned earlier, my favorite is *How to Write a Good Advertisement* by Victor O. Schwab.

What a Winning Ad Must Do

First, the ad must capture the attention of readers, preferably those who have some interest in the product or service being offered. (In the sales trade, this is called qualifying the prospect.) The first words are responsible for creating this interest immediately. The beginning of the ads above clearly accomplish this. "STOP SMOKING" would catch the eye of anyone who wants to quit smoking. "LOSE WEIGHT?" would attract anyone who wants to take off extra pounds. "ACNE? ARTHRITIS?" would interest anyone who has any of the medical problems mentioned and would like to get rid of them. "MAKE EXTRA MONEY" would appeal to anyone who wants more money.

Now let's talk about the last ad. Why do you think I used "FREE, INTERESTING" as the opening words? Who would be attracted to this ad? Might more people read the body of the ad than would have if I had begun with "SELF-IMPROVEMENT BOOK CATALOG"? Which opening do you think would pull a larger response?

Second, an ad must give enough information to motivate the reader to act. Which catchy words and phrases in the body of our sample ads would likely get readers to take action? We'll talk more about this as we progress through this chapter.

Two Types of Classified Ads

THE ONE-STEP METHOD

The first three ads we've been discussing are one-step ads. They sell the product directly from the ad. The risk with this method is that you may not be able to include enough information to motivate the reader to buy. You can't use testimonials or illustrations or give explanations of what the product does or how it works. Remember, every word you use costs you money.

The trick with a one-step ad is to achieve a balance between saying enough to be effective and not saying so much that you drive up your costs too high. Inexpensive products (less than $12.00) that need no explanation lend themselves well to the one-step method. Coming up later in this chapter are tips on words and phrases that will help you get a powerful message across in as few words as possible.

Many mail order companies use one-step ads with a slightly different twist. They offer a single item, usually at a low price, primarily as a means of getting leads for the more expensive items that comprise the major part of their business activity. The sale of the advertised item is not their main concern. In each outgoing order, they enclose a brochure or catalog for their main items, which are usually more expensive than the leader and harder to market using classified ads. For example, the "ACNE, ARTHRITIS?" ad says it's selling special reports. Its main purpose, however, is to sell more expensive products which are described in a catalog or brochure sent with the special reports.

When deciding whether or not to use the one-step method, remember that a good classified ad should do all of the following:

1. Capture attention.

2. Create interest in the product or service.

3. Describe product benefits.

4. Create the desire to purchase.

5. Offer a guarantee.

6. Tell the price.

7. Call to action.

8. Have a key in the address.

If any of these items cannot be included, it may be better to use a two-step ad.

THE TWO-STEP METHOD

The last two ads are examples of two-step ads. Notice that they do not attempt to sell directly from the ad. Instead, they solicit inquiries. Direct mail literature is then used to convert these inquiries into sales. This method will be discussed in detail in a later chapter. The two-step plan is the most popular method. It allows you to do a good selling job with follow-up literature and a cover letter, rather than having to squeeze the information into the ad, itself. As you'll see in the sample ads, I use the two-step approach to sell books.

You can experiment with both the one- and two-step methods to see which pulls best for you. However, I strongly suggest that you try the two-step method first. It's usually less costly and promises the best chance for success. The proof of this is its extensive use by successful mail order entrepreneurs. Now, let's get down to business—the business of actually writing your ad.

Headlines Carry the Greatest Impact

The headline generates 75% of the impact of an ad. In classified ads, the beginning words serve as a headline, making them extremely important. For this reason, most publications set them in all capital letters. The first few words can serve several purposes:

1. To get the attention of your best prospects.

2. To promise a benefit.

3. To encourage the reader to read on.

Tap into the reader's self-interest. Tell him immediately what your product or service can do for him.

The Body Delivers the Message that Makes or Breaks the Ad

The best message is the promise of a benefit to the reader—preferably an irresistible one that satisfies one of the eleven basic human desires listed in chapter three. Here's where you sell them on the dream.

Four Rules for Writing the Body of a Powerful, Money-Making Ad

1. WRITE SUCCINCTLY AND TO THE POINT.
   Remember, the fewer words you use, the lower the cost. Eliminating the words you don't really need can mean a savings of hundreds or even thousands of dollars a year. A

good trick is to pretend you're writing a telegram. Make every word count. I could, for instance, condense what I've just told you into five words: Save money. Use fewest words.

2. USE HOT-BUTTON WORDS AND PHRASES.

Some words evoke a better response than others. Here are over 40 hot buttons you should press as often as possible.

FREE

Free is one of the strongest words you can use. It's so powerful, in fact, that the creative director of a large mail order agency once issued the following directive to his staff: "If you can use the word *free*, and don't . . . you're fired!"

Everyone likes to get free things. That's why catalogs or literature that are offered free get a substantially larger response than those that require even a minimal payment. Here are a few ways the word *free* is used in mail order advertising:

Free Information

Free Details

Free Catalog

Free Gift

Free Trial Offer

NEW

Anything new is newsworthy. Just about everyone is interested in what's new; that's why we have *new*spapers. Here are some variations on the same theme:

Now

At Last

Never Before

SAVE

People like to save money, time, wear and tear, work, grief, and hassle. Here are a few variations of the word *save* and some key phrases that appeal to these desires:

Sale

Discount

Introductory Offer

Sold Only by Mail

Buy Direct and Save

Fast

Easy, Easy-to-Follow Instructions

Step-by-Step Instructions

Freedom

Prevent

Protect

Relief

MONEY

Because most everyone, it seems, wants to make more money, hot buttons relating to money are used frequently.

Extra Income

Make Big Money

Wealth

Financial Freedom

Cash, Checks, and Money Orders

Riches

Unlimited Income Potential

HOW TO

Research shows that ads promising useful information have, on the average, 75% greater readership than those offering a product. That's why so many successful book titles start with "How to," as in *How to Win Friends and Influence People.*

MONEY-BACK GUARANTEE

This is mandatory. You must promise "satisfaction or your money back" for any product you sell. It can be for 10 days, 30 days, 60 days, or more. Some mail order entrepreneurs guarantee satisfaction by allowing the purchaser to postdate his check for 30 days. If the product is not to the customer's liking, he can ask for his check to be returned or he can stop payment on it.

I sell some of my books on a 365-day money-back guarantee. I do it to lend credibility to my offer, and I have yet to receive one request for a refund for any of these offers. It may sound incredible, but it's a fact.

If your product or service is worthwhile, the chances of a refund request are negligible. Always include the guarantee in your literature. If you do get a request for a refund, send back the money immediately. Include a self-addressed, stamped envelope, and politely ask the customer why he was dissatisfied, explaining that if there is a way to improve the product, you would appreciate his letting you know. If you have very many requests for refunds, it's an indication that something is wrong with your product. It is up to you to do something about making improvements or corrections.

Other hot-button words:

Exciting

Amazing

Wanted

Secret (as in "Secrets of Success")

Learn

Do-it-Yourself

Romance

Self-Improvement

Sex

Power

Success

No Risk

3. Include complete information on where to send payment.
   This should appear at the end of the ad.

4. Key all your ads.
   This is a must. You have to be able to track your ads to determine which are winners.

Where Not to Advertise

Where should you not advertise? In daily newspapers. Classified ads in dailies generally do not pay off. The reason is twofold. First, the life expectancy of a newspaper is, at most, one day. That means that the paper is not lying around for weeks on a coffee table or in a magazine rack where it may be picked up any number of times by any number of people, each time providing a new opportunity for your ad to be seen. And second, as a rule the general public is not in the habit of looking for mail order merchandise in a newspaper's classified section. Remember, you are best off not advertising where people don't usually look for your type of offer.

Fish Where the Fishing is Good

It is best to advertise in magazines that other mail order companies use. Magazines that consistently run mail order ads are the survivors of trial and error. The advertisers have tested the various magazines, and you can learn from their experience which are the best. That doesn't mean that you can't experiment. Hunches and long shots have been known to pay off. But customers, by habit, have become programmed to look in certain publications for classified offers, and you would be well advised to use them if you want the largest possible audience.

In time, you'll discover which mail order companies have the most successful advertisements and in which publications they appear. They will repeat their ad runs. This indicates that the ads are making money. Mail order advertising must pay off or the ads will stop. A non-paying ad—even though you like it—should be pulled. My advice is to rewrite the ad.

Test the Water Before You Plunge In!

Run one ad in the best publication that seems likely to produce orders for you. If appropriate, consider the *Star* or the *National Enquirer*. They have a 65% female readership. I like them because their closing date is only six weeks, rather than the eight weeks required by most publications. That means you'll be able to test your offer in a short time. It's not necessary to run in both publications. Choose one or the other for your test.

The Best Times to Advertise

Many products have a well-established seasonal period. Don't try to buck it. If you are selling a product for the rainy season, for instance, it will sell best during the winter when problems associated with rain are on people's minds. But with some creative thinking, you could extend that season considerably.

If your business is seasonal, do some brainstorming to come up with innovative ways of stimulating sales during slow periods. I.J. Fox, a Boston furrier, turned the months of July and August into his biggest months for sales of fur coats. How? By offering incentives to prospective buyers; mainly, saving money. He undertook an aggressive radio and newspaper ad campaign and it paid off. People got the message that summer was the best time to purchase furs.

Generally the following months, ranked in order, are considered best for mail order sales:
1. October
2. November
3. September
4. January
5. February
6. March

Mail order companies usually do the largest percentage of their business during the months of September, October, and November due to holiday season purchases. It's the time of year when people are in the mood to buy gifts. The first three months of the year are also great mail order months because people are home much more during the winter than at other times of the year. That means more time for reading and for acting on New Year's resolutions for self-improvement.

In planning your advertising campaign, bear in mind that most national monthly publications require that your ad and remittance reach them by the 10th of the second month preceding publication. That means your ad must be delivered to the publication office by

January 10th for the March issue, February 10th for the April issue, and so on.

How Much Will it Cost?

As I mentioned previously, often the publication will tell their advertising rates at the beginning of the classified section. It will read something like this: $5.00 per word. Minimum words—15. You can write to the publications you are interested in and ask for their classified rates, or get a fast, overall view of magazine classified rates by writing to: National Mail Order Classified, Dept. A-l, 2628 17th Street, Sarasota, Florida 34230. Telephone (941) 366-3003. Ask for Marilyn. She'll send you free information about hundreds of magazines you would not otherwise know about.

It's Time to Run the Ad

Run the ad one time and one time only. Then sit back and watch the results. You'll waste money if you run more than once for testing purposes. Generally, the ad will not pull better with repetition. Running one time gives you the opportunity to revise and strengthen your ad as soon as you've determined it needs improvement. The rule in mail order is to keep testing to minimize your losses and maximize your earnings.

You've Got a Winner! . . . What Do You Do Now?

You're going to keep doing what you've been doing—only do more of it! Run the ad again and gradually expand your coverage until it's running in as many magazines as you can manage. If appropriate, you might want to test the same ad in several classifications in the same publication. The readership varies from one classification to the next. The prudent way to expand is to use a large part of your profits generated by ads to run more ads. In choosing where to run, remember to look for long classified sections. Watch those keys and keep careful records of profits generated by each publication so you aren't continuing to run in any that are not making money for you. At the same time, try to improve your response by adding a few hot-button words.

How to Track Your Results

You are going to keep an accurate account of every inquiry and order you receive. If you are running a one-step ad, you will count how many sales each of your ads generated in each publication for each day that it ran.

If you are running a two-step ad, you'll count the inquiries for each publication each day the ad ran, then you will count the sales that result from the inquiries. If you recall, my own ad—the last one in the list at the beginning of this chapter—used the number key "Suite

711" as part of the address, which indicates the magazine in which the ad ran. I can easily tell how well that publication pulled by simply counting the responses with that key on them.

Unobtrusively write the same key you are using for the publication that generated the inquiry on your follow-up literature order form or on your return envelope if you are using one. Then when each order comes in, it will be clear which publication generated the original inquiry.

Whether you use a computer or a manual filing system to keep your records, you should be able to quickly and easily trace orders back to the original inquiries. File all original inquiries by state, in alphabetical order by the customer's last name. Using the same system, in separate file boxes, file all original orders. Envelope boxes with dividers that have the states on them serve this purpose nicely. This system makes large numbers of inquiries and orders manageable and provides valuable information about which parts of the country are responding best to your offer. Always keep a running list of inquiries for future use as mailing list.

You've Got a Loser. . . . What Do You Do Now?

Analyze why your ad isn't working. Here are some things to consider:

1. You may be advertising in the wrong publication for your type of offer.

2. There may be too much competition for the product, causing sales to be watered down.

3. Your price may be too high or too low.

4. Your follow-up literature may not tell the story fully and convincingly.

5. The offer may not be believable.

6. Your advertising copy may not generate excitement.

7. Your response to inquiries may take too long. A good rule of thumb is to answer each inquiry the day you receive it. Remember, you are competing with others who have the same product. You want to get there first with the best.

Finally, if you don't think any of these are the reason your campaign didn't work, then sadly, it's time to consider the possibility that you've simply picked a loser. If it turns out that you have, try not to feel too bad. Even the most experienced mail order people sometimes pick losers. Accept the loss as part of the expense of doing business and go on to the next project. A losing campaign is always a learning experience. And sometimes you can salvage some good elements from it that will help a new campaign become a winner.

Self Quiz and Assignments

For this quiz you will need to examine the classified sections of at least six current national magazines, which can be found at the library. You'll also need an issue of the *National Enquirer*, the *Star*, or the *Globe*. All three are available at grocery store check-out counters and newsstands.

1. Did you notice that some publications have large classified ad sections and others have rather limited sections? Which would you advertise in, and why?
    A. Those with large sections.
    B. Those with short sections.

2. Look at the capitalized or emphasized words at the beginning of the ads. List the ones that quickly grab the attention of people interested in the products being advertised. Also make a list of words that motivate the reader.

3. Find and list at least ten hot-button words and phrases in the ads you are examining.

4. Why is it important to write succinctly and to the point?

5. Why should you key your ads?

6. Is it a good idea to advertise in a daily newspaper? Why or why not?

7. In order of importance, list the best six months in which to advertise.

8. What should you do if you have a winner?
    A. Continue to run the same ad in the same publication.
    B. Gradually expand into other publications and perhaps other classifications of the same publications.
    C. Both of the above.

9. What should you do if you have a loser?
    A. Try to improve the ad.
    B. Drop it immediately.
    C. First try to improve the ad, then drop it if it still doesn't pay off.

Answers

1. *A.* Generally you should choose publications with large classified ad sections. It's an indication that advertisers are getting results.

2. Your first list should contain words such as hemorrhoid sufferers, bald men. Your second list, words such as stop dandruff, relieve itching, stop bed-wetting.

3. This list should contain such words as free, new, save, how to. See complete list of more than 40 earlier in this chapter.

4. Because you're charged by the word and you could save thousands of dollars a year.

5. So you can trace which ads and which publications produced the best results.

6. No. They usually don't pay off because people aren't used to finding mail order merchandise there. Also the life expectancy of a newspaper is usually only one day.

7. 1. October, 2. November, 3. September, 4. January, 5. February, 6. March

8. *C.* Pat yourself on the back. You're on the way to mail order success.

9. *C.* Don't be discouraged. Remember, ads that don't work are a part of the business. Success awaits you if you persevere. Simply find a different product and start again.

IT COULDN'T BE DONE

Edgar A. Guest

Somebody said that it couldn't be done,
    But he with a chuckle replied
That "maybe it couldn't," but he would be one
    Who wouldn't say so till he tried.
So he buckled right in with the trace of a grin
    On his face. If he worried he hid it.
He started to sing as he tackled the thing
    That couldn't be done, and he did it.

Somebody scoffed: "Oh, you'll never do that,
    At least no one ever has done it;"
But he took off his coat and he took off his hat,
    And the first thing we knew he'd begun it,
With a lift of his chin and a bit of a grin,
    Without any doubting or quiddit,
He started to sing as he tackled the thing
    That couldn't be done, and he did it.

There are thousands to tell you it cannot be done,
    There are thousands to prophesy failure;
There are thousands to point out to you, one by one,
    The dangers that wait to assail you.
But just buckle in with a bit of a grin,
    Just take off your coat and go to it;
Just start to sing as you tackle the thing
    That "cannot be done," and you'll do it.

Reprinted from *The Collected Verse of Edgar A. Guest*
Copyright 1934 by Reilly & Lee Company

Chapter Five

What I've Learned from Running Thousands of Classified Ads Month After Month, Year After Year

Will anybody really notice your little two- or three-line ad buried in columns of similar ads, at the back of some magazine or tabloid? . . . My answer is a resounding, yes, absolutely!

Some people read classified ads to find a particular item or service but many others read them because they have an intellectual curiosity about what they may find. They enjoy the experience of scanning the columns for little treasures. They consider it fun. And they are ready to respond with an order or request for information to any ad that strikes them as interesting. They approach the ads with a willingness to act on anything that appeals to them.

Chances are that you are a reader of classified ads. And you probably have responded to some—perhaps even to one of mine. I know it's likely because you are interested enough in classified ads to be reading a book about how to make money with them. Of all the ads you have read, something prompted you to answer particular ones. What is it that motivated you to act? Do you scan all the ads or only a particular category, as many people do?

Think of other people doing as you have done—reading every ad in a category they like, or in an entire publication. If you were to have an ad running in the section they are reading, they would see it for sure. They wouldn't be able to miss it. The point is that when you run a classified ad you have a captive audience—one that's reading your ad by their own choosing. Give them what they are searching for, and you'll have an advertiser's dream—a customer eager to respond to your offer. Here's a perfect example.

For many years I ran a one-step classified ad in numerous horse publications for a book I publish called *Practical Guide to Horseshoeing*. (There are 125 publications devoted to horses.) It was the perfect product in the right publications and the ad was clear. It read:

PRACTICAL GUIDE TO HORSESHOEING Guaranteed. $7.00 postpaid. Wilshire Books, 12015 Sherman Road, North Hollywood, California 91605

In response I sent them the book and my catalog of horse books. Back came more orders for various horse books. I also successfully ran the following two-step ad:

FREE FASCINATING HOW-TO BOOK CATALOG. Write: Wilshire Books, 12015 Sherman Road, North Hollywood, California 91605

Here's an ad that seems to work everywhere both as a classified and display ad. I've seen it, and variations of it, for as long as I can remember.

PLAY GUITAR IN 7 DAYS or your money back. Special introductory offer includes 66-page book, 52 photos, 110 songs. $9.98 postpaid. Ed Sale Guitar, Studio 15-A Main Street, Grand Island, Florida 32735

See the display ad on page 88. Note the nice illustration. The ad copy reads: 1,000,000 people of all ages have learned to play guitar thanks to Ed Sale's amazing secret system. (Just think of that number!) That's powerful copy. Included is a $3.00 gift certificate. He promises you'll be able to play any song by ear or note in 7 days. Who can resist that promise? I like his key: Studio 15-A instead of Dept. 15-A.

Here's a one-step ad that I run periodically in various magazines with good success.

HOW TO SELF-PUBLISH YOUR BOOK. Have the fun and excitement of being a bestselling author. Famous publisher of multi-million bestsellers reveals his marketing secrets in 240-page book. Send $22.00 to: Melvin Powers, 12015 Sherman Road, North Hollywood, California 91605. Or call (818) 765-8579 for credit card orders.

This offer has a fabulous back end. After reading my self-publishing book, writers contact me to print their books. Because of the volume of books I run, I get them the best possible prices and they also benefit from my book publishing expertise. It's a win-win situation. See page 240.

How to Make a Good Ad Even Better

Over many years of running classified ads, I've learned that no matter how much one learns about this business or how long one is in it, experimenting with advertising copy is still necessary. Trying to make ads better is a never-ending job even for the most experienced, most successful mail order entrepreneur.

How can you make your ad better when you think you have already done a good job on it? One way is to look at competition's ads that successfully run again and again, and try to improve upon them by analyzing what elements make them winners and working those elements into your own ad. Do it well and you have the potential of pulling more orders than your competitors. Even when your good results become excellent results, keep trying to improve the ad. Don't stop until you are completely satisfied you've done your absolute best.

The Right Item At the Right Time Is Magic!

Some years ago when there was a gas shortage, I published a book called *How to Save Up to 50% on Gas and Car Expenses*. It flew out of the warehouse because of the following classified ad I ran in numerous magazines and tabloids.

GUARANTEED! SAVE 50% on gas and car expenses. Only $6.00 postpaid. Write: Wilshire Book Company, Dept. 713, 12015 Sherman Road, North Hollywood, California 91605

There was no need for further elaboration. Not only did I sell lots of books, but as a result of a lead that developed from the ad, I established contact with a company that bought 8,000 copies to use as a premium. That was an unexpected bonus, but it wasn't all that unusual. When you're out there, things like that sometimes happen.

Your Lack of Interest Can Cost You a Fortune

Some time ago, I produced a 30-minute infomercial selling an automotive engine treatment called SLICK 50, before such products became well-known. My show helped promote the product nationally, contributing to its present popularity. Although my offer was for one quart of SLICK 50 at $29.95, I was surprised when 50% of the customers calling the 800 number ordered two quarts. Why did they do it? Because I had instructed the 800-number operators to offer callers free shipping and a free gift—a book on how to save gas—if they would order two quarts. Interestingly, I later received many additional orders for the book from these SLICK 50 customers.

I should have developed a catalog of automotive aftercare products, auto-related items, and books. I never did. I was busy with other projects at the time and told myself that I didn't have the time to devote to it. But in retrospect, it seems that it was my lack of enthusiasm for the automobile aftercare industry that caused me to miss out on the all-important back end of a business that was generating thousands of initial orders. The truth is that I just didn't have the inclination to be in an automobile-related business. I'm not much interested in cars. To me, they are nothing more than a means of transportation. I'm happy driving most any kind and I don't take care of it myself. (So much for taking my own advice!)

A Little-Known Secret of Mail Order Success

The secret is that there is a correlation between excitement and money that can get you a lot of both. Over the years, I have found that generally my enthusiasm for the products I sell has been reflected in their sales. When I'm hot about an item or book, sales are usually terrific. When I'm lukewarm about it, sales are usually lukewarm. And when I used to feel indifferent toward an item or book, sales were usually slow. (I learned early on not to try selling anything I didn't personally find interesting and feel some enthusiasm for—even if the product seemed to have good market potential.)

Don't Fall in Love

One of the times when falling in love can cost you dearly is when you fall for a product that ultimately doesn't make money in the marketplace. Once you've given the relationship your best effort and it didn't work, you must be strong enough to say goodbye. Every so often, it happens—even to me. There have been times when a project couldn't be saved no matter how excited I had been about it, nor how much time, energy, and money I had invested in it. I pushed it aside and moved on.

Don't let your ego or your feelings of attachment run your business. It's a sure way to fail at making it in mail order, or in any commercial or professional endeavor. You can't have a winner every time and it's no reflection on you personally or on your creative ability. I know lots of hit songwriters and bestselling authors. They all recognize that every song can't be a chart song and every book can't be a bestseller. And highly acclaimed movie producers know that every film can't be a box office hit. When one of their projects doesn't prove profitable, they move on to the next one. And so must you.

Look for Gems
In Other People's Rubble

My expertise in book publishing is to find other publishers' books that haven't made it in the market place and turn them into bestsellers. I have done it numerous times. A change of title and cover design, a foreword by yours truly, an aggressive advertising campaign, and help from my numerous domestic and international book outlet contacts all work in conjunction to transform a dud into a winner. I find it fun and challenging, and most rewarding. Keep your eyes open. Watch the marketplace for what's working and what's not. You may find a treasure being tossed into the trash.

E. Joseph Cossman, author of *How I Made a Million Dollars in Mail Order*, bought rights to products that other people had been unable to make profitable and sold millions of them by using his creative ability. His book tells about his advertising and promotional campaigns in detail. I highly recommend that you read it, as it will ignite the creative talent in you. See pages 90 through 93.

Test . . . Test . . . Test

I recently published a new positive-thinking, motivational book called *Think Like a Winner!* by Dr. Walter Doyle Staples. Leading authorities in the motivational field have praised it, and the sales to individuals and corporations have been exceptional. Some multi-level (network) marketing companies have placed the book at the top of their "must read" list, which consists of such books as *Think & Grow Rich* by Napoleon Hill and *The Magic of Thinking Success* by Dr. David Schwartz. Some of the motivational gurus have made *Think Like a Winner!* required reading for their staff. That's quite a compliment.

How did I accomplish this feat? I had the author on numerous radio talk shows and had a comprehensive promotional campaign going. Then I began my mail order campaign. What type of ad do you think I decided to run? Why, classified, of course. Here is the first one I ran.

THINK LIKE A WINNER! by Dr. Walter Staples. Exciting, new motivational book can accomplish wonders for you. Endorsed by leading authorities. Send $12.00 to Wilshire Book Company, Dept. 422, 12015 Sherman Road, North Hollywood, California 91605

Do you think this ad pulled in lots of orders? If you said no, you are correct. In retrospect, it had some of the right elements, but it wasn't my best effort, which was reflected in the fact that it failed to produce enough sales to make a profit. As soon as I saw the ad wasn't doing well, I looked it over and found numerous ways to improve it. (Can you?) But I decided, instead, to run a two-step ad, asking the reader to send for free information. It worked perfectly.

MAKE YOUR DREAMS YOUR GOALS! Psychologist's powerful new book shows you how to accomplish whatever you want. Send for free *Think Like a Winner!* literature. Melvin Powers, Suite 423, 12015 Sherman Road, North Hollywood, California 91605

In response, I sent out two different two-page circulars, each to half the inquiries. They are shown on pages 94 through 97. Note that they were keyed so I could count the orders. Which circular do you think pulled best? The one on pages 94 and 95 out-pulled the one on pages 96 and 97 by two to one. Do you have any idea why? Because it has more sizzle to it. The circular on pages 96 and 97 sells the steak. A well-known rule in mail order advertising is to sell the sizzle, not the steak. But every so often, it seems, I have to prove it to myself all over again.

A high percentage of those who order *Think Like a Winner!* reorder multiple copies to share with family, friends, and business associates. And those who receive the book from others, order copies for others. That's how a book, movie, or product takes off. It's usually by recommendation. Word-of-mouth is the best possible advertising. Notice that the book carries a lifetime guarantee. (Not one person has returned it and asked for a refund.) What is your reaction to the lifetime guarantee?

To Charge or Not to Charge . . .
That is the Question

My mail order students invariably ask if they should charge for the literature they send out. Whether they should ask the reader to send a self-addressed, stamped return envelope? They say the literature costs money and figure that if readers are really interested, they'll send the stamped envelope. In most cases, I tell them not to ask for it. Why not? Because you want as many people as possible to respond to your free offer, and asking for a SASE (self-addressed, stamped envelope) cuts down significantly on the number of responses.

I recently experimented with charging $1.00 for my one-hour audio tape and accompanying literature that sell my Mail Order Millionaire program. Where normally I receive 100 requests for information from my ads when the tape is free, I received only 10 requests when I asked for the dollar. Since I know the tape and literature do a good job of pulling in orders, I want as many people as possible to receive them. Needless to say, I dropped the request for $1.00 from my ads. Here's how the two ads read:

FAMOUS MAIL ORDER MILLIONAIRE reveals money-making secrets. Send for free, exciting, one hour cassette tape. Write: Melvin Powers, 12015 Sherman Road, North Hollywood, California 91605

FAMOUS MAIL ORDER MILLIONAIRE reveals money-making secrets. Send $1.00 for exciting, one-hour cassette tape. Write: Melvin Powers, 12015 Sherman Road, North Hollywood, California 91605

How did I figure the bottom line? Let's suppose that my follow-up tape and literature convert into sales of 20% of the 10 people who send in $1.00. Those two customers would pay $107 each for my course. That would bring in $214. If we add the $10.00 I received from the 10 people who sent for my tape and literature, that makes a grand total of $224.

Now let's suppose that 20% of the 100 people who responded to my ads that offered free information ultimately purchased my course. Those twenty people would bring in $2,140. The difference of $1,926 way more than covers the cost of my sending out 100 sets of tapes and literature. What I spend on advertising, follow-up tapes and literature, and envelopes and postage pays for itself many times over.

When is Enough, Enough?

I am often asked how long a classified ad should run. The answer is, as long as it is making money. If you are keeping careful records, you will notice when your inquiries or orders are slowing down. When that happens it may be time to cancel the ad. But first, ask yourself how much money you are making on the back end. Can you afford to lose some on the front end in order to get the names of customers who order additional products from you?

Most of my ads run on a TF (till forbid) basis. You may have seen some of them running month after month, year after year. I am so sure that I will make money from the advertising space that I pay for it a year in advance, taking advantage of discounts offered for up-front payment. The ads can be changed at any time. So if responses slow down, at some point, I can replace it with another one. However, before stopping an ad, I always figure out how much money it is generating in back-end business. Remember, sometimes it is worth it to lose a little on the front end in order to obtain customers who order and reorder additional products from your catalog.

A New Spin on Classified Ads

I'm always looking for products to sell on television on a two-minute spot or half-hour infomercial. One of the ways I search is to run a classified ad. My ad appears below. It is straightforward and brings in excellent responses. Also see page 98.

TELEVISION MARKETING COMPANY SEEKS UNIQUE PRODUCTS. Write or call: Melvin Powers Television Marketing, 12015 Sherman Road, North Hollywood, California 91605. Telephone (818) 765-8529

Once you know how to write effective classified ads, you can use them for a variety of purposes, some you may have never thought about before. For example, if you are in multi-level sales or are thinking about getting into it, be sure to read the next chapter. It could make a big difference in your life.

Discover how the Internet can put you on the fast track to making money . . .

INTERNET MARKETING
Frank Catalono & Bud Smith

How to Sell, Advertise, Publicize, and Promote
Your Products and Services

The Information Superhighway is an exciting promotional vehicle for anyone interested in mail order. It gives you access to millions of potential customers, no matter what your product or service. Home-based businesses as well as companies of all sizes are using the Internet and online marketing services to reach a diverse audience, often finding it less expensive and more effective than conventional media.

Internet Marketing for Dummies guides you through the essentials of online marketing. It shows you how to take advantage of the Internet's incredible profit-making power. Whether you are considering supplementing your current income or creating an entirely new, full-time business, this practical, easy-to-understand book contains all the information you will need to start generating revenue online. It tells you how to combine your interests, knowledge, and skills with online technology. You'll find it a fun, exciting adventure to develop an online business that you can run at your convenience.

YOUR BLUEPRINT FOR SUCCESS

• Brings you up to speed on the Information Superhighway

• Gives sound, practical, down-to-earth advice to help you create a successful online business and launch a marketing program that will make money day and night

• Shows how to enhance your marketing program and build customer loyalty with services available online, such as support centers and electronic mail

• Provides real-world examples of how companies, big and small, promote their products and services online, so you can follow their success

START THOSE ORDERS ROLLING IN

Order *Internet Marketing for Dummies* today and get started right away. You won't believe how excited you'll get when you open your electronic mailbox and find it filled with orders! Take the attitude that if others are doing it, so can you. Why not open up a whole new world of possibilities? Stimulate your creative thinking. You'll become excited with your newfound knowledge and unlimited potential for success.

320 pages . . . $24.00 postpaid (CA res. $25.60)

Send orders to: Melvin Powers, 12015 Sherman Road, No. Hollywood, CA 91605
For credit card orders: Telephone (818) 765-8579. Fax (818) 765-2922.
E-mail: mpowers@mpowers.com

89

HOW I MADE $1,000,000 IN MAIL ORDER

by E. JOSEPH COSSMAN

- HOW YOU CAN GO INTO THE MAIL ORDER BUSINESS
- HOW TO FIND NEW PRODUCTS
- HOW TO TEST YOUR PRODUCTS
- HOW TO DEVELOP AND PRODUCE YOUR PRODUCTS
- SELLING YOUR PRODUCTS
- ADVERTISING AND PROMOTING YOUR PRODUCTS
- TEN SECRET RULES TO WIN SUCCESS IN MAIL ORDER
- HOW TO GET THE MOST FROM TRADE SHOWS
- CASE HISTORY OF A MAIL ORDER SUCCESS
- MY BEST 35 MAIL ORDER LETTERS
- 23 TRADE SECRETS AND IDEAS
- HOW TO SELL YOUR PRODUCT OVERSEAS
- A SIMPLIFIED SYSTEM FOR KEEPING MAIL ORDER RECORDS
- HOW TO USE A BILLBOARD TO SELL YOURSELF AND YOUR BUSINESS

Preface, Introduction, Index

"The ideas in this book—and the practical, step-by-step system explained in detail—will give anyone who has an atom of persistence and creative imagination the key to financial independence in his own mail order business."

Elliott A. Meyer
President
NATIONAL DYNAMICS CORP.

"Joe Cossman is one of the two authentic geniuses I have met in 14 years in the business. Not only does he have an almost prophetic sense for picking winning items, even when they have been discarded as "worthless" by so-called experts, but he has an uncanny knack of squeezing the absolute maximum dollar profit out of each of them. If this book can convey even a fraction of 1% of his money-making ability, it will be worth 100 times its cost."

Eugene M. Schwartz
President
EXECUTIVE RESEARCH INSTITUTE, INC.

ABOUT THE AUTHOR

Mention E. Joseph Cossman in mail order circles, and you get a reaction similar to mentioning Thomas Alva Edison to an electrical engineer. Joe Cossman is rightfully regarded as one of the "miracle men" of the field because of his amazing record of resounding successes.

Starting in his spare time, with a kitchen table for an "office", Joe Cossman built an international mail order empire that has made him a millionaire. He learned the ins and outs of mail order the hard way...and you can benefit from his experience in these pages. Here Cossman tells you how he thought up—tested—marketed—produced—and sold his products. His mail order methods pulled an astounding total of *ten million sales* on six products alone—and that was just the beginning!

Today, Joe Cossman knows that anybody can find, advertise and sell a product in mail order. Capital—experience—even the product—all these are of secondary importance. The important thing is to know how to go about it—and that you will discover, spelled out in fascinating detail, in this book. Let this book be *your* first step towards starting your own company—in your spare time. In just a few years you may be wealthier than you ever dreamed!

30-DAY TRIAL PERIOD

As Joe Cossman says: "*I know of no business in the world that requires such a small investment to start, and yet holds promise of such tremendous financial gains as mail order!*"

The greatest business opportunities in the world today are in the booming field of mail order. That's the only field in which you can start small—with a minimum capital outlay—and build a fast-growing, money-making business right at home.

Joe Cossman, one of the biggest men in mail order, can tell you exactly how to do it. He shows you how to think up a product (with an infallible system responsible for his own list of successful products)—how to test the product—how to get lists—how to produce and sell the product...and all of this can be done right in your own home!

Here are the professional "trade secrets" of a mail order giant who started small and wound up with one of the biggest mail order companies in America. He shows you how to do it, every step of the way. From getting the original idea, and writing the advertising, to how and which lists to rent, and where to get them. He details for you other successful mail order campaigns—shows you how other men started small and founded a booming business.

Cossman gives you valuable tips and pointers on how to produce your product inexpensively—and how you can branch out and develop new products.

If you've ever wanted to start your own business—here's the chance for you. Opportunities are actually unlimited in mail order. Nobodies have become millionaires overnight—and if anybody can show you how, Joe Cossman can.

If you follow his tested, fool-proof rules, you can start with little cash—working even in your spare time—and build a good income out of mail order. In a short time you can achieve the financial independence you have dreamed of...and be your own boss, with your own business. This is your chance to break out of the old rut and hit the big time years earlier than you ever dreamed you would!

Contents

HOW I MADE $1,000,000 IN MAIL ORDER

tells how

YOU CAN MAKE $1,000,000 IN MAIL ORDER

WHAT THIS BOOK CAN DO FOR YOU

If you want to break out of the old rut—start your own business with little or no capital necessary—and be your own boss at last—mail order is the greatest business opportunity that can do this for you.

In this book I will show you how to think up a mail order product and test it inexpensively (following the advertising system given in these pages), produce it and market it. Starting with just one product, and working in your spare time or just on weekends, it is actually possible to bring in several thousand dollars a day in cash-in-advance orders!

That is what makes mail order the fastest-growing and most profit-making business in the world today. This book will show you how to go about it, from getting the first idea right on through to establishing an entire line of successful merchandise for your own mail order business.

I started out using the kitchen table as a desk and working on weekends while keeping my regular nine-to-five job. Today I own the office building in which I work and sit behind a $1,000 desk.

In these pages you'll discover how with common sense, imagination, and perseverance you can do the same, building a business with unlimited potential and adventure.

E. JOSEPH COSSMAN

"I have been in the mail order business for 40 years and during this time I have read every book I could find on the subject. In my opinion, Joe Cossman's book, **How I Made $1,000,000 In Mail Order,** is one of the best mail order books ever written."

Melvin Powers

MAIL NO-RISK TRIAL COUPON TODAY!

Please send your order to:
Melvin Powers
12015 Sherman Road
North Hollywood, California 91605

Gentlemen: Send me a copy of *How I Made $1,000,000 in Mail Order* by E. Joseph Cossman. $15.00 postpaid.

I will use this book for 30 days entirely at your risk. If I am not thoroughly pleased, I will simply return it for a full refund.

Enclosed is my check ( ) money order ( ) for $15.00.
California residents please send $16.07.

Name _____
(Please print)

Address _____

City _____ Zone _____ State _____

Nothing is more exciting than the realization that you can accomplish whatever you want....
And nothing is more life changing than the tools to accomplish it.

THIS BOOK IS GUARANTEED
TO
CHANGE YOUR LIFE!

I am excited to announce I've just published a new book that has the rare elements necessary to propel it into the elite category of all-time, bestselling motivational classics. It's called *Think Like a Winner!* by Dr. Walter Doyle Staples, a highly acclaimed authority on human potential.

For years I have been fascinated by how some people become successful, while others in the same business or profession never quite seem to make it, no matter how hard they try. I wanted to know what sets them apart.

LEARN THE SECRET OF SUCCESS

I found that many successful people credit the shaping or changing of their thinking for putting them on the road to personal and financial success. Most remember a specific book that had great influence on their manner of thinking.... That's exactly what had happened to me. I read *Think & Grow Rich* by Napoleon Hill when I was only 16 years old, and I've never forgotten the impact it made.

I have been a book publisher for more than 40 years, specializing in motivational books. I've published such multi-million bestsellers as *Psycho-Cybernetics*, *The Magic of Thinking Big*, and *Think & Grow Rich* (which I published in trade paperback years after first reading it in hardcover). And I've read almost every motivational book that's been on the market. Though many have been interesting and helpful, only a handful have attained true greatness. *Think Like a Winner!* is destined for such greatness. Those who read it are profoundly affected. It's only a matter of time until *Think Like a Winner!* is cited by successful people as the book that changed their lives.

Of the many motivational books available, *Think Like a Winner!* has been chosen as the Bible of the Melvin Powers Wealth-Building Team—a group of motivated entrepreneurs participating in my money-making opportunities. Why are we using this particular book?... Because it teaches people how to think like winners and get the concrete results that winners get.

TECHNIQUES OF THINKING LIKE A WINNER

How do you think like a winner if you haven't been as successful as you'd like? In *Think Like a Winner!* Dr. Staples explains how the mind functions and specifically how you can achieve your personal and financial goals—even if you've repeatedly been unable to do so in the past. You'll learn how to reach your full potential, resulting in psychological and physiological changes that create a win-win life.

Dr. Staples compares the mind to a giant computer. Both are neutral. Both put out what has been put into them. Garbage in, garbage out—an expression well known to computer users—also applies to the human mind. Negative suggestions and experiences are the garbage that get programmed. Dr. Staples tells how to change one's programming so that what comes out is life enhancing ... the stuff of winners.

94

THE MOST IMPORTANT CHOICE YOU'LL EVER MAKE

What is the most important choice you'll ever make?... Your manner of thinking. And it is a *choice*. By choosing to think like a winner, you'll be choosing personal and financial success. You'll be open to opportunities that come your way—motivated and diligent in your pursuit of them. Eventually you'll catch the brass ring. I've seen it happen again and again with readers of my books and people who participate in my business opportunities. You are not only what you are today, but also what you choose to become tomorrow.

YOU'RE IN THE RIGHT PLACE AT THE RIGHT TIME FOR SUCCESS ... RIGHT NOW!

How many times have you heard that success is being at the right place at the right time? Well ... you're in luck. At this very moment you are at the right place at the right time. Begin to think like a winner and seize this opportunity to get on the road to success.

LEADING AUTHORITIES IN THE MOTIVATIONAL FIELD PRAISE *THINK LIKE A WINNER!*

Anthony Robbins — Author, *Unlimited Power*
"Helping people discover their richest possibilities and reach their greatest heights is an extraordinary gift, and the one that Dr. Staples shares."

Dr. Robert Schuller — Founding Pastor, The Crystal Cathedral
"If you want to maximize your life's potential and at the same time enhance the lives of others, *Think Like a Winner!* is vital reading."

Denis Waitley — Author, *The Psychology of Winning*
"A complete 'how to' success system for reaching new heights of personal excellence."

Dr. Norman Vincent Peale — Author, *The Power of Positive Thinking*
"*Think Like a Winner!* is a scholarly motivational book. It convincingly presents workable formulae for releasing your potential."

Dr. Kenneth Blanchard — Co-Author, *The One Minute Manager*
"Leaders are those who have a vision of excellence and have acquired the necessary skills to help themselves and others reach their full potential. By applying the principles of this book, you are taking a major step in this direction."

James Newman — Author, *Release Your Brakes!*
"The years of study and exploration which have gone into your book, *Think Like a Winner!* have produced a terrific course for personal growth. It will make a positive contribution to the life of every person who reads it."

Brian Tracy — Author, *The Psychology of Success*
"This book is a veritable encyclopedia of success ideas and concepts, and anyone could benefit by applying these ideas to his or her life."

A LIFETIME MONEY-BACK GUARANTEE

You'll be given a tested, proven blueprint for success. Follow it and your life will change forever. Order *Think Like a Winner!* If it isn't all I've said it is—and more—you can return it for a full refund at any time. Send $10 (CA res. $10.83) plus $2.00 shipping and handling to:

Melvin Powers
12015 Sherman Road
No. Hollywood, CA 91605

THINK LIKE A WINNER!

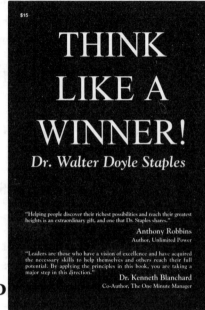

Dear Friend:

I am Melvin Powers, president of Wilshire Book Company. I've had the pleasure of publishing such multi-million bestsellers as *Psycho-Cybernetics*, *Think & Grow Rich*, and *Magic of Thinking Big*.

I've just published another book of the same stature, which I predict will be a perennial bestseller. It's *Think Like a Winner!* by Dr. Walter Doyle Staples, a leading authority on human potential.

It isn't often that a publisher can honestly say that the book he is promoting is the best one on a particular topic that he's read in his entire publishing career. (For me that's 40 years.) This is one of those rare occasions. Watch *Think Like a Winner!* climb the bestseller list.

GIANTS IN THE MOTIVATIONAL FIELD PRAISE *THINK LIKE A WINNER!*

Anthony Robbins — Author, *Unlimited Power*
"Helping people discover their richest possibilities and reach their greatest heights is an extraordinary gift, and the one that Dr. Staples shares."

Dr. Robert Schuller — Founding Pastor, The Crystal Cathedral
"If you want to maximize your life's potential and at the same time enhance the lives of others, *Think Like a Winner!* is vital reading."

Denis Waitley — Author, *The Psychology of Winning*
"A complete 'how to' success system for reaching new heights of personal excellence."

Dr. Norman Vincent Peale — Author, *The Power of Positive Thinking*
"*Think Like a Winner!* is a scholarly motivational book. It convincingly presents workable formulae for releasing your potential."

Dr. Kenneth Blanchard — Co-Author, *The One Minute Manager*
"Leaders are those who have a vision of excellence and have acquired the necessary skills to help themselves and others reach their full potential. By applying the principles of this book, you are taking a major step in this direction."

Art Linkletter — Author, lecturer, and television personality
"Dr. Staples has written a complete manual for personal and professional development. It will surely help many reach the pinnacle of success."

James Newman — Author, *Release Your Brakes!*
"The years of study and exploration which have gone into your book, *Think Like a Winner!* have produced a terrific course for personal growth. It will make a positive contribution to the life of every person who reads it."

Brian Tracy — Author, *The Psychology of Success*
"This book is a veritable encyclopedia of success ideas and concepts, and anyone could benefit by applying these ideas to his or her life."

THINK LIKE A WINNER! HAS A PROFOUND EFFECT ON ITS READERS' LIVES

"If you want to get the results winners get, you must think like a winner thinks!" This is the premise of this lively and motivational book on how to achieve success in the 1990s. *Think Like a Winner!* is an upbeat guide for everyone who wants to be successful.

How do you think like a winner if you haven't been as successful as you'd like? In *Think Like a Winner!* Dr. Staples explains how the mind functions and specifically how you can achieve your personal and financial goals—even if you've repeatedly been unable to do so in the past. You'll learn how to reach your full potential, resulting in psychological and physiological changes that create a win win life.

Think Like a Winner! clearly explains in an entirely new way the profound effect on our lives of our core beliefs and values. Throughout the book there are engaging exercises and relevant quotes by some of the most successful people who have ever lived. You can literally turn to any page and find something new, or a new twist on an old idea. *Think Like a Winner!* is a fascinating adventure toward a better understanding of how the human mind functions, and what specific steps each individual can take to turn his or her life around. It is quickly becoming the standard reference text for personal and professional growth.

PARTIAL TABLE OF CONTENTS

What Makes People Successful?
The Key to Success. The Process of Thinking. What Are You Telling Your Mind?

Principal Influences in Your Upbringing
What Are Your Beliefs? Abundance Is Everywhere. Can One Idea Change Your Life? Risk and Change.

A Model of Human Behavior
Humans Versus Animals. The Formula. You Are Greater Than the Sum of Your Parts. Total Success. Your Basic Hardware: The Mind/Body Connection. The Genius in Creativity.

The Power of Perception
Conscious and Subconscious Thought Processes. Testing Your Perception. Mental Images. The Power of Suggestion.

The Human Success System
Your Built-In Success System. Your Success System Never Fails. Self-Concept. Self-Image. Self-Esteem.

How the Mind Works
Five Mental Laws. Mental Attitude. The Learning Process. Inherent Versus Learned Drives. The Two Principal Fears: Failure and Rejection. Freedom from Fear.

Reprogramming Your Mind for Success
Your Mental Room. How Have You Been Programmed? Your Mental Light Switches. Autogenic Conditioning. Your Book of Beliefs. The Power of Affirmations. Breaking Through Fear. You Control Your Life. The Ultimate Secret of Success.

This Powerful Book Can Change Your Life. Order *Think Like a Winner!*
304 pages. $10 plus $2 postage. Send to:

Melvin Powers
12015 Sherman Road
North Hollywood, CA 91605

12015 Sherman Road
No. Hollywood, CA 91605

(818) 765-8529
FAX (818) 765-2922

$10,000 Reward

Dear Friend:

$10,000 will be paid to each person who sends in a video of a product we use on TV in a "successful" two-minute direct response commercial or half-hour infomercial.

Just video tape the hottest selling item or items from your fair and send us the tape. If we like the product, obtain rights to it, and go national as described below, you get your $10,000 reward. If you submit more than one "successful" product, you will receive $10,000 for each one.

Why are we offering this reward? Because we need your help. Although we spend a great deal of time every year searching fairs, trade shows, and publications, and reviewing submissions to find new products to present on television, it is impossible to find every potential winner that may be out there.

Each video tape submitted must be clearly marked with submitter's name, address, and telephone number and must list names of products and demonstrators. Each video tape must be submitted with an attached list that sets forth the following:

1. Submitter's name, address, and telephone number.
2. Product names, manufacturers' names, addresses, and telephone numbers.
3. Demonstrators' names, addresses, and telephone numbers.
4. Date sent or delivered.

Terms and Conditions

Melvin Powers Television Marketing (MPTM) is continuously searching the marketplace for new products in connection with its video marketing programs. This is not a contest or sweepstakes, but a nationwide search for products. We spend thousands of dollars in our search, and we are willing to pay a "reward" to individuals who provide us with a video demonstrating a "new" product. "New" means that the product has not appeared on national or regional cable television. There is no limit on the number of tapes that can be submitted, but the format must be VHS or 8mm. All tapes submitted become the property of MPTM. Submitter warrants and represents that he or she has the legal right to make such submission and will hold MPTM harmless against any third party claim. In the case of duplicate products being submitted, MPTM will be the sole judge of the recipient of the $10,000 reward. In the case of multiple "successful submissions" of distinctly different products, multiple rewards will be awarded. To qualify for the reward, the product submitted must be accepted by MPTM, and at the sole discretion and judgment of MPTM, after appropriate evaluation and testing, be aired on national cable as paid programming for at least 12 consecutive weeks as a two-minute direct response commercial or half-hour infomercial. The $10,000 reward is completely separate of any ongoing royalty or similar arrangement that may be negotiated with and paid to the actual owner of the rights to the "successful" product. MPTM has the right to require the name and photograph of reward recipients for use in its future promotional activities as a condition to the reward. Any dispute, controversy, or claim between submitter and MPTM will be arbitrated in Los Angeles in accordance with the rules of the American Arbitration Association, and judgment upon may be entered in any court having jurisdiction thereof. Submitter must be over 18 years of age and this offer is not valid in states or territories where it would be prohibited.

Chapter Six

Classified Ads Can Help You Make Big Money in Multi-Level Programs

Whether you are currently involved in a multi-level program or are serious about wanting to make extra money or a career change, this chapter will be of great help in achieving your goals.

Unfortunately, many people have a closed mind when it comes to the subject of multi-level marketing. I suggest that you keep an open mind. There's a very positive side to the business that is often overshadowed by false preconceived notions. Multi-level marketing has been wrongly associated with pyramid schemes which suggests to people that they can make money without working or that the entire thing is a scam, but I know for a fact that there are companies out there that have bona fide programs and sales into the multi-millions. They offer one of the best business opportunities available for financial security and personal freedom.

What Can Multi-Level Marketing Do for You?

Making big money in multi-level takes hard work, but how many people do you know who already work hard, yet struggle to make a living? They could be putting the same effort into multi-level sales and be rewarded with great wealth and the satisfaction that goes with being highly successful. Multi-level is a golden opportunity that can transform a person's life, regardless of educational background, race, religion, gender, age, or health status. I have seen ex-waitresses and bartenders, school teachers and postal employees, bus drivers and department store employees, small business owners and police officers—people from all walks of life—make $3,000, $5,000, 10,000 to $100,000 a month, and more. The stories go on endlessly of those who have made it. With determination and a willingness to do what it takes, anyone can be successful in multi-level. Why not you?

What's the Secret of Success?

I've sold millions of copies of my motivational books to multi-level companies and have been involved in several different programs. I am most familiar with health-related companies and personally know individuals who are making a million dollars a year. I've asked them their secret of success. Their answer invariably is: consistency of purpose. I've also talked to key people in various types of multi-level companies about who becomes successful in their programs. As in most endeavors, it's the person who takes the challenge seriously, learns the techniques of making money from people who have done it, and does what's been proven to work. The secret is no secret. It's just good, old-fashioned, consistent work.

Your Money-Making Mentor

There is a tremendous amount of personal and corporate help for those who want to succeed in this business. It's a rich training ground for any type of entrepreneurial success. Supervisors teach, guide, encourage, and help those whom they introduce into the business. They provide invaluable help in numerous ways, including:

1. Teaching entrepreneurial business techniques that are invaluable no matter what one ultimately does in life.

2. Helping people to develop a winning mind set that makes great accomplishments possible.

3. Teaching a specific, proven system of making money.

4. Offering emotional support.

5. Giving continuous help.

Supervisors become mentors, holding people's hand and guiding them steadily toward their personal goals. Why are they so good to those they introduce to the business? Because they have a vested interest in their people's success. It's that simple.

I can tell you firsthand that multi-level marketing has tremendous power to create wealth and a lifestyle that most people only dream about. When you make your dreams your goals, they become attainable. If you just do what it takes, exactly what you are taught, there is nothing to stop you from achieving everything you ever wanted. There are no ceilings on how much you can make. It's all there for the taking. Everything you ever wanted. Your success is entirely in your hands.

A Never-Ending Source of New Leads

As you know if you are already in multi-level, one's circle of influence—friends, relatives, business associates, and casual acquaintances—is the first place to look for customers and recruits. But once they have been approached, there is a need for new means of generating leads. That's when classified advertising can make all the difference. It can supply a steady stream of people interested in what is being offered.

Let's look at some interesting ads that successfully generate leads for new customers and potential recruits. The following recruiting ads and similar ones are working very effectively for Don Hart, a dynamic Las Vegas-based multi-level supervisor and seminar instructor. You can use these same ads or variations of them for your own multi-level business.

Basically, Don is asking for a phone call to introduce himself and his program to prospective, motivated individuals. Those who join the program can use the same ads and techniques to build their business. An unusually successful marketing program has helped his company grow in sales every year. It's quite a credit to the marketing skills of everyone involved.

Ads that Work

Here are some of Don's ads. Notice they include his Web site address. They all sell the sizzle. As we analyze them, see if you can improve them.

A FREE 3-MINUTE PHONE CALL can dramatically change your life! Call (800) 299-3491 www.hireyourboss.com

A FREE 3-MINUTE PHONE CALL can dramatically change your life! Call (800) 299-3491. Don Hart, wealth builder. www.hireyourboss.com

What impression do you think the reader gets from the first ad without Don's name? The second, with his name added? Does it matter either way as long as the message is clear? Remember, the reader has no idea what type of an ad he is answering. Don elected to use his name in this particular ad. I like it because it makes the ad more personal. You know who is running the ad.

Don has an exceptionally high closure rate and teaches people how to accomplish the same. He's cheerful, friendly, and eager to share his techniques of running a home-based part-

or full-time business. He tells those who respond to his ads that the program can work like a charm if they follow the company's step-by-step instructions—a statement he knows to be absolutely true.

Here's a variation of the same ad:

A FREE 3-MINUTE PHONE CALL can dramatically change your personal and financial life! Call (800) 299-3491. www.hireyourboss.com

He is now giving further information, telling the reader the call has to do with one's personal and financial life. By doing so, he is further qualifying the caller. He offers the opportunity right on the phone and helps the person get started immediately.

I list my phone number in some of my ads to sell my mail order course. It's very effective and the personal touch invariably makes the sale.

What do you think of the following ad compared to the previous three?

YOU CAN BECOME WEALTHY! Money making secrets revealed! Call (800) 299-3491. www.hireyourboss.com

I like the bold statement "YOU CAN BECOME WEALTHY!" It's not saying maybe or that it might work. His ad states it as a fact. I also like "MONEY MAKING SECRETS REVEALED." I've been using this tried, tested, and proven ad copy for years to sell my mail order course. Don adapted it to promote his program.

Here are three variations on the fourth ad. As you read them decide which ad or ads attract you. Which would you run?

BECOME WEALTHY before it's too late! Money making secrets revealed. Call (800) 299-3491. www.hireyourboss.com

YOU CAN BECOME WEALTHY. Money making secrets revealed. Before it's too late, call (800) 299-3491. www.hireyourboss.com

BEFORE IT'S TOO LATE, let me help you become wealthy. Call (800) 299-3491. www.hireyourboss.com

Which ad do you think pulled best? Why? What do you think of the phrase "BEFORE IT'S TOO LATE"? What message does it convey? Do you like it? Dislike it? Does it sound sincere? Would you use it in your ads? Would you answer an ad that had that phrase?

As you can see, writing good ad copy is part art and part science. It's a wonderful feeling to get the response you want, and even better to exceed your expectations. As a songwriter, I knew when I had a hit song as soon as I had written the title and the first few lines, just as I have often known I have a winning ad by the headline and the first few paragraphs. Yet, one never knows for sure how any creative effort will fare until you put it to the test. The effort that goes into creating a successful ad is well worth it. It's fun knowing you can hit the jackpot at any time, and when you do, it's exciting and rewarding.

Here are two of my favorite ads. What do you think of them? Do they sound sincere? Would you answer an ad like this? Would you be curious to know what it is all about?

I MADE LOTS OF MONEY last month lying around my swimming pool every afternoon and working only when I wanted! I can positively teach you to do the same. Call (800) 299-3491.www.hireyourboss.com

I MADE $8,793.23 LAST MONTH going skiing and working only when I wanted! I can positively teach you to do the same. Interested? Call (800) 299-3491.www.hireyourboss.com

It's great advertising copy and it does it all: tells the amount of money made, paints a glorious picture of lying around a swimming pool or going skiing, assures the reader he can do the same, and calls for action. You could use a variation of these ads, perhaps substituting another activity for skiing, such as fishing, golfing, playing tennis, sailing, horseback riding, skin diving, bowling, gardening, or working out at the gym. Try it. The ad works perfectly.

The questions I've asked you to answer as we discussed these sample ads are precisely the ones you should ask yourself when writing your own classified ads. Your answers will help you to see how readers of your ad will perceive it. Analyze, rewrite, test. Then analyze, rewrite, and test again, forever trying to improve your return. That's what mail order is all about.

In response to people answering my various business opportunity classified ads, I offer the opportunity to work with Don Hart in his program. See pages 104 through 107 for my four-page letter. You are welcome to use this layout and adapt its copy, if appropriate, for your own program

......I've been asked many times to recommend a network marketing program that offers excellent financial opportunities, proven products, and has an outstanding track record. This is it!

TWO MARKETING EXPERTS CAN DRAMATICALLY INCREASE YOUR INCOME!

Dear Friend,

I'm going to give you some great news that will make it possible for you to make more money, sooner than you ever thought possible. But first, I want to tell you about the three elements that can guarantee your success.

Three Golden Keys to Getting Rich

Have you ever wondered how so many people who start with nothing, become financially successful?

1. They look for a good opportunity until they find one.
2. They get someone to teach them what to do.
3. They do it.

You can do as they have done. You will need an opportunity and a teacher. But just *any* opportunity won't do, and neither will just *any* teacher. Your chances of success are best if the opportunity is unique, powerful, easy, and proven to work—and if the teacher is experienced, successful, and dedicated to helping you make it.

Here's your chance to seize the *right* opportunity and the *right* teacher. It couldn't be any easier. I've already found them both for you! All you have to do is take advantage of the opportunity being offered to you.

Your Own Personal Teachers Will Stand by Your Side And Help Make You Successful

Have you ever had a successful person say to you, "I'm going to teach you how to become financially successful and guide you every step of the way"? Well now someone is saying *exactly* that. Don Hart, a dynamic, full-time, Las Vegas multi-level supervisor and seminar instructor and I are dedicated to helping people who dream of riches and want to get their bank accounts to overflow with cash, checks, and money orders. Like so many other things in life, it seems so easy when you know how...and so difficult—sometimes impossible—when you don't.

Most individuals who achieve success are "ordinary people." They start out with dreams, probably much like yours. Dreams of extra money to buy larger homes, new automobiles, travel, and pay for their children's college education. Dreams of becoming their own boss and working as much or as little as they want. Dreams of finding their work rewarding, challenging, and fun.

This Opportunity Has Every Element Necessary to Qualify It As a Virtual Gold Mine

There are thousands of millionaires in the United States. Interestingly, many of them made their fortunes in the last twenty years in multi-level sales. In fact, more millionaires have been created in the last two decades by network marketing than by any other form of business.

The company I am excited about and enthusiastically recommending is a multi-level marketing company. This means that in addition to making a profit from selling products yourself, you can make money on other people's sales.

Every one of your future happy customers is a potential distributor as he or she enthusiastically tells amazing success stories to friends and relatives.

Infinite Level Bonus Plan Helps Set A New Industry Standard for Distributor Compensation

The money-making opportunity is great because of the company's lucrative marketing plan. It provides an infinite level bonus, rather than the three to five levels offered by most other multi-level companies. The plan can dramatically increase the amounts of money you earn over what you would with the traditional limited level plan.

Many Motivated Entrepreneurs Have Been Transformed into Millionaires

Many of the individuals who learned of this innovative company's products when first introduced, and who chose to put their energy into marketing them, have already become rich. They knew the time was right for what they had to offer. And once again, the time is right.

The company is on the cutting edge of scientific technology. They have years of invaluable experience with substances from the plant world that medical researchers are now looking to for solutions to our most puzzling health problems. The scientific community's interest in preventative health care and natural means of dealing with illness and disease is growing larger every year...and health care is now one of the largest industries in America. Market conditions couldn't be better.

They Have Changed Their Lives Forever And It Can Happen to You!

Thousands of people have had the foresight to recognize this opportunity as the life-changing event it truly is. Students, homemakers, accountants, engineers, teachers, police officers, construction workers, waitresses, market checkers, truck drivers, retired and disabled people have taken control of their lives. They found out what works from someone who knows, and they did what it takes to make it. As a result, they have achieved financial freedom while doing something they find satisfying and which makes a worthwhile contribution to mankind. You can do as they have done.

You Will Become Valuable

Do you know how much you are worth in the marketplace? <u>You are worth what you're being paid</u>. How valuable do you think you are? Why do you think corporation presidents are paid hundreds of thousands or millions of dollars a year? Because they are valuable!

<u>Don Hart and I will teach you skills that will make you valuable</u>. You will bring value to the marketplace...with products that make people feel great...and with an opportunity that helps others to change their lives, follow their dreams, and take control of their futures. All you need is a good attitude, a willingness to take direction, a desire to take control of your life, and a dedication to consistency and perseverance.

Rich People Are No Smarter Than You

They just know the techniques of making money. <u>Don and I will teach you how to be a money maker</u>—and how to have a Rolls Royce mentality, rather than that of a wage earner. You'll develop the Midas touch and have a winning attitude in everything you do. <u>You are no different from those who are making unbelievable sums of money</u>. What's their secret? They are motivated for success and are willing to follow a proven plan while keeping their sights on their long-term goals.

You'll Be Given a Tested, Proven Blueprint to Follow

<u>Don and I will give you a plan that works—a plan that has already made many people wealthy</u>. If you do what they did, you'll get what they got—and more—because we have committed our years of successful marketing experience to multiplying the earning potential of the plan.

<u>*Your* success will be *our* success. We will be available to help you every step of the way</u>. We'll hold your hand and guide you as you build your business from the first day on—for as long as you want our help. This plan makes sense. It's working. It's growing every day.

What Is the Secret of a Winning Team?

It has been our experience that the most successful teams are comprised of members who believe in their ability to be successful, are enthusiastic about the project at hand, have pride in a job well done, and have a vested interest in the outcome of their efforts. In plain language, this means that <u>each person has a positive attitude, works hard to do his or her best, and has the opportunity to share in the profits</u>.

An Unusual Promise When You Join
The Powers-Hart Wealth-Building Team

<u>Don and I are inviting you to take a wealth-building journey with us that will change your life in ways you may never have imagined</u>. Becoming more valuable, making a lot of money, and feeling satisfied with what you have chosen to do in life are only part of what the wealth-building team offers. As a member, you will get a sense of belonging to a new family that is supportive of

106

your goals and self-development. A family you will find psychologically uplifting. A family with an ongoing personal growth program that will empower you to reach both your personal and financial goals. The continuing personal contact with us will help you become a winner in this endeavor...and in life.

Don't Neglect Your Future

If you want your life to change, you must change. If you want things to be different, you must do something different. Be good to yourself—allow yourself to be a winner. You have the chance to associate with winners and to be part of a winning team.

Where will you be one year from today if you don't join us? Two years from today? Take responsibility for where you are and where you want to be. Take charge of your future. Remember, you are not only what you are today but also what you choose to become tomorrow.

Think Like a Winner...
You Are at the Crossroads of Success

Don't lose one precious minute! Those who get in on the ground floor of this once-in-a-lifetime opportunity will flourish. Don't be left out.

Be ready to feel great. Be ready to spread the word to others. Be ready to be successful faster and easier than you ever imagined possible. Be ready to have others spread the word for you. Be ready to cash in on your mounting sales and on the sales of others. Be ready to take loads of cash, checks, and money orders to the bank. And be ready to lead the life you've dreamed of, but never really thought possible to attain.

This Is the Moment of Truth
A Pot of Gold is Yours for the Asking

If wishing could make money for you, you'd already be rich. Now is the time to do what it takes to get what you want. You have the opportunity to join a winning team. Create a miracle in your life by taking the steps that have made fortunes for others. Do yourself a favor that can dramatically change your life! Order your *Wealth-Building Start-Up Kit* for $5.00. Send your order to Don Hart, 4542 E. Tropicana, Suite 205-A, Las Vegas, Nevada 89121. Find out how you can get started making money immediately. You have a wonderful adventure in store for you!

Don and I look forward to welcoming you to our wealth-building team.

Melvin Powers

P.S. The secret of success in life is to be ready for opportunity when it comes. I hope
      you're ready...because it doesn't get any better than this! Good luck.

MAKE YOUR DREAMS YOUR GOALS

Chapter Seven

Two-Step Classified Ads
Made Me a Multi-Millionaire
They Can Do the Same for You!

The beauty of classified ads is that they are relatively inexpensive compared to display ads. Once they work, you can run them on a TF (till forbid) basis, as I explained in chapter six, paying in advance and having them run continuously until you stop them. I've sold millions of dollars worth of my book *How to Get Rich in Mail Order* and my audio tape program called *Mail Order Millionaire* using both one- and two-step classified ads on a TF basis. The same techniques that have made this campaign successful can be used to sell all types of products.

Libraries have a reference series called *Subject Guide to Books in Print* which I mentioned briefly in chapter one. It lists over 1,000,000 books in numerous categories and gives the title, author, price, and name and address of the publisher. If you are interested in any of the listings, you can write to the publisher telling him you are in the mail order business and would like to sell those particular books. Ask for his catalog, advertising literature, price schedule, and any additional information you might want. He'll be pleased to work with you.

The Secret Weapon that Drives Response Rates Up

For years I ran the following classified ad and variations of it in the Business Opportunities section until the pulling power diminished:

HOW TO GET RICH in Mail Order. An expert's step-by-step guide. Money-back guarantee. $22.00 postpaid. Melvin Powers, Suite 905, 12015 Sherman Road, North Hollywood, California 91605

Now I'm running an ad that doesn't tell specifically what the offer is for. People are curious about it. I've received many letters and phone calls from readers telling me they have seen my ad for years, and because of its longevity, finally decided to send for the cassette. The ad reads as follows:

FAMOUS MAIL ORDER MILLIONAIRE reveals his money-making secrets. Free, exciting details. Write: Melvin Powers, Dept. 853, 12015 Sherman Road, North Hollywood, California 91605

An improved version that greatly increased the inquiry response, and consequently the number of orders reads:

FAMOUS MAIL ORDER MILLIONAIRE reveals his money-making secrets. Free, exciting one-hour cassette. Write: Melvin Powers, Dept. 375, 12015 Sherman Road, North Hollywood, California 91605

I send the same literature as before with the addition of the audio tape. What percentage increase in orders would you guess was the result of adding the tape to the offer—10%, 20%, 25%, 50%, 75%, 100%? The answer is 400%! That's because I have a captive audience for one hour and can tell my story. The prospective customer also hears the actual voices and success stories of many of my students who have become successful following my instruction. (They were glad to share their experiences and encourage others to do as they have done.) It all adds credibility and excitement to the offer. This approach is heads and shoulders above selling the book and course from a classified ad alone or sending out the four-page sales letter by itself. The combination of ad, tape, and literature does the job.

I had such success with audio tapes that I experimented with using video tapes to sell some of my business opportunities. The results were good, however, I watch the bottom-line carefully to make sure the campaign continues to be profitable, as video tapes are more expensive than audio tapes to duplicate and mail.

Creative Thinking Can Save the Day . . . and the Offer!

One of my television infomercial clients was trying to sell a business opportunity. They had tested various prices but none worked. They were about to drop the show after spending a great deal of money. I suggested that they go after leads only, using an 800 number, and follow up with a half-hour audio cassette, four-page sales letter, and other literature. They took my advice and the offer is now working perfectly—and very profitably! The point is that you must think creatively and test changes in your approach to any campaign before abandoning it.

Although sending out a tape doesn't lend itself to all offers, do it whenever appropriate. At my suggestion, a number of my mail order students have begun using a half-hour audio cassette. In nearly every case, it at least doubled their response. To inexpensively test the use of audio cassettes for your offer, you can record your message on a home tape recorder, duplicate it yourself, and try it out with your literature. It gives your offer a personal touch and can do wonders for your response rate. Or if the offer warrants it, you might want to consider using an inexpensive video tape.

The Magic Number is Four

Often students assume that long copy is a negative; that people will be too busy to spend the time to read it. But the opposite is true. Long copy works well because consumers are hungry for information. And they won't buy unless all their questions have been answered and all possible objections overcome. For example: What will your product do for me? Why do I need it? How does it work? How does it look, feel, sound, or smell? What sizes and colors does it come in? How long does it last? Is it easy to use? To maintain? etc. Why should I buy your product rather than your competitor's? How do I know you are telling the truth? How much does your product cost? Is it worth the price? Have other people been happy with it? How can I order? Can I get my money back if I don't like it? And on and on. This information must be provided specifically, completely, interestingly, and clearly. Most mail order companies choose four-page sales letters to accomplish this task, having found that they work best.

I have included in this chapter two samples of four-page sales letters that I'm using in my follow-up literature to my "FAMOUS MAIL ORDER MILLIONAIRE" ad. See if you can determine which letter is working better and why. See pages 121 through 124 and pages 125 through 128.

I received a very favorable review for my book *How to Get Rich in Mail Order* by Og Mandino, author of *The Greatest Salesman in the World*. See page 129. When I began enclosing this reprint in my sales literature, the sales increased measurably. If you have not read *The Greatest Salesman in the World*, I highly recommend that you do. It's one of the best books I've ever read. You will be in for a real treat and you'll thank me for it. Millions of copies have been sold and it has been translated into numerous languages. It's available in paperback at bookstores and libraries. If you would like to read another of my favorite books, try *The Knight in Rusty Armor* by Robert Fisher, also available in paperback.

Books have always played a very important part in my personal and business growth, and I love to share them. That's the reason for my enthusiasm for the books I publish on self-development. It's also the reason for my outstanding success in this area of book publishing. I once had three books on the bestseller list all at the same time. (I'm still dreaming about it!) I believe that achieving success in any endeavor is due more to attitude than to what you do or don't do. Rich people are no smarter than anyone else. They just have a good attitude about themselves and the tasks they undertake. They proceed logically, finding out all they can, they plan, and they execute their plan, all the while believing that there is every reason to expect success. You can expect success if you follow their example.

I tested an eight-page circular for the "FAMOUS MAIL ORDER MILLIONAIRE" ad and it would have worked fine, I decided, as a single mailing piece. But I ended up cutting it down to four pages because I was offering several different business opportunities in the same package, and I didn't want it to overshadow the others. What do you think of offering several business opportunities at the same time rather than only one? What do you think of offering more than one product or book at a time?

Early in my career I found four-page sales letters to be the magic length. They helped me to sell millions of copies of the book *Psycho-Cybernetics* by Maxwell Maltz, M.D. Here's how my two-step ads ran.

MAKE YOUR DAYDREAMS your goals! Amazing new science of mind shows you how. Write or call for fascinating information. Melvin Powers, Dept. 7, 12015 Sherman Road, North Hollywood, California 91605. Telephone: (818) 765-8579

DOCTOR'S AMAZING, NEW science of mind helps you achieve all your goals! Financial security, personal power can be yours. Write or call for fascinating details. Melvin Powers, Dept. 120, 12015 Sherman Road, North Hollywood, California 91605. Telephone: (818) 765-8579

When I saw the gigantic number of orders the circular was pulling in, I rented thousands of names of people interested in self-improvement, and I sold hundreds of thousands of books. It was easy. I had found the winning formula—great ad copy. It was as if I had my own gold mine. When I had sold 1,000,000 copies of the book, I wrote a special foreword that helped increase sales even more. I was on a winning streak! To date, I've sold about 5,000,000 copies!

My first printing of *Psycho-Cybernetics* was for only 3,000 copies, even though I was certain I had a big winner. I took my own advice of initially printing small quantities until the results of my first sales efforts were evaluated. I knew I could run more when I was positive I could sell them. I remember telling my printer that I would be printing millions of copies of the book in subsequent runs. He wanted to know why I felt that way and I told him it was a gut feeling. I just knew it! In later years, we reminisced about that conversation many times, especially when I was giving him a print run of 250,000 copies.

Now that I think about it, I often had the same gut feeling during my songwriting career. I'd call my songwriting partner, Tommy Boyce, and say, "I just got an idea for a hit song." Then I'd proceed to sing and play the song for him on my guitar.

A Hit Ad Sold Tons of Hit Songbooks

When the book *How to Write a Hit Song and Sell It* by Tommy Boyce first came out, I sold it successfully from a one-step classified ad that read as follows:

FAMOUS SONGWRITER for the Monkees, Tommy Boyce, with 22 gold records such as "Last Train to Clarksville," "Come a Little Bit Closer," tells you how to write hit songs and sell them. Send for exciting new book, *How to Write a Hit Song & Sell It*. Guaranteed or full refund. $12.00 postpaid. Also order Songwriters Rhyming Dictionary $12.00 postpaid. Write to: Wilshire Book Company, Dept. 713, 12015 Sherman Road, North Hollywood, California 91605

More than half the sales were for two books. I had great sales to libraries for both books. See page 130 for my full-page ad. From the classified ads, I went directly to full-page display ads in country western music magazines. They did well. I also ran in various songwriting magazines and did PI (per inquiry) deals for many years. The magazines ran the ads and I paid them $5.00 for each book I sold. They were paid once a month.

PI deals are wonderful. The magazine runs the ad and you pay them a percentage of each order. The ads are keyed, so you know how many orders you are getting from each source. Payment is made on the honor system. I'm always delighted to pay. It means I'm making money, too. And with a PI deal, I can try new ads without risking a cent. The magazines are delighted too, as my ad helps fill up their unsold advertising space and attracts other advertisers. It's a win-win situation.

After advertising in a particular publication for awhile, you may become friendly with the publisher or advertising manager, who may then be open to a PI deal. Usually, all it takes is asking. They usually want full-page ads although I have had—and still have—deals for smaller space. I've had arrangements for years with various publications for one-step PI deals for books. How sweet it is!

Over the years, I've purchased distressed space (also called remaindered space) in numerous magazines and most tabloids. It usually goes for half the normal rate or less. That's a great buy. You can make money at those rates even with ads that are marginal. Think about it, have you ever seen a magazine or tabloid run with a blank page? The advertising department of the publication needs to fill blank space and will gladly call you the last minute when they have space they can't sell. Simply ask.

Sometimes Less is Plenty

Now that I've told you four-page circulars are the magic length, I'm going to qualify that statement by saying it isn't always necessary to use four pages. If the advertiser's complete story can be told in less space and if the copy is powerful, two-pages can work admirably. I'm having fun experimenting with two-pagers and testing them against four pagers. It has become a creative challenge to make the short versions pull as well as the long ones. Here's one of my ads that is followed-up with a two-page sales letter.

900 TELEPHONE NUMBERS can make you a bundle of money. Fascinating book tells how. Send or call for free information. You'll be glad you did! Melvin Powers, Dept. 128, 12015 Sherman Road, North Hollywood, California 91605. Telephone: (818) 765-8579

I tried various one-step classified ads for the book but they didn't pull well enough to keep the ad running. Finally I resorted to the two-step technique and it worked beautifully. In response to the inquiries, I send out a two-page circular and a page of testimonials. They do a great selling job. See pages 131 through 133.

Use testimonials whenever you can get them. Be sure to obtain the people's written permission to use them. At most, give first names and last initials only, and the city. In my ads and literature, I use success stories of many of my students. To make them completely believable, I used to give each one's full name, street address, city, and state. But they began to get phone calls all hours of the day and night from people asking if the testimonials were true and questioning them about how they developed their businesses. Sometimes the callers spent more money on the phone call than it would have cost them to purchase the book. Isn't that funny?

What do you think of the layout and copy of the circular? Does the full page of testimonials lend credibility to the book? How would you improve the advertising copy? I love the headline, "He's Sailing Off Maui, Making Money Around the Clock!" That's like Don's classified ad reading, "I MADE $8,793.23 LAST MONTH skiing and working only when I wanted!" Both ads paint powerful visual images that help excite readers to action. These advertisers both follow the rule of selling the sizzle rather than the steak. But to make a sale, there must also be convincing copy that supplies information and provides an excuse to buy.

What do you think of adding a picture of a couple lying on the beach in beautiful, romantic Hawaii holding tall, cool drinks? The headline could read, "They're making money around the clock while working on their tans, enjoying their favorite drink, and munching Macadamia nuts."

Here's a two-step classified ad that works just great.

THREE MAGIC WORDS will bring you everything you ever wanted. Over 1,000,000 people have already learned an incredible, life-changing secret from this bestselling book. Send or call for free details. Melvin Powers, Dept. 3, 12015 Sherman Road, North Hollywood, California 91605. Telephone: (818) 765-8579

In response, I send the two-page circular on pages 134 and 135. As a result of their reading this book, the customer invariably orders other books that the author has written, including *Secret of Secrets*, *Magic in Your Mind*, *Greatest Power in the Universe*, *Success Cybernetics*, and *The Secret Power of the Pyramids*. A large percentage of readers order additional copies of *Three Magic Words* to give to family and friends. That's part of the secret of my success.

I have a very high re-order rate for some of my books and those sales add up. Because it's impossible for bookstores to carry a comprehensive selection of books on every subject, I have a thriving mail order book business in specialized categories. My sales are big in Canada, England, Australia, New Zealand, Singapore, and Hong Kong.

You could be doing the same thing in any category that is of interest to you. And you could be selling audio and video tapes, too. A list of 50,000 audio cassette titles can be found in a library reference book called *On Cassette*. *Bowker's Complete Video Directory* and *Variety's Video Directory Plus* each contain 50,000 video titles. There are also directories of computer software. Zero in on a subject you like, make yourself knowledgeable about it, and become a worldwide source for books, audio and video cassettes, and software programs in that field. Give good service, and you'll develop a substantial mail order business.

Here's a very good classified ad that's right to the point.

Largest selection of gambling books, computer software, videos, and supplies. Write or call: Reno Gambler's Bookstore, Dept. 711, 135 N. Sierra Street, Reno, Nevada. (800) 323-2295

In response to inquiries, the company sends a 48-page catalog that lists 1,500 titles. It's a winning operation. If interested, send or call for their catalog.

Another very successful mail order operation catering to gamblers is Gambler's Book Club, 630 South 11th Street, Las Vegas, Nevada 89101. They have the largest bookstore in the world for people interested in gambling. For their free catalog, call (800) 634-6243. If further interested, visit their stores when you are in Reno or Las Vegas. It's all part of your research. The point is pick a category and become well known in that area. Before long you'll be getting orders from all over the world. You will be delighted with the mail that you will get, especially if you are a stamp collector.

Several of my students have started mail order operations with small classified ads selling horse-related books, videos, equipment, and gifts. Since I own several horses, I was pleased to purchase items from them. It was convenient and I was delighted to give them the business. Incidentally, there are 125 different horse magazines and numerous regional publications.

I've had other individuals specialize in dog and cat products. One is doing a great job with cat art, gifts with the cat motif, and cat decorations. Woman's Day magazine gave her a three-page, full-color write-up that resulted in her receiving several hundred-thousand dollars worth of orders. Other students are specializing in health products for cats, dogs, and parrots.

I buy most of the food for my home at a health food chain in the Los Angeles area called Mrs. Gooch's. They also sell big bags of dry health food for dogs and cats. Their sales for these products are excellent. It's a natural product for people interested in good health. I see customers buying them all the time. I print a book for one of my students called *Pet Allergies.* It's a good seller. Another student has a mail order course that instructs how to teach tricks to parrots. Someone else sells food for parrots. I buy organic carrots for my horses. (I hope they appreciate it!)

There is no end to what you can sell via mail order using the two-step approach. You must be personally interested in the products, be willing to spend the research time, and then begin in a small way to start your mail order career.

Individuals come to my office with lots of money to invest in a mail order program. I tell them the same thing I've been telling you, namely to be slow to spend their hard-earned money. To take one step at a time and learn as they go along. And to read every mail order book they can get their hands on. Sometimes, they'll say, "I've read your book and listened to your tape program. Isn't that enough?" My answer is always, "You can never learn too much. It's good to read what other authors have to say. Why not have the advantage of their experiences, too."

A few years ago, I took a class at UCLA in starting and running an infomercial business. Some of my mail order students were also enrolled. Before class started, they asked if I was going to be lecturing. I told them I was, however, I was also enrolled as a student and planned to attend all of the class meetings. Why not? I was there to learn as well as to contribute. In any endeavor, one's education is never over.

Give Them a Lift

Haven't you received with mail order offers a little note that says "Read This Only if You Have Decided Not to Order"? And haven't you read it out of curiosity? It is known as a "lift letter," and what it does is to give the mailer another opportunity get his message across. Using a lift letter is like adding a P.S. It usually either cements the readers decision to purchase or makes him question his reasons for not doing so. Be sure to use a lift letter whenever it seems appropriate to your offer.

Selling to the Rich and Famous

There's a monthly magazine called *Robb Report*. It has a circulation of 110,000 and caters to individuals leading affluent lifestyles. It's a great mail order publication for expensive products. Price is no object! Some of the products sold are exotic cars, sports cars, luxury cars, airplanes, boats, cowboy boots, expensive wrist watches, jewelry, writing instruments, personal computers, paintings, sculptures, sports memorabilia, stamps, coins, personal protection products, and trained security dogs.

Every month there are full-color ads for miniature horses. See page 136. Obviously it's making money. Miniature horses sell for thousands of dollars. I would have never thought of selling them in this publication. But someone else has, and is doing well. I wish I had thought to run ads in the publication when I was in the Arabian horse business. It would have been a better place to advertise than in the regular Arabian horse publications which were jammed with ads from the competition.

I'm also surprised by an ad that has been running for a long time for an electronic lock pick. It sells for $199. See page 137. Notice the ad says, "Send $5.00 for a complete list of locksmithing tools." I can't figure out why this publication is a good place to advertise for this product. Can you? I'm curious.

If you are interested in selling expensive products and might want to place an ad in the *Robb Report*, send for a review copy and advertising rate card to: *Robb Report*, One Acton Place, Acton, Massachusetts 01720-9988. They also have a classified section.

800 Phone Numbers . . . Do You Need Them?

At one time I used 800 numbers in my classified ads but I have stopped for the most part. Do you have any idea why? I'll give you a hint. Having an 800 number makes it easier to call. Can you think of any reason why that might be a negative? What about the fact that it's so easy that people don't even have to decide whether they think the call is worth paying for. They can grab the phone and call, prompted by nothing more than a little curiosity about the offer. Few of these calls result in sales. I track every phone call and all leads from magazine ads and know the exact percentage of closures for ads with and those without an 800 number. Believe it or not, the ads with 800 numbers produce the lowest number of sales at the highest cost. (You get charged for every call received on your 800 number whether or not it results in a sale. If lots of people call and few order, it doesn't take long for the non-productive calls to eat up your profit.)

A better lead results when the reader is sufficiently interested in the offer to pay for the call or when he takes the time to send for the information. If you get these qualified responses and don't make many sales, what do you know is wrong? It must be your literature. People were interested enough to inquire about your product but apparently were not sufficiently persuaded to buy. Although it isn't realistic to think you can sell everyone, a viable campaign should be able to pull in enough money to pay for your ad, literature, and postage, and still make a profit.

Your Product on TV? . . . It Could Happen!

I sold thousands of copies of my *Mail Order Millionaire* course on TV through one-hour and half-hour infomercials and two-minute commercial spots. It was an exciting experience to be checking results and figuring out the profit generated by my own programs, rather than those of clients as I had done in the past. I used an easy-to-remember 800 number, and a service bureau handled all the calls. If you ever think about running on TV, don't even consider taking the calls yourself, unless perhaps you are testing your offer in a small local area—and even then, it's risky. If a caller gets a busy signal, your sale goes the way of the wind. And experienced telephone marketers are a big help when fielding responses to TV advertising.

After awhile, the responses to my shows slowed down, which was no surprise as all ads eventually lose their pulling power. When my two-minute spot began to flounder, I decided to use it to generate leads and follow up with the same literature I was using successfully with my two-step classified ads. The response rate of the TV offer turned out to be much lower than that of the ads. I finally took the program off the air.

If you find you have a product that's selling great from classified ads and you dream of putting it on TV, get educated as to what criteria a product should meet in order to have a chance of making it. Analyze infomercials as I have been suggesting you do with classified ads. Call for information. Listen to the sales pitches and the upsells. You may want to purchase some of the products, get on the advertisers' mailing list. Use a key as you do in your ads and track what happens to your name. Keep track of which shows appear often and remain on for a long time. Also observe which do not. Keep your eyes and your mind open. Some people have made fortunes on TV. Why not you?

What Works . . . And What Doesn't

Do you think you could sell a $195 travel agent course directly from a classified ad? The answer is no. Did I try? No, I didn't. Why not? Because I knew that although I might get a few orders here and there, there wouldn't be nearly enough for a continuous ad program to pay. How did I know this without testing? One of the facts of classified advertising is that the higher the price, the more difficult it becomes to sell any product directly from a classified ad. Although this product wouldn't work as a one-step, I am running it as a two-step with great success, alternating headline copy as shown below. Do you think it makes any difference? Which ad do you think might pull better and why?

BECOME A TRAVEL AGENT, make extra money, see the world at a fraction of the non-agent cost. Work from home or local travel agent's office part- or full-time. Enjoy huge discounts on hotels, resorts, condos, cruises, transportation, and car rentals. Get priority, VIP treatment. Go on lavish for-agents-only familiarization trips at incredibly low prices or free. Travel is the easiest sale ever. Customers call you to buy. Money-back guarantee. For details, call (818) 765-8529 or write to Melvin Powers, Dept. 101, 12015 Sherman Road, North Hollywood, California 91605

MAKE EXTRA MONEY and see the world at a fraction of the regular cost. Become a travel agent part- or full-time. Work from home or local travel agent's office. Enjoy huge discounts on hotels, resorts, condos, cruises, transportation, and car rentals. Get priority, VIP treatment. Go on lavish for-agents-only familiarization trips at incredibly low prices or free. Travel is the easiest sale ever. Customers call you to buy. Money-back guarantee. For details, call (818) 765-8529 or write to Melvin Powers, Dept. 101, 12015 Sherman Road, North Hollywood, California 91605

In response to inquiries, I send a four-page circular. The conversion rate is excellent, and I'm delighted to be helping people enter a wonderful new profession that they can easily learn and can do at their own pace. I receive upbeat letters, phone calls, and personal visits all the time from new travel agents who have taken advantage of my offer. They share stories of where they have been, interesting people they have met, fun they are having, and money they are making. It's gratifying to hear the excitement in their voices and to hear about the profound changes becoming a travel agent has made in their lives. Here is an example of a two-step classified ad that is working perfectly.

The product I offer teaches everything necessary for the customer to get started as a travel agent and sets them up in business quickly. I also encourage them to read trade magazines and attend educational seminars and trade shows around the country to enhance their knowledge and skills. Travel-related events are tremendously informative and fun. I attend them myself. The most recent one was a travel convention in Palm Springs sponsored by TravelAge West magazine. I met part-time travel agents who were having the time of their lives traveling the world and making lots of money. Several said they had all the business they could handle and weren't taking on any more clients! Agents who spoke a foreign language said they had a special bond with their foreign customers, whose loyalty they said was assured by the camaraderie and ease of communication.

As you can see, when I sell a product I become knowledgeable about the industry it is a part of, and I recommend you do the same. There is no substitute for being well-informed about what is going on in the minds of people interested in or involved with your type of product.

To help you keep current with what's going on in the world of mail order, I highly recommend that you subscribe to the monthly magazine *Direct Marketing*. It's full of helpful "how-to" articles and very interesting "how-we-did-it" case histories about successful direct marketers. It covers products, techniques, issues, and events you should know about, including postal issues, copywriting, and new technology. The magazine includes a list of terrific books and new releases of audio and video tapes covering recent conferences and seminars and on current hot topics. If you are serious about your commitment to the mail order business, it is important that you keep abreast of things with this professional publication. I always recommend *Direct Marketing* to my students and they love it.

FREQUENTLY ASKED QUESTIONS AND THE ANSWERS THAT WILL HELP YOU START TO MAKE MONEY IN YOUR OWN PROFITABLE MAIL ORDER BUSINESS

Question: Can the average person make money in mail order?

Answer: Yes. There is nothing unique about the thousands of individuals who are successfully making extra money in mail order. They are following sound mail-order techniques--techniques you can learn from my book *How to Get Rich in Mail Order* or audio cassette program *Mail Order Millionaire*, which includes a copy of my book. If you are willing to invest the time necessary to attain your financial goals, I'm willing to help you.

Question: Do I need an office?

Answer: No. Conduct business from your home until your volume necessitates moving into business quarters. Keep overhead to a minimum.

Question: How can I find products to sell?

Answer: My book contains numerous sources for suitable mail order products. Simply zero in on something you would like to sell.

Question: How do I know how much inventory to order?

Answer: Initially, whenever possible, make arrangements to have merchandise drop-shipped until you can estimate how much inventory to carry. Drop-shipping means that orders are shipped to your customer by your supplier upon receipt of your instructions and payment. This is done only after you receive payment from your customer. Thus, you avoid spending money on inventory and can concentrate on sales.

Question: Can you recommend a supplier of gift items who will drop-ship merchandise?

Answer: I enthusiastically recommend Specialty Merchandise Corporation. This company was founded in 1946 and has supplied mail order dealers with a reliable source of products from all over the world. You can select from over 3,000 items. Write to: Specialty Merchandise Corporation, Mail Order Dept. 322, 6061 De Soto Avenue, Chatsworth, California 91365. If you are in the Los Angeles area, you can visit the showroom and see merchandise on display. The showroom is open Monday through Saturday.

Question: In which magazines should I advertise?

Answer: The same ones that other mail order companies use to sell products similar to yours. These magazines, which consistently run the same ads, are the survivors of the trial-and-error method of choosing media employed by successful advertisers. That doesn't mean you can't experiment. Hunches sometimes pay off. But customers, by habit, have become programmed to look in particular publications for specific types of merchandise. I advise you to take advantage of the publication's ability to attract a large audience that is interested in the type of merchandise you have to sell. Then your challenge will be to attract the attention of potential customers and sell them your product or service from the ad, or motivate them to send for further information.

Question: I have heard that some magazines will run a free advertisement on a product. Is this true?

Answer: Yes. In my book, I devote a chapter on how you can get free ads to put you on the road to riches. You should also try to get free publicity in your local newspapers. An excellent book on the subject is *Publicity: How to Get It* by Richard O'Brien.

Question: Should I run a classified, or display ad?

Answer: My advice is to begin with a classified ad.

Question: Should I sell directly from the ad, or offer free literature?

Answer: I suggest you offer free literature. It takes too many expensive words to write a classified ad that will convince people to send money. Once you draw the inquiries, send advertising literature to do the selling.

Question: What should I include in the advertising literature?

Answer: As much concise information as possible about your product or service. Stress the benefits to be derived and support them with testimonials from authorities in the field or from satisfied customers. Include illustrations and specifications, if the items call for it. State price, postage, and guarantee. Don't forget to ask for the order!

Question: I'm using the two-step approach to sell my product. What is the optimum sales literature package?

Answer: The literature that comprises the classic response to an inquiry is a sales letter, advertising literature that includes photographs or art work of the product, testimonials, guarantee, credit card option, toll-free 800 telephone number, postage paid reply envelope, and an incentive (such as a gift) for prompt response.

However, it may not be necessary to use the optimum literature. This is something you need to find out because of the expense involved in printing, envelopes, and postage. Your objective is to develop a mailing package that will generate maximum response at the lowest cost. Keep testing until you are satisfied that you have achieved this. For example, you might not need four-color circulars to sell your product or expensive coated stock for your mailing pieces.

Question: Can you recommend a source that has non-fiction books and will drop-ship single orders?

Answer: My own Wilshire Book Company drop-ships and can supply beautifully illustrated brochures like the ones enclosed, advertising 300 books on a wide range of subjects, such as astrology, chess, cooking, gambling,health, hobbies, humor, hypnotism, marriage, sex, parenthood, metaphysics and occult, self-help and inspirational, sports, pets and horses.

In my book, I tell in detail how I created a bestseller that took exactly one day to write and 50¢ to produce. Following my instructions, you could do the same. I also give you sources for out-of-print books, records, and tapes in perfect condition at a fraction of their original cost. These items are excellent for mail order as they are highly profitable.

Question: What is the best way to get started selling books?

Answer: Choose a category and contact publishers selling that particular type of book. You'll find them in *Subject Guide to Books in Print*, a reference guide found at all public libraries. Inquire whether the publishers will drop-ship books for you. If not, order the books as you receive the orders. When you determine which books are selling well, order small quantities and gradually build your inventory. Advertise the same way you would for a product.

Question: I think I have a good mail order idea and want to run a display ad. How many ads should I run to begin with?

Answer: Run one advertisement in the best of the publications that you think would logically produce orders for your type of product. Although you would get a better advertising rate by committing to running three times in succession, I advise against it. If your first ad doesn't pay off, you'll be wasting money by running the next two. Generally, ads do not pull better with repetition. Running one time gives you the opportunity to revise and strengthen your ad as soon as you have determined that it needs to be improved. The rule in mail order is to keep testing to minimize your losses and maximize your earnings. If you have written an ad that pulls well, your potential customers will still be there when you run your ad again.

Question: What are the best months to advertise?

Answer: The best mail order months are September, October, November, January, February and March. The first three months of the year are great because people are home much more during the winter than at other times of the year. That means more time for reading and activating New Year's resolutions for self-improvement. Many companies do the greatest percentage of their business during the months of September, October, and November. These months produce a great volume of orders, as people buy gifts for the holidays. Some products have a well-established seasonal period. If yours is one that does, accept it, and advertise accordingly.

Question: I have found a product and have written an ad. How do I know I've written a good one that will pull?

Answer: Do market research on it by asking friends and family what they think of the ad. In time, you'll develop a sixth sense about what works. Keep in mind that your success depends not only upon finding a product, but in developing and recognizing copy that will sell it. Advertising copy is the catalyst that makes your operation go. Spending small amounts of money on good ads will lead to success. Spending a fortune on ads that don't have a chance will spell disaster. Don't fall in love with your advertising copy. Be willing to change it to make it better. My favorite book on advertising is *How to Write a Good Advertisement* by Victor O. Schwab. If your local library or bookstore doesn't have it, you can obtain a copy from my office for $22.00 postpaid.

Question: How can I further develop a sense of what might be a good mail order product?

Answer: By studying the repeat advertisements in publications, analyzing the direct mail that you receive, reading success stories in publications, and reading books dealing with all phases of mail order. Eventually, you'll develop that indefinable sixth sense for knowing what is right.

Question: What are some of the reasons people are not successful in mail order?

Answer: I have found the common denominators to be a lack of information and conviction as to what makes a good mail order product. People often have perfectly good products, but lack persuasive advertising copy. Poor returns cause them to doubt their products and give up before they find out they have winners.

Question: I have an uneasy feeling that I will not be successful even though I understand the principles and procedures to follow. Do you have any comments about this?

Answer: Fear of failure is a common apprehension among beginners in any field of endeavor. Success seems so far down the road. It may be difficult to imagine yourself as being successful, but your potential for success is as great as anyone else's. Don't worry about it. Proceed one step at a time, initially setting only small goals. You'll be exhilarated when the first order puts you into the mail order business. Belief will come with experience.

Question: What's the first step to start making money in mail order?

Answer: Read my book *How to Get Rich in Mail Order* published by Wilshire Book Company. It is carried by B. Dalton, Walden, Crown, and most independent bookstores. It's 8½" x 11" and contains 352 pages and 200 illustrations. The book is jam-packed with details and examples of my own successful and not so successful media advertising and direct mail campaigns--all used as teaching aids that give you the benefit of my 40 years of mail order experience.

Mail 30-Day No-Risk Coupon Today

YES, I want to invest in my future.

( ) Please send me *How to Get Rich in Mail Order*. $20.00 plus $2.00 S&H. (CA res. $23.65)

( ) Please send me the *Melvin Powers Mail Order Millionaire Course*, which includes the book *How to Get Rich in Mail Order*, 11 cassette tapes of practical instruction and the special bonus tape, *50 Proven Mail Order Products*. $100.00 plus $7.00 S&H. (CA res. $115.25)

Enclosed is my ( ) check ( ) money order for $_____ payable to Melvin Powers.
Charge to my ( ) Visa ( ) MasterCard. Or call (818) 765-8579.

Number_____ Expiration Date_____

Name_____ Date_____
                    (Please print)

Address_____
            (Give street address for UPS delivery)

City_____State_____Zip_____

Mail to: Melvin Powers, 12015 Sherman Road, North Hollywood, California 91605

12015 Sherman Road
No. Hollywood, CA 91605

(818) 765-8579
FAX (818) 765-2922

I CAN HELP YOU
ACHIEVE YOUR FINANCIAL GOALS

Sound like the impossible dream? It's a dream that positively can come true for you. Why am I so sure? Because I've taught many people who once only dreamed of riches, how to start and operate a successful mail order business. **Like so many other things in life, it seems so easy when you know how; so difficult, sometimes impossible, when you don't.**

I've made millions starting with less than $100. As president of Wilshire Book Company, I've published such multi-million bestsellers as *Psycho-Cybernetics* by Maxwell Maltz, M.D.; *The Magic of Thinking Big* by David Schwartz, Ph.D.; *Think and Grow Rich* by Napoleon Hill; and millions of copies of other titles—most of them through the mail. I started my mail order career with one book. How did I do it? I spent 40 years developing a mail order system that works, and I use it faithfully.

I'm not the only one who has become rich using this mail order system. As a mail order consultant, I used my system with many businesses. I saw them flourish. As a college instructor, I taught my system to thousands of students. Many started with little money and became successful. As an author, I wrote about my system in my book *How to Get Rich in Mail Order*, read by tens of thousands of people. As consultant to top cable television marketing companies, I applied my system to direct response TV. As a direct response TV product marketer, I offered my course of instruction on a show called "Mail Order Millionaire" which aired nationally.

The individuals who have achieved success are "ordinary people" who used my system to carry them along the road to riches. They started out with dreams, probably much like yours—dreams of extra money to buy larger homes, new automobiles, travel, and pay for college educations. Dreams of becoming their own boss and working as much or as little as they wanted. Dreams of finding their work rewarding, challenging, and fun. Dreams of achieving financial security that would guarantee comfort in their later years. And dreams of a mail order business that would dramatically change their lives forever. Today these "ordinary people" are living their dream lives.

The testimonials on the next page are from people like you. Their results could be your results. The money they made could be money you've made. Here is authenticated proof that my system works. **These success stories are on file in my office, as required by law.**

125

CERTIFIED SUCCESS STORIES

$7,000 IN 2 MONTHS
"Made over $7,000 in two months using your advice."

S.M. Manhattan Beach, CA
J.F.B. Levittown, PA

$8,230 IN 1 MONTH
"You have whet my appetite for success. Following your suggestions, I did $8,230 worth of business in just one month."

T.C. Utica, NY

$18,000 IN 3 WEEKS
"You changed my life. I followed your instructions. The results—$18,000 in the first three weeks! I know that I am on my way to riches! Those checks look so beautiful. Thank you, Mr. Powers."

V.W. Carpinteria, CA

$20,000 IN 6 MONTHS
"By using only a couple of your suggestions, I personally made $20,000 in a six-month period. Melvin...priceless and highly recommend it to anyone."

S.M. Manhattan Beach, CA

$30,000 IN 1 MONTH
"Following your advice, I did $30,000 worth of business in one month. Many thanks."

J.W. Los Angeles, CA

$40,000 THE FIRST MONTH
"The tips and instructions grossed me $40,000 the first month and the money is still rolling in."

G.B. Canton, MI

$93,000 IN 28 DAYS
"I earned over $93,000 in one 28-day period using your techniques. Never before have I made so much money with so little effort. Thanks for your good advice."

S.H.N. Indianapolis, IN

$100,000 IN 4 MONTHS
"Using your techniques and expertise, I made over $100,000 in four months. Keep up the good work."

B.K. Grand Rapids, MI

$1,000,000 IN 5 MONTHS
"I was completely broke and in the depths of depression when I read your material. Believe it or not, in five months I did $1,000,000 worth of business, and I am now in the process of purchasing a building worth close to $500,000. My whole life has been changed due to you. How can I ever thank you?"

G.C. Los Angeles, CA

How can you duplicate these peoples' success? By duplicating their attitudes and actions. That means thinking as they thought and doing as they did. They didn't just sit around wishing for success. They developed a belief in their ability to be successful, and they put forth a sustained effort using the Melvin Powers program to create wealth. Now you have the opportunity to do the same.

Don't let your psyche sabotage your success. Most people are defeated before they ever begin—not by a lack of ability, talent, knowledge, time, energy, contacts, and/or money, but by a lack of belief that they can be successful. In any endeavor, people most often fail because of self-doubt. They scare themselves into mediocrity by listening to an insistent inner voice that relentlessly tells them the task that lays before them is too difficult; that successful individuals

126

have something they lack; or that the program, method, or system that repeatedly has been effective for others probably won't work for them. Some people never try at all; others give up too soon, often just as they are unknowingly on the verge of success.

I understand the self-doubt you may have if you have never been your own boss, but just because you haven't done it yet doesn't mean you can't. It does mean, however, that you may have great difficulty believing that you can be successful in your own business. Why? Because <u>you haven't yet proven to yourself that you can do it.</u>

Only experiencing success will completely convince you. In the meantime, pretend that you already believe you can do it. Think and act just as you would if your belief had already grown strong. Decide to give yourself a vacation from the most treacherous of all saboteurs—self-doubt. Pack it away until you experience your first few successes. You'll be amazed how easily success will wipe out even the most stubborn feelings of insecurity. <u>Give yourself a gift of time—time to get yourself on the road to riches without your concerns and fears holding you back. That's when you will know in every fiber of your being that you positively can and will be every bit as successful as the individuals whose success stories you have just read.</u>

Three secrets of success guaranteed to make you a winner.
1. Nourish the belief that you can be successful.
2. Put forth a sustained effort toward your goal.
3. Use a system that has created wealth for others.

Being your own boss in a successful business is one of the greatest joys in life. It's unlikely you will become wealthy working for someone else. The only way to achieve financial security for you and your family is to become your own boss in a substantial business that you control. It is the best way to achieve financial independence, and it allows you to work when you want, live where you want, have time to enjoy your family and recreational activities, and feel good about yourself. <u>When you become your own boss, you take control of your life and build the secure future you once thought was beyond your reach.</u> Only then are you truly free. If you will do your part, <u>my mail order course will give you that freedom.</u> <u>That's my promise.</u>

The system that has worked for others can work for you as well. The *Melvin Powers Mail Order Millionaire Course* turns road blocks into stepping stones to success. <u>The question is not whether the system will work for you, but will you work the system?</u> Whether you want to earn extra money working part time or yearn to become wealthy—you can do it. <u>Rich people are no smarter than you.</u> They have simply learned and applied the techniques of making money. You can do the same.

Professionals acclaim the *Melvin Powers Mail Order Millionaire Course*. They call it the Rolls Royce of mail order instruction courses. Why? Because it's loaded with practical information based on many years of successful personal experience.

This is the moment of truth. Do you really want financial independence? Do you want to have the money, peace of mind, and time necessary to enjoy life with your loved ones? If your answer is Yes, it is time for you to take the first step. Send now for the *Melvin Powers Mail*

Order Millionaire Course. It consists of my bestselling book, *How to Get Rich in Mail Order,* and a comprehensive cassette tape program filled with many hours of detailed information describing the techniques that have made me and others rich. You will learn my secrets of hitting the jackpot again and again, raking in millions. My course gives easy-to-follow, step-by-step instructions on how to get your hands on those stacks of mail full of cash, checks, and money orders that represent your future financial independence.

Picture yourself opening envelope after envelope and shaking out more money than you ever imagined possible. Can it ever really happen to you? It sure can—just as it has for others who once had your same doubts, but refused to let that stop them. Remember: You are not only what you are today, but also what you choose to become tomorrow.

Take that first step along the road to riches by picking up your pen and filling out the coupon below or by calling (818) 765-8579 and using your Visa or MasterCard. Do it right now. And do it with complete peace of mind knowing that I unconditionally guarantee my course will show you how to make money in mail order. I'm so sure it will bring you the riches you've dreamed of that you can postdate your check or money order for 30 days. If, for any reason, you decide to return the course, I'll send back your uncashed check or money order or credit your account immediately. Fair enough?

Don't procrastinate! It takes more than dreaming to achieve success. Order my course and change your life.

Mail No-Risk Money-Saving Coupon Today

SAVE $25   **40th YEAR IN BUSINESS**   **SAVE $25**
                      SPECIAL ANNIVERSARY PRICE

Please send me the *Melvin Powers Mail Order Millionaire Course*, which includes the book *How to Get Rich in Mail Order*, 11 cassette tapes of practical instruction and the special bonus tape, *50 Proven Mail Order Products*. Regularly $100.00. Special anniversary price $75.00 (CA residents $81.19) plus $7.00 S&H.

Enclosed is my ( ) check ( ) money order for $_____ payable to Melvin Powers. Charge to my ( ) Visa ( ) MasterCard.

Number_____ Expiration Date_____

Name_____ Date_____
                        (Please print)
Address_____
                (Street address for UPS delivery)
City_____State_____Zip_____

Mail to: Melvin Powers, Dept. 9, 12015 Sherman Road, No. Hollywood, California 91605

How to Get Rich in MAIL ORDER
by Melvin Powers

352 pages, 200 illustrations
$22.00 postpaid

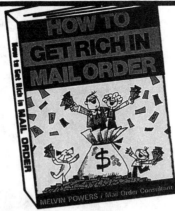

I have always been fascinated by those individuals who begin with little more than an idea and a dream and eventually convert those two unrefined bits of ore into a fortune.

Leonard Carlson took a $1 personalized rubber stamp and parlayed it into Sunset House, the multimillion-dollar catalog-sales firm.

Anastasios Kyriakides came here from Athens at age 15 with only $72 in his pocket and is now the "father" of the *Lexicon*, that amazing little computer translator which can be a lifesaver when you're traveling in a foreign country.

Frederick Mellinger, nearly broke in 1947, decided to design women's clothes from a man's point of view, and now his California-based Frederick's of Hollywood grosses millions.

Joseph Sugarman failed, time and again, until he began to sell low-cost pocket calculators and digital watches, and now this young marketing guru is the head of a $50 million-plus consumer-electronics organization.

These four entrepreneurs, and hundreds of others in our country, have something in common. They became success stories after they learned how to sell their products to the consumer by *mail order*.

Selling by mail (either through advertisements in the media or direct mail) is one of the last American outposts of free enterprise where an individual can begin on little more than a shoestring and, with persistence, motivation and luck, become wealthy. How wealthy? Estimates vary, but it's safe to figure that approximately $200 billion of merchandise is being sold directly to consumers at home each year, and that may be conservative.

If you've ever had an itch to look into this lucrative field and didn't know how to begin your exploration, let me recommend a new book that will answer every question you ever had about mail order and plenty you never thought about. *How to Get Rich in Mail Order*, unlike many books on the subject that are so replete with charts and diagrams that one dozes before page nine, was written by a talented mail-order expert with a long and successful track record. Listen to him, from his opening chapter:

I am Melvin Powers—writer, editor, publisher, lecturer and executive head of the Wilshire Book Company, specializing in self-improvement books. I have been a book publisher and mail-order entrepreneur for more than 25 years, selling millions of dollars' worth of books and products, utilizing mail-order techniques almost exclusively.

During those years, I have learned that the mail-order business, despite its mundane image, is a highly creative endeavor. You will better understand this once you start to open the envelopes and watch the money pour out.

Like most businesses, the world of mail order is one in which there is a direct correlation between what you are prepared to put into it and what you will eventually take away from it. But unlike many, it is a game unfettered with restrictions and qualifications—and for that reason, it could be the best game in town. The opportunity for success is available to all. There is no distinction in terms of social background, job or affluence. No particular skills are necessary, nor is education required beyond that which is provided in my book and the supplemental-reading program suggested. Play by the rules, follow the guidelines, meet the challenges squarely, and the only limit on how much you can earn is that which you set.

As with anything else, the prime catalyst for accomplishment in the mail-order field is *motivation*. Given this incentive, the determination to succeed and the guiding hand of one who has already successfully established a business, and you are well on your way.

In this large-format book, crammed full with fascinating examples and illustrations as well as sage advice, the author provides a firm guiding hand while mincing no words. If you're looking for an easy way to earn a fast buck, this is not the book for you. Throughout the book, you will, again and again, encounter statements that sound as if they sprang from a master of self-help, and that's only natural, I guess, when you consider that Mel Powers's publishing company, Wilshire, over the years, has published such success classics as *Think and Grow Rich*, *I Can*, *Psycho-Cybernetics* and *The Magic of Thinking Big*. For example:

Each of us is unique. Each of us has a personality and temperament distinct from others. We each have individual hopes, desires and ambitions. It is by virtue of these individualities that each of us brings to a business venture a different approach from that used by someone else. It is this uniqueness I want to encourage and develop, for it is the element which will eventually spell success. If you have not yet been as successful as you would like to be, don't be discouraged. In reading this book, at least you are doing something about it—taking constructive steps to bring it about. A failure in the past does not preclude a future that can be extremely successful. Monetary and personal success begins with a correct mental attitude. Knowing someone is successfully mail ordering lobsters from Maine . . . or selling apples from the state of Washington should be good news for you. If he can do it, so can you.

Just a few of the chapter titles will give you some idea of how much this book can teach you: "How to Make Money With Classified Ads," "The Unlimited Potential for Making Money With Direct Mail," "How to Start and Run a Profitable Mail-Order Special Interest Book or Record Business," "Melvin Powers's Mail-Order Success Strategy—Follow It and You'll Become a Millionaire," "How to Get Free Display Ads and Publicity That Will Put You on the Road to Riches," "Questions and Answers to Help You Get Started Making Money in Your Own Mail-Order Business." After you have read this book, written in a style that is never dull or stodgy, you just might get the urge to try what you've been talking about for years—starting a business of your own. And here's one that you can test while you're still working at your regular job.

Famous songwriter reveals secrets:

Would you like to write a hit song? If your answer is yes and if you are willing to devote some time to a pleasant and fun-filled hobby, you can be successful in the exciting world of music. Your dreams of songwriting success can come true! Listen to this.

Songwriter with 22 Gold Records Tells You How

Tommy Boyce, an internationally known hit songwriter, who has earned millions of dollars in royalties, has written a book called *How to Write a Hit Song and Sell It*. It's a complete course of instruction in which he reveals professional songwriting tips for the beginner and up-and-coming songwriter. You'll find out how he wrote six of his biggest hits, see step-by-step how the music and lyrics were developed, and learn how you can use the same techniques to write your own hit songs.

This one-of-a-kind book tells it all. It even includes some of Tommy's actual royalty statements from around the world—something that has never been published in any other book. And you'll see personnal photographs of Tommy and many of his celebrity friends.

Here are some of the songs that Tommy Boyce has written: *Last Train to Clarksville, Come a Little Bit Closer, I Wanna Be Free, Valleri, I Wonder What She's Doing Tonight, Lazy Elsie Molly, Be My Guest, Pretty Little Angel Eyes, Alice Long, I'm Not Your Stepping Stone, Peaches 'N' Cream, Words,*

She, the Monkees' theme song, and the theme song for the ever-popular TV show "DAYS OF OUR LIVES."

Here are the chapter titles:
1. Who Am I? 2. Can the Amateur Songwriter Reach Stardom? 3. How to Begin with or without a Musical Background. 4. Moods, Titles, and Melodies 5. Where Do Songs Come From? 6. Which Comes First, the Lyrics or the Melody? 7. Analyzing Hit Songs. 8. What Makes a Hit Song? 9. Professional Songwriting Tips for the Amateur and Up-and-Coming Songwriter. 10. How I Created Six of My Hit Songs. 11. Evaluating Your Music. 12. Rewriting Before Presenting Your Song. 13. Promoting Your Own Songs 14. Copyright, ASCAP, BMI. 15. The Business Side of Music. 16. How to Sell Your Songs in Person or by Mail.

The Easy Way to Rhyme Lyrics The Songwriter's Companion

Songwriters' Rhyming Dictionary, which contains thousands of rhymes, will be of tremendous help with your lyrics. Organized for quick reference, it contains rhymes for single and multiple syllable words.

Amateur Songwriter Hits it Big

Melvin Powers, publisher of Tommy Boyce's book, was fascinated by the manuscript when it was first presented to him. As a direct result of reading the book in its manuscript form, he

wrote two country-western songs that made the charts. His song *Mr. Songwriter* was recorded by Sunday Sharpe on United Artists Records and *Who Wants a Slightly Used Woman?* was recorded by Connie Cato on Capitol Records. He even won an award from ASCAP for *Who Wants a Slightly Used Woman?*. What this remarkable, instructive book did for new amateur songwriter, Melvin Powers, it can do for you.

Don't delay. Get started in the fascinating, fun world of songwriting and music. Send for both books: *How to Write a Hit Song and Sell It -* $12.00 postpaid and *Songwriters' Rhyming Dictionary -* $12.00 postpaid.

130

How to Succeed With Your Own 900 Number Business

"Nothing will guarantee success in this business, but reading this book will go a long way toward maximizing the chance for success."

W. Brooks McCarty, President
Information 900 Services Corp., Palm Springs, CA

Four Facts You Should Know About 900 Numbers:

1 Dial-a-porn is on the way out, and even now accounts for only 3% of 900 programs. The future in this industry will be with legitimate information and entertainment services with good perceived value.

2 Many new 900 programs fail because they are launched by people who have not done their homework to learn the business or to find out what it takes to succeed. Because the 900 business has so many truly unique advantages, the lure of easy profits has been irresistible, and too many would-be entrepreneurs have jumped onto the bandwagon completely unprepared.

3 There is a lot of hype and blatant misinformation out there surrounding the 900 industry, perpetuated by snake oil hucksters who are fleecing naive opportunity seekers. For example, you cannot "own" a 900 number, and the government does not limit the quantity of 900 numbers that are available.

4 Established businesses are getting into the 900 industry in ever growing numbers. Virtually every business has access to unique, timely or specialized information that can be sold by means of a 900 number. A 900 number is a convenient, efficient information delivery medium, for both the caller and the information provider.

Here's a partial listing of only a fraction of the well-known companies and organizations that have joined the 900 industry:

Sports: ....*USA Today*, *Sporting News*, *Sports Illustrated*, Coors
Financial: ....H&R Block, AM Best, *Fortune*, Dow Jones & Company
Entertainment: ....MTV, HBO, *Spin Magazine*, NBC, Paramount Pictures
Health: ....Whitehall Laboratories, PMS National Network Support Assoc.
Consumer help: ....*Consumer Reports*, *Car & Driver*, Better Business Bureau
Technical advice: ....Novell Netware, Technical Software, Inc.
News & Politics: ....ACLU, *Newsweek*, Freedom International, Inc.
Fundraising: ....March of Dimes, Amnesty International, World Vision

About the Author
Robert Mastin

Robert Mastin is an entrepreneur in the truest sense of the word. For more than 15 years he has run several successful small-business enterprises based in Newport, Rhode Island. His achievements include the organization of a residential design and development firm whose projects have been featured in *Popular Science Magazine*, *Builder Magazine*, and *The New York Times*. Mr. Mastin has successfully developed his own 900 number information service and currently has several more under development.

A graduate of the U.S. Naval Academy and the recipient of a master's degree in accounting from the University of Rhode Island, Mr. Mastin began researching the 900 pay-per-call industry with a view toward launching a tax preparation service. Quickly he discovered that reliable, honest information about the 900 industry was scarce — and difficult to find, at best. After establishing his own 900 number business, he decided to write a book about his knowledge and experience: ***900 KNOW-HOW***.

With acknowledged expertise in the area of telecommunications and voice information, Mr. Mastin is currently working on yet another book; this one about launching an 800 number order-processing service.

A Personal Note From The Author

"When I first got into the 900 business, accurate information was scarce and very difficult to find. As I waded through all the hype and misinformation, I decided that serious entrepreneurs needed honest, useful information about the industry. That's why I wrote 900 KNOW-HOW — for people like me. I wish such a book had been available when I jumped into the business myself - it would have saved me a lot of time, effort and money."

He's Sailing off Maui, Making Money Around the Clock!

The Ideal Home Business

Launch your own 900 number business and sell pre-recorded information over the telephone to a national market—24 hours a day, 365 days a year.

Learn the secrets to one of the most exciting business opportunities of the century—this industry exploded from zero to $975,000,000 in only four years! And it has only just begun.

Easy to Start

You will be amazed how easy it is to start your own 900 number business. Very low start-up costs. Work part-time from home, from anywhere in the country. The only equipment needed is a touch-tone telephone.

Enormous Potential

Your potential market is huge - the entire country - only a telephone call away. And best of all, the telephone company collects all your money for you—collection costs are zero!

Learn How

To launch a profitable 900 program, you must learn the secrets to success. What 900 programs work, and why. What pitfalls to avoid. You need honest advice from experts—people who have seen the mega hits as well as the flops.

You need **900 KNOW-HOW: How to Succeed With Your Own 900 Number Business**. This new book is crammed with 174 pages of honest, straightforward, nuts-and-bolts information.

Endorsed by Experts

Here's what some of the leading industry experts say about **900 KNOW-HOW:**

"I have been involved in the audiotex industry for over 5 years and 900 KNOW-HOW is one of the best books on the pay-per-call industry that I have seen. The information provided is accurate and concise. This book is a must for anyone contemplating getting into the business."

Bill Gundling, Vice President
The Nine Call Corporation, Newton, MA

"Well written and informative for new or experienced IPs (Information Providers). We even use it as part of our training for new salespersons."

Robert Bentz, Director of Marketing
Advanced Telecom Services, Wayne, PA

Ironclad Guarantee

You can't lose. If not 100% satisfied with your copy of 900 KNOW-HOW, simply return it within 30 days for a full refund. No questions asked.

Act today! Join other successful entrepreneurs in this explosive industry. Earn money while dozing on the beach, while playing tennis, or while vacationing at Disney World. But you can't get started until you know how.

( ) YES! Please rush my copy of 900 KNOW-HOW. I'd like to learn more about the 900 business. If I'm not completely satisfied, I can return the book for a full refund.

Enclosed is my ( ) check ( ) money-order for $20.00 (CA res. $21.65) plus $2.00 postage.

Name_____

Address_____

City_____ State_____ Zip_____

Please make your checks payable to:

Melvin Powers
12015 Sherman Road
North Hollywood, CA 91605

132

Here's What They're Saying About *900 KNOW-HOW:*

"It was only a matter of time until somebody wrote a frank, no-hype book on launching a 900 pay-per-call business. The author is experienced 900 number entrepreneur Robert Mastin and the title is '900 KNOW-HOW'...."
--Joyce Lain Kennedy
Nationally Syndicated Careers Columnist

".... a superb job of gathering and conveying the information....crammed full of information which is concise and accurate....I highly recommend it for anyone contemplating going into the 900 number business...."
--Ed Durham, Editor
Home Income Reporter

".... Solid advice to anyone wanting to start-up the business....a good starting place for 'infopreneurs' who want to get in the game....presented in a factual, concise manner that can be easily understood and digested...."
--Bruce Jones, Book Reviewer
Mailer's Review

"The book is fantastic....the answers you need for going into this business....I am glad to recommend this book to you because it contains the information you need to become successful in your own 900 number business...."
--Bob Barnes, Book Reviewer
Jackpot magazine

".... This book provides HONEST information about what it takes to be successful in this business....Get the REAL facts...."
--Bob Riemke, Editor
The Real Entrepreneur

".... 900 KNOW-HOW explores this explosive industry in-depth, including how to start and operate a 900 business, what pitfalls to avoid, the costs involved, and what kinds of 900 programs have been successful...."
--Business Bookshelf
Business Opportunities Journal

"Medium-to-small businesses could profit from the acquisition of a 900 number, and this title is a good place to begin. It's a detailed examination of the 900 pay-per-call option which offers detailed advice on how to succeed with a 900 number -- and what to avoid...." --The Bookwatch
The Midwest Book Review

".... Really offers the readers non-biased information....This has to be one of the best, well written and informative books on the subject.... 900 KNOW-HOW is a must...."
--John Moreland
The Dream Merchant

"Everything one needs to know to start a 900-number phone service is surveyed ....Starting a 900 number service is relatively easy, but its success depends on the additional factors of marketing research, customer service, and costs which are also dealt with in this introductory guide."
--The Small Press Book Review

"Here's an exploration of one of America's growth industries. The author covers how to start and operate such a business, pitfalls, costs and marketing....a good primer on starting a business based on the 900 telephone numbers...."
--Jeff Rowe, Business Book Editor
Orange County Register

"The book provides honest information about what it takes to be successful in this business, and clearly debunks some of the hype and blatant misinformation surrounding the 900 industry...." --MAIL PROFITS Magazine

".... a good primer if you have ever dreamed of making your fortune with a 900 number.... This book will help focus your thoughts and give you the resources to study how to build a successful 900 number service...." --Kathy Mathews
Stepping Stones

".... you'll get a nuts-and-bolts guide to starting and operating a 900 service....start-up and monthly operating costs....ways to effectively market a 900 service....details on types of services that are successful...."
--Barbara Kaplowitz, Editor
What's Working in DM and Fulfillment

"This is the bible of an industry that shot from $0 to nearly $1 billion in annual sales in only four years...."
--Duncan Anderson, Book Reviewer
SUCCESS Magazine

"....explores the pay-per-call industry in depth....and what makes a successful 900 program...." --FOLIO Magazine

"... 900 KNOW-HOW is a comprehensive guide that helps the start-up information provider..."
--The Newsletter on Newsletters

".... the author shoots straight from the hip in his clearly understandable approach to the business, showing you what can and cannot be done, how and how not to do it... an extraordinary accomplishment... read it before you act..."
--Entrepreneur's Digest

"If you're interested in launching a 900 pay-per-call information or entertainment service, you will find this book helpful." --Galen Stilson, Publisher
The DIRECT RESPONSE Specialist

"This is a valuable book to have on your bookshelf."
--Mail Order Entrepreneur

"... provides in-depth coverage of the 900-number industry..."
--Sales and Marketing Strategies & News

"... the first comprehensive how-to book about launching a 900 pay-per-call business... explores the ever growing pay-per-call industry, including pitfalls to avoid, effective marketing, the most successful programs to start, and much more." --Income Opportunities magazine

Three Magic Words Will Bring You Everything You Ever Wanted

Three Magic Words is a ground-breaking book about the greatest idea in the world—a secret revealed in just three words—an idea so simple, so startling, so wonderful that it can start you on an adventure that will forever change the way you see yourself, others, and life. Knowing the secret opens up a whole new world of contentment, fulfillment, joy and abundance.

What Are You?.... Why Are You Here?

This is the age of uncertainty. This is the time of emotional upset and nervous instability. This is the era when man, surveying the universe from atop the heap of his material accomplishments, sees his insignificance in comparison to the stars, understands how puny is his strength in comparison to nuclear power. This is the time when man, in his headlong rush to master the elements and harness nature's energies, has come far enough to know that he treads the wrong path to his own security. For there is no security in machines or electricity or electronics or nuclear power.

What am I? What caused me? Why am I here? Where am I going? These are the questions of the human soul that demand an answer.

For man is not an animal that exists upon the earth for a day, a freak of existence in a maelstrom of chaos. The human soul does not exist who at some cloistered moment has not reached out with timid fingers and touched God.

No circumstance or fact or event or thing exists that does not have a reason, and so it is with man. All harnessing of nature's elements and powers, all creation of material wealth and possessions are but passing fancies, things of the moment, for man enters into life naked, and naked he departs. The only thing, the single most important thing that concerns his existence on earth, is the discovery of his soul.

For man is not body alone. No human being can bear to live who regards himself as only a freak occurrence in a freak circumstance. Man is spirit, clearly and without dispute. Man is the essence of the mighty intelligence that guides and controls the universe. Man lives in this

134

intelligence; he is a part of it and the whole of it. He is as small as his temporal life and as great as his spiritual life, for the intelligence from which he comes is greater than all, greater than the far reaches of space, greater than the power that holds the planets in their courses. This intelligence is man's to use as he sees fit. It is God-given, a divine birthright, and is denied to no man except by himself.

Your Unlimited Power Over All Things

In the pages of *Three Magic Words*, you will learn of the unlimited power that is yours. You will learn how you can turn this power to work for you, here on earth, to make your life majestic and overflowing with good. *Three Magic Words* is not a religion or a sect or a society. In its entirety it is a series of essays aimed at revealing to you your power over all things. You will learn that there is only one mover in all creation and that mover is thought. You will learn that there is only one creator and that creator is the Universal Subconscious Mind, or God. You will learn that this creator creates for you exactly what you think, and you will be shown how you can control your thoughts, not only to obtain answers to your problems but to create in your experience exactly what you desire.

It requires only a few minutes of your time each day, a few minutes that will reward you with greater vistas in life, greater hope and promise than has ever been dreamed.

There is a cause! There is a reason! There is a power greater than you are, of which you are a part, that you can use to make your life good and great and vigorous and full of abundance!

A Promise of Success

If you read this remarkable book through, and do what it tells you to do, you cannot fail to accomplish what it promises. *Three Magic Words* is a book that many people carry with them for years, referring to it again and again to remind themselves of its powerful, life-changing message. Your life, too, will be affected, for once you learn the three magic words, you will feel compelled to live by them, every day of your life.

LIFETIME MONEY-BACK GUARANTEE

Please send me *Three Magic Words* by U.S. Anderson on a money-back guarantee basis. Enclosed is my check or money order payable to Melvin Powers for $14.00 postpaid (CA residents $14.99 postpaid).

Name_____ Date_____
                       Please Print

Address_____

City_____ State_____ Zip_____

Mail to: Melvin Powers, 12015 Sherman Road, North Hollywood, CA 91605

136

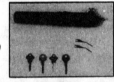

Specially Targeted Catalogs of Catalogs

FREE National Advertising

THE BEST
MOVIE & VIDEO
CATALOGS

THE BEST
SPORT
CATALOGS

THE BEST
COUNTRY & VICTORIAN
CATALOGS

THE BEST
GARDENING
CATALOGS

THE BEST
CHILDREN'S
CATALOGS

THE BEST
WESTERN
CATALOGS

THE BEST
CRAFT & HOBBY
CATALOGS

Plus Many Others —
See Inside

Choose From 24 Targeted Publication Titles To Advertise Your Catalog And Reach Millions Of Known Catalog Buyers. . . Risk FREE!

SPECIALLY TARGETED CATALOGS OF CATALOGS

We Target Our Mailings To Select Individuals!

The right audience generates the right catalog requests. We've created 24 niche publication titles to match each catalog advertiser to the right audience. Each of our publications is mailed to a very targeted mail order buyer and is the best kind of media source for producing qualified inquiries. A skillfully created listing of your catalog will make these niche publications work well for you!

Using an affinity approach to marry catalog advertisers with publication titles is where we start. We use a sophisticated database modeling and profiling process to match each publication to a unique market segment of known catalog buyers who are responsive to your offer. These unique market segments represent consumers who have indicated particular interests and activities that relate closely to the products in your catalog. This vivid portrait of lifestyle and behavior, coupled with a profile of your catalog, identifies consumers with a higher propensity to respond to your catalog offer and make purchases. **NOW, THAT'S TARGETING!**

Free Help With Ad Design And Media Consultation!

Our advertisers are always the first consideration. We are extremely careful about the way our advertisers are presented and in which Publication Title they are placed. We absorb all the cost associated with color separations, copywriting, ad layout, and design of your listing.

Reach Millions Of Known Catalog Buyers Nationwide... Without Risking A Dime!

The circulation of our "Catalogs of Catalogs" is national. Your catalog will be presented to the most affluent catalog buyer households in the world. They are interested in your products, and have an average household income of $50,000. You'll get all this and more for only sixty cents per inquiry with no cost for advertising, printing, or postage.

Regardless of your marketing objective or your target audience... whether they be avid outdoor enthusiasts, crafts or collectibles hobbyists, fashion minded consumers, or consumers with home decorating interests... we have the targeted niche publication that's right for your catalog.

You'll Benefit By Years Of Experience!

In 1981, the principals of **Publisher Inquiry Services, Inc.** conceived the concept of cost per inquiry programs in a Catalog of Catalogs to develop qualified requests. Over the last 16 years, catalog request programs have consistently delivered qualified catalog requests that convert at a profit and become repeat buyers for catalogers.

We understand catalog marketing, and the challenges of today's economics. Let's face it, with rising paper, production, and postage costs, it's too expensive these days to mail your catalog to non-responsive prospects. We use sophisticated database modeling and profiling techniques to identify the interest and behavior of known catalog buyers for our targeted Catalog of Catalogs mailings. We don't pull any punches in our quest to generate highly qualified prospects for over 1000 of our catalog advertisers.

We Are Tough On Detail!

We use accurate pictures and descriptions to make sure the consumers who request your catalog do so for all the right reasons. This process generates catalog requests that convert at profitable rates the first time mailed, and many new customers become valuable repeat buyers.

CALL TODAY 1-800-455-7929 FOR THE CLOSING DATE OF OUR NEXT ISSUE!

REACH THE RIGHT AUDIENCE!!!

GET MORE QUALIFIED BUYERS!

1. Just choose the publication titles ideally suited for your catalog.
2. Make your first and second choices.
3. Mail this page — along with the General Information & Application, and the Advertising Agreement forms in the postage-paid return envelope.

Check Your First And Second Choices For Publication Titles

1st Choice / 2nd Choice	1st Choice / 2nd Choice	1st Choice / 2nd Choice
THE BEST ART & MUSEUM CATALOGS	THE BEST BOOK CATALOGS	THE BEST WOMEN'S CRAFT CATALOGS
THE BEST MEN'S CRAFT & HOBBY CATALOGS	THE BEST AUTO & SPORT VEHICLE CATALOGS	THE BEST CHILDREN'S CATALOGS
THE BEST MOVIE & VIDEO CATALOGS	THE BEST MUSIC & AUDIO CATALOGS	THE BEST MILITARY CATALOGS
THE BEST TOOL & HOBBY CATALOGS	THE BEST MEMORABILIA CATALOGS	THE BEST WESTERN CATALOGS
THE BEST IMPORT CATALOGS	THE BEST GIFT CATALOGS	THE BEST HOME DECOR CATALOGS
THE BEST FOOD & CULINARY CATALOGS	THE BEST GARDENING CATALOGS	THE BEST COUNTRY & VICTORIAN CATALOGS
THE BEST PET & ANIMALS CATALOGS	THE BEST WOMEN'S FASHION CATALOGS	THE BEST MEN'S FASHION CATALOGS
THE BEST SPORTS CATALOGS	THE BEST HEALTH & FITNESS CATALOGS	THE BEST GIFT FOOD CATALOGS

I would like to see my catalog placed in your targeted publications

NAME OF MY CATALOG _____

COMPANY OR CORPORATION NAME _____

TELEPHONE _____ FAX NO. _____ PERSON TO CONTACT _____

SIGNATURE _____ DATE _____

CALL TODAY 1-800-455-7929 FOR THE CLOSING DATE OF OUR NEXT ISSUE!

When You Participate In The Largest And Most Prestigious Catalog Request Program In The World, You'll Be In Good Company!

Adirondack Design
African Connexion
Alsto's Handy Helpers
America
American Science & Surplus
Angels And More
Anticipations
Antique Hardware & Home
Archival Company, The
Art & Artifact
Art Institute Of Chicago
Atkinson Country House
Audio Editions
Australian Catalogue Co., The
Aviation Book Co.
Back In The Saddle
Back To The 50's
Barnes & Noble Book Sale
Barrie Pace Ltd.
Barrons
Bart's
Bathroom Machineries
Baths From The Past
Bear Creek Nursery
Beauty Boutique
Bedroom Secrets
Biltmore Estate Catalogue
Bits & Pieces
Blue & Gold Sports Shop
Body Shop By Mail, The
Body Time
Boundary Waters Catalog
Brainstorms
Brigade Quartermasters
Brownstone Woman
CR's Bear and Doll Supply
Carolee Creations
Caswell-Massey
Cat Claws
Cats, Cats & More Cats
Celebration Fantastic, The
Charrette
Don Francisco Coffee Traders
Ebbets Field Flannels
Edmund Scientific Co.
Elderberry Collection, The
Embossing Arts
Emerald Collection, The
Enchanted Doll House
Enco Manufacturing Company
Enterprise Art
European Heritage
Everything Roses Catalog, The
Exposures
Five Star Stamps
For Counsel
Fran's Wicker And Rattan Furniture
Frank Lloyd Wright Museum, The
Frederick's of Hollywood
Galligaskins Alaska Collection
Garden Solutions
Gardener's Supply Company
Gazin's Cajun Cole Cuisine
Gemmary, The
Gooseberry Patch Co.
Graceland Gifts
Griot's Garage
H.J. Saunders U.S. Military Insignia
Hampton Art Stamps
hanna Andersson
Harbor Freight
Harvard Square Records
Harvest Direct
Heavenly Handicrafts
Herrschners
Hobby Builders Supply
HomeSmart
Importers Bel Vasaio
improvements

In The Air
In The Swim
Initials
International Male
Into The Wind
J & R Mega Catalogue
J. Marco Galleries
J.C. Whitney & Co.
J.C. Whitney Motorcycle Parts
JCPenney
JCPenny Big Kids Catalog
Jackson & Perkins'
Jackson Hole Traders
Janet Coles Beads
Jazzertogs
Jeffers
Jerry's Catalog
Jos. A. Bank Clothiers for Men
Jos. A. Bank Clothiers for Women
Just Between Us
Just My Size
Kaiser Crow Gatherings
Keepsake Quilting
Ken Pierce Books
King Size
Kirchen Bros.
Kitchen Etc.
Lands' End
Lands' End Coming Home
Lavender Lane
Light Impressions Corp.
Lilliput
Limoges Encore
Linen & Lace
Long Elegant Legs
Lucasfilm Fan Club, The
Mach 1, Inc.
Magellan's "Essentials For The Traveler"
Martin Rochelle
Masters' Collection, The
Medals of America
Mepps Fishing Guide
Metropolitan Museum of Art, The
Micro • Mark
Miller Stockman
Minnetonka
Motherwear
Movie Book, The
Movies Unlimited Video Catalog
Mule Creek Mercantile
Museum of Modern Art Gifts
Music Barn, The
Music Direct
Musicmaker's Kits, Inc.
Musser Forests, Inc.
Myson
Mysteries By Mail
Nancy's Specialty Market
National Music Supply
National Safety Equipment
Nature By Design
Newport News
Noble Collection, The
Norfolk Lavender
Nostalgia Family Video
NuTone
Nutrition Headquarters
Old Telephones
Old Time Radio
Old Wagon Factory, The
Omaha Vaccine Company
On Paper
Once In A Blue Moon
One Step Ahead
Optional Extras, Inc.
Outlet Catalog
Oxfam America Trading
Paisley Panda Home Collection, The
Patterncrafts

patternworks, inc.
Paul Fredrick
Pendery's
Penn Herb Co. Ltd.
Pentrex Catalog
Petdoors U.S.A.
Pet Warehouse
Petals
Peter Pauls Nurseries
Phoenix
Pieces of History
Pintchik Homeworks
Piquant Pepper
Porter's Camera Store
Principal Secret
Pro Team
Pueblo to People
Quartermaster
Radio Spirits, Inc.
Radio Yesteryear
Rand McNally
Real Goods
Reasonable Solutions Software
Red Rose Collection
Reggio Registers
Reliable Home Office
Renovator's Supply, The
Reverie
Rhino Records
Rick's Movie Graphics
Ritchie
Road Runner Sports
Rose's Doll House
Roslyn Nursery
Ross-Simons
Royal Doulton Collectors
Royal Silk
Rue de France
Sadigh Gallery Ancient Art
Salsa Express
Sampler Records Ltd.
Samurai Armour
Science Fiction Collectibles
Science Fiction Video Collection, The
Scottish Lion Import Shop, The
Script City
Seasons
Shareware Express
Sheplers
Shillcraft Latch Hook
Short Sizes
Signature Basket Co.
Silhouettes
Silk Collection, The
Silver Spring

Silverts Clothing For Seniors
Simply Tops
Simply Whispers
Smith & Noble Windoware
Sony Signatures
Sound Choice
Southwest Indian Foundation
Speedgear
Spice Merchant
Spices etc...
Sport Europa
Stamp of Excellence, Inc.
Star Pharmaceutical
Stash Mailorder
Stash Tea by Mail
State Line Tack Discount Western Catalog
Storybook Heirlooms
Strasburg, Inc.
Sturbridge Yankee Workshop
Sundance
Sunshine Discount Crafts
Sur La Table
Tailwinds
Taos Drums
Tasha Tudor
Teas Orchid & Exotic Plant Supply
Tiger Software
Times Past
Tree Book, The
Tucker Electronics
Tweeds
U.S. Cavalry
Undergear
Upstairs Records
Video Age, Inc.
Videos For You
Vintage Video
Walnut Acres Organic Farms
Warner-Crivellaro
Watch Depot
What on Earth
Whole Work Catalog, The
Winfield Collection, The
Wonder Laboratories
Woodcraft
Woodworker's Supply Catalog
Woodworkers' Store, The
Work Out Music
Worldwide Collectibles & Gifts
Worldwide Treasure Bureau
Yankee Pride
Yield House

and many others!

"If you want high conversions on leads that turn to multi buyers then we at Stash Tea recommend **The Best Catalogs In The World**™ We've been extremely happy with the results of advertising in **Best Catalogs** and look forward to a long profitable relationship..."

Sunday Doane
Stash Tea

CALL TOLL FREE 1-800-455-7929 FOR MORE INFORMATION OR TO RESERVE SPACE FOR YOUR CATALOG LISTING.

THE BEST CATALOGS IN THE WORLD™ • **PUBLISHER INQUIRY SERVICES, INC.**
951 Broken Sound Pkwy. NW, Building 190, P.O. Box 3008, Boca Raton, Florida 33431

SUCCESS

Success is in the way you walk
   the path of life each day;
It's in the little things you do
   and in the things you say.
Success is not only in getting rich
   or rising high to fame;
It's not alone in winning goals
   which all men hope to claim.
Success is being big of heart
   and clean and broad of mind.
It's being faithful to family, friends,
   and to the stranger, kind.
It's in the children whom you love
   and all they learn from you;
True success depends on character
   and everything you do.

Chapter Eight

One-Inch Display Ads
Can Work Wonders

If the publication in which you want to advertise doesn't have a classified section, you might want to consider running a one-inch display ad. You would basically use the same advertising copy as for a classified, but have the advantage of using graphics, a variety of typefaces, and reverse white copy on black. Another plus is that the ad will be seen by more readers, as display ads stand out.

Since small display ads have these advantages over classifieds, why not use them all the time? Because they cost more, which may be worth it for some offers, but not for most. And the classifieds may be seen by different people than see the display ads. Using both gives you good readership coverage. The most reasonably priced, easiest to create ad is still a classified, and as you will see, there is simply no substitute for these little gems.

One Step or Two? . . . How to Decide

You might be tempted to sell a product off the one-inch ad, but in my experience, the space is too limited to do it profitably. There just isn't enough room to provide all the information necessary to prompt a sale. Of course, as with most general rules, there are exceptions. A product that pulls in orders from a one-step classified should work as a one-inch display, as well. Use the classified ad criteria in chapters four and seven to decide whether or not a one-step display ad has a reasonably good chance of producing results.

One-Step Display Ads . . . How Big to Pull Big?

The minimum space that usually works as a one-step ad is 2 ¼" wide (one column) x 5" high. That is equivalent to one-sixth of a page or one-half of a column in height in a 7" x 10" magazine. Should you ever run an ad this size, don't make the mistake of taking

143

up precious space with a coupon even though you have probably seen it done over and over again. Why repeat other people's errors? Use all the available space to sell your product.

See page 146. NEW CONCEPT is using a sixth-of-a-page ad to secure leads for their lingerie mail order program. The part that is interesting is that they offer the option of a complete kit which includes a video for $20.00. That's an excellent lead. Someone is paying $20.00 to listen and see the potential of the business opportunity. It doesn't get any better than that.

Display Ads . . . Do They Get Better Results than Classifieds?

I have run classified ads and one-inch display ads at the same time in the same publications, and of course, tracked the responses. The display ads have always out-pulled the classifieds because there's a better chance of them being seen. Which do you suppose produces a better lead, classified or display?

On top of page 147 is a one-inch display ad I have used for a long time. It works perfectly. Can you tell why? Incidentally this ad has been copied dozens of times by my competitors and it's also working for them. Look how much information I've put into this small space. The ad says it all.

Can you find the key that identifies for me in which magazine I'm running the ad? It's the kit number. Each time I run, I change the number. No matter which kit number is ordered, I send the same one. There is only one! But the customer doesn't know that little secret. Only I do—and now you do, too, of course. Because I'm still running this ad successfully, you know it's a good layout. It works. You are welcome to adapt it to your own product.

If you would like to contact a graphic artist to inquire about having him do some work for you, call me at (818) 765-8529 or write me at 12015 Sherman Road, No. Hollywood, CA 91605.

Look at the bottom ad on page 147. Do you think this ad was profitable for me? I stopped running it. Have you any idea why? The answer is that I didn't receive enough one-dollar bills. The same ad in the classified section was more cost effective without asking for $1.00, and I'm currently running it in numerous magazines.

A Great Team . . . Full-Page Ads and Classifieds

Many mail order companies use full-page ads to get leads for their programs, preferring two-step ads rather than one-step, even though they have plenty of room in the ad to give information and do a good selling job. Why do they choose two-step ads over one-step? Because they have more to say about their offer than can be presented in one page. They've found that their follow-up literature packages pull best. They even use the two-step method in their two-minute television spots and 30-minute infomercials.

One company that has been very successful in using this technique is Specialty Merchandise Corporation. Interestingly, the company also runs numerous classified ads as part of their advertising campaign. Their full-page ad is on page 150. It's doing an outstanding job for them. As a matter of fact, it's one of the best-pulling ads in their 40-year history. Can you tell why? What do you think of the headline? Do you like that it asks a question? Can you guess the answer? Doesn't the headline draw the reader right into the body of the ad? Identify key elements that make this ad a winner. Every time you analyze a successful ad, you are developing your instinct for what works.

Look at the people in the ad. Do you see Finn Skeisvoll? He is a very astute mail order entrepreneur. He's also one of my students, I'm proud to say. It's obvious that he did his homework. Be sure to do yours, too. It pays off handsomely. Do you recognize anyone else?

146

Click and Connect

to the World of Direct Marketing on Target Marketing's Web Page

http://www.targetonline.com

Search the Toolbox for ideas you can take to the bank
Join a lively online forum
Explore an industry Buyers Guide
Link to other direct marketing resources
Get advertising and subscription information
And more!

TARGET
MARKETING

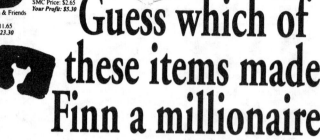

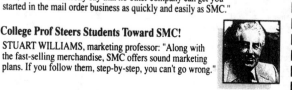

Chapter Nine

Full-Page Display Ads Can Make You A Fortune Overnight

Let's assume you have run a two-step classified ad offering free details. It pulled lots of inquiries. You sent out a two- or four-page sales letter extolling your product's virtues. It pulled in a substantial number of orders and you were very pleased with your profit. Then you ran the ad in another publication, then in others, pyramiding your earnings. Now what do you do? Full-page display ads pop into your mind. It's only natural to want to run them. They're the dream of every mail order entrepreneur. But should you risk it? My answer is a qualified yes. Run it, but only after you have tested it and know it's a winner. How can you test an ad without running it? That's what we are going to discuss next.

How to Make Sure Your Full-Page Ad Is Going to Be a Winner

First choose a layout that you like. Then take the most pertinent copy from your sales letter and redesign it so that it includes a strong headline, good subheads, compelling copy, a good money-back guarantee, and a coupon with a key. Your typesetter or graphic computer service can do this for you, or you can do it yourself if you have a computer with desktop publishing capabilities. When you finish the ad, live with it for a few days and try to get some feedback from other people.

Should you now spend thousands of dollars to test your ad? No, not yet. One of my money-saving techniques is to mail out your one-page display ad instead of your two- or four-page sales letter in response to people who answer your classified ad. Track the results. See if the number of orders is the same, less, or more than it would have been had you used the sales letter as follow-up literature. If it is lower, redesign and/or rewrite the ad and try again. If it's the same or more, you are ready to test your full-page ad in an appropriate publication.

Now listen carefully to what I'm telling you. Run one full-page ad one time and one time only in magazines where similar ads have appeared. Most magazines will give you a discount if you run three times. Don't do it! A representative of the magazine may tell you it's necessary to run three times to do a valid test. Don't believe it. If the ad doesn't hit the first time out, something isn't working right. Go back to the drawing board.

Here's another way I recommend to test the pulling power of a full-page ad before running it. Rent a small number of names. Then evaluate your response. What percentage of names resulted in orders? Did you make money, lose money, or were the results marginal? If you lost money or if the results were marginal, you should think twice about running the full-page ad as is. If you made money or the results were marginal, purchase more names and do another mailing. Tabulate the results again. When you have made money sending out a thousand or more pieces of mail, it is reasonably safe to run a one-time test of your full-page ad. Good luck!

How to Get Rich in Mail Order

A very favorable review of my book *How to Get Rich in Mail Order* appeared in *Entrepreneur Magazine*. It resulted in thousands of orders. What did that tell me? That *Entrepreneur* was the right publication in which to sell my book. I subsequently ran full-page ads every month for four years in *Entrepreneur* and in all of the other business opportunity magazines and all weekly tabloids. I also ran in numerous newspapers around the country including the Los Angeles Herald Examiner in which I ran a full-page ad every other week for five years. I was on a roll!

I experimented with different ads and various prices for the book. I found that the price was not the deciding factor for readers. I did not sell more books at $10.00 than at $20.00. Ordinarily you would assume you'd sell more books at the lower price. That wasn't my experience. I believe that if the price is within reason, you'll make the sale. When people want something, they spend the money. Many big mail order and TV infomercial products sell better at the higher price when prices are tested. And think of the hundreds of dollars people spend on tickets to concerts. Some world-class entertainers command even more, yet time-after-time the tickets sell out.

Turn to page 160 to see one of the ads that sold over a million dollars worth of *How to Get Rich in Mail Order*. Originally the headline read: How to Get Rich Starting from Zero! The results were excellent, but when I added the two words *this year*, it pulled even better. I love the lead into the headline: Don't wait for success. Make it happen! My favorite saying is under the headline: You are not only what you are today, but also what you choose to become tomorrow! And isn't that true? We have the option every day of changing our life. I ran the ad without these attention grabbers and the results were not as good.

How to Get the Best Spot

In magazines, I always insist on a right-hand page. It's easier to see than the left. I also place the coupon on the outside of the page so that it's easy to clip out. Another problem with running on the left is that the reader must struggle with the binding (also called the gutter). Give your ad every chance of success. Put it in the best place.

A Few Words Can Make All the Difference

In the coupon of my full-page ad selling the *Mail Order Millionaire* course, I changed the wording slightly and it resulted in thousands of dollars in extra sales. My original offer read:

Send for Melvin Powers *Mail Order Millionaire* course, which includes the book *How to Get Rich in Mail Order* and 12 audio tapes. $107 postpaid.

The subsequent offer read:

Send for Melvin Powers *Mail Order Millionaire* course, which includes the book *How to Get Rich in Mail Order*, 11 audio tapes, and the special bonus tape, 50 Proven Mail Order Products. $107 postpaid.

The respondents to both ads received the same package. Obviously, the idea of the bonus tape had an impact. I tested the change of copy in a 50,000 mailing to the same list; 25,000 received the first copy and 25,000 received the second. The second copy pulled a higher return. That translated into thousands of dollars. Since then I have been using the bonus tape copy.

The point I'm making is that whether you are using display ads or direct mail, a few strategic words can make a significant difference. Overall, it's brought in hundreds of thousands of dollars that I would never have seen if I hadn't thought to change the order form slightly. Your challenge is to do the same with your advertising copy.

Split Runs Give Indisputable Answers

Some publications are willing to print two different ads in the same issue so the advertiser can test which copy pulls better. This is known as a split run. Let's assume a publication has a 500,000 circulation. They'll run 250,000 with one price in the coupon and 250,000 with the another price. The advertiser uses different keys in each of the two coupons so the number of orders at each price can be counted. When I was deciding how much to charge for my book *How to Get Rich in Mail Order*, I tested $20.00 against $15.00 in several publications and found there was no difference in the return. I did more split runs, testing $20.00 against $10.00 and again, it didn't make any difference what the price was. The returns were the same. How much did I finally settle on for a selling price? Twenty dollars, of course.

Tova Borgnine sold a facial creme called "Facelift in a Jar" via full-page mail order ads. To determine the best price to charge, she did a series of split runs. She tested $9.95 versus $19.95, then $19.95 versus $29.95, $29.95 versus $39.95, and finally $39.95 versus $49.95. The magic number turned out to be $39.95. That was the perceived value of the product. How do you account for her selling more jars at the higher price?

Split runs are very useful for testing both headlines and body copy, but not at the same time. You can only test one element with each run or you won't know which was responsible for the change of response rate. I constantly wrote new ads and tested them against the ad I had been using, changing headlines, types of guarantees, and other ad components. That's what I recommend you do, too.

An Unusual Money-Back Guarantee

A friend of mine named Joe Karbo, author of the book *The Lazy Man's Way to Riches*, was running full-page ads that stated, "I'll hold your check for 30 days. If for any reason you are unhappy with my book, return it and I'll send back your uncashed check. Fair enough?" When he substituted this statement for his usual 30-day money-back guarantee, his sales increased 25%.

I borrowed his guarantee idea for my ads and my response rate also jumped 25%. After many years, I'm still using this copy in some of my ads and sales literature. I have also begun to use a lifetime guarantee for some of my books, but for some inexplicable reason I'm not completely comfortable with it, even though so far not a single book has been returned. What message does this guarantee convey? Is it favorable? Would you feel comfortable using it in your own advertising?

Although I have sold hundreds of thousands of mail order books and courses, I rarely have them returned. This is also true of the hundreds of books that I publish. Come to think of it, I can't remember the last time someone returned a book. On the rare occasions that I do have something returned, I always respond immediately, refunding the purchaser's money and asking the reason for the return. I include a self-addressed stamped envelope for the reply. This feedback is valuable. If you ever get too many returns on an item, feedback from dissatisfied customers will pinpoint the source of the problem so you can get to work on it.

Get the Best Ad Placement on the Best Days

In newspapers, request the front page of the classified section. It gets a higher readership than the middle of a section. Although some newspapers won't do it, many will—so ask. My experience has proven the best-pulling days to be Monday, Tuesday, and Wednesday—in that order. I always ran my ads on Monday because people are generally home after the weekend, and the newspapers are smaller which means the ad has a good chance of being seen. Don't run on Thursday, Friday, or Saturday. People may be preoccupied with the coming weekend and not be as receptive. Some advertisers love to run on Sunday because the circulation is higher. But the advertising rates are also higher. I usually don't run on Sunday because the paper is so large that the ad may not be seen.

Creativity Can Turn One Hot Offer
Into an Entire Industry!

I ran a full-page ad for my book *Secret of Bowling Strikes* and it was a big, big winner! After that, I ran the ad every month in *Bowling Magazine* and in other bowling publications for ten years! On the back end, I was selling a record called "The Secret of Bowling Strikes." The conversion rate was extremely high. I was also selling a book called *How to Bowl Better Using Self-Hypnosis*. Naturally, I had a record on that, as well.

I knew there were many sports enthusiasts in addition to bowlers who were serious about wanting to improve their game, so I decided to use the same sales technique to do a campaign on the mental side of golf. I began with a book called *The Secret of Perfect Putting*. The ad worked like a charm. Naturally, I followed up with a record called "The Secret of Perfect Putting." I also published a book called *Psych Yourself to Better Golf* that sold extremely well. I even published a book called *How to Play Better Golf Using Self-Hypnosis*. I had already developed the market for this type of book, and I kept adding new products that were exactly what I knew these people were looking for. Since my customers were interested in the mental side of golf and had an insatiable appetite for books on the subject, I began to sell golf books published by other companies in addition to my own.

An article appeared in one of the major golf magazines about using the techniques of *Psycho-Cybernetics* to improve one's golf game. That brought an avalanche of orders for the book. It seemed there was no end to the sale of books and records. To give even more impetus to my sales, a book came out on the mental side of tennis called *The Inner Game of Tennis* by W. Timothy Gallwey. When it hit the bestseller list, my sales increased even more.

But I didn't stop at books and records. I figured my avid golfing customers would purchase other golf-related items. I made arrangements with a golf ball company to personalize a dozen golf balls, gift-box them attractively, and enclose a gift card in every order. (At that time, personalized golf balls were not readily available.) I also arranged for the manufacturer to drop-ship the orders for me. I designed a circular and included it in all my outgoing orders for golf books and records. It suggested that people purchase the personalized golf balls for themselves and to give as gifts for Father's Day, Mother's Day, Valentine's Day, anniversaries, birthdays, Chanukah and Christmas presents, and other special occasions. The literature worked beautifully.

I received many multiple orders and the reorder business was great. I sold thousands of sets. I even got large orders from major corporations. The sale was going so well, I began including the circulars in all of my outgoing mail, even if it wasn't related to golf. Responses were good. To top it off, I ran display ads selling the imprinted golf balls. They worked, too, and on the back end I included circulars for my books! There was an avalanche of orders! What a thrill! Big money can be made with full-page ads. All it takes is creative thinking, knowledge of the mail order business, and having the attitude that you can and will do it. Your turn will come.

When you have an offer that's working, ideas flow. They pop up effortlessly—sometimes while you sleep. I've had the experience many times of waking up in the middle of the night with a new idea or the answer to a previously perplexing problem. I have had it happen numerous times when I was writing lyrics or a new book. The experience is common. You have probably had a similar experience at some time, perhaps when trying to remember a person's name. You can't seem to think of it and then suddenly, when you least expect it, it pops into your mind. That's how ideas will come to you once you're focused on your mail order business.

Does Setting a Time Limit on an Offer Move Readers to Action?

It seems that the urgency implied in setting a time limit to order would have the effect of moving readers to action, and many successful mail order entrepreneurs use this technique. I don't use it in my literature because somehow it sounds insincere to me to be saying, "You must respond within 15 days to take advantage of this offer." Or: "This special price good only this month" (or until a specific date). If you feel comfortable with it, you may want to test it with your offer and see if it makes any difference in your response rate.

What Full-Page Ads and Direct Mail Pieces
Must Do to Be Successful

Remember, products that promise to satisfy any of the basic human desires or needs stand a good chance of being sold, as long as the advertising copy does what it is supposed to do. Here's the formula for writing successful display ads and direct mail pieces that uphold their important part in making an offer work.

1. Capture the reader's attention with an eye-catching headline.

2. Generate interest by persuasively describing product or service benefits.

3. Stimulate desire with proof, testimonials, and/or a further explanation of benefits. (When using classified and one-inch display ads, insufficient space requires that this information be put into follow-up literature.)

4. Offer a guarantee.

5. Solicit the order.

Readers Will Instantly Recognize These Elements
That Can Make or Break an Offer

By now you are well aware that doing a complete and easily understandable job of presenting the product or service story is critical to an offer's success, but there is something else that is of the utmost importance in making an offer work. It's the tone of the advertising copy. What do I mean by tone? Primarily believability, authoritativeness, and the all-important sincerity. How can you get these intangible elements into your advertising copy? By simply telling it as it is. That's where these elements come from.

1. Believability comes from being honest about what a particular product or service will do. It is the result of telling the truth about your offer.

2. Authoritativeness comes from knowing your product or service so thoroughly and completely that it's obvious you know what you're talking about.

3. Sincerity comes from believing that the product or service you're writing about really can help readers. That you are doing them a favor by introducing them to your product or service.

157

Being honest, knowledgeable, and believing in the good of what you are doing in the world not only makes mail order offers successful, it also makes for a satisfying, fulfilling, positive feeling about oneself and one's life. Knowing that I have for my entire career made available books, tapes, and other products that have helped people to improve their personal and business lives in many ways (some quite dramatically) is one of the great joys of my life. I wish that joy for you. The joy that you've made your fortune by doing good.

Business Opportunity

POSTAL LISTS

AAA Financial Corporation Profitable Business Opportunity
75,189 Masterfile Buyers...............@$85/M

America's Classifieds Opportunity Seekers
779,736 Masterfile ....@$80/M

American Business Ventures Opportunity Seekers
2,422,994 Opportunity Seekers ......@$80/M

American Business Ventures Enhanced Lifestyle Database
2,300,000 Enhanced Seekers ....@$80/M

BizStartup Business Opportunists
199,513 Total Buyers......................@$90/M

Business Opportunists
200,000 Total File ....@$85/M

Business Opportunity Digest
963,015 Total File ....@$85/M

Continental Book Buyers
292,612 Total File ....@$80/M

Coupon Connection of America Business Start-up Program
393,469 Total File Buyers ....@$80/M

D'Aracangelo Seminars
688,671 Seminar Attendees/Buyers@$85/M

Direct Franchise Management Services
470,347 Total Paid Responders ......@$85/M

Emerald Coast News
65,320 Active Subscribers..............@$90/M

Electronic Medical Billing Home Based Business
109,320 Total File Buyers...............@$80/M

Entrepreneurs at Home Buyers
3,858,373 Total File ....@$80/M

Financial Gains
40,629 Buyers ....@$85/M

First American Publishing Business Opportunity Book Buyers
252,769 Last 12 Month Buyers ......@$80/M

Postal and Email Lists Available from VentureDirect Worldwide

Franchise & Investment Expo
139,400 Total File ....@$100/M

Futurewealth Strategies Business Opportunists
638,350 Total Buyers......................@$85/M

Hi-Tech SOHO Computer Product Buyers Enhanced Masterfile
4,450,472 Hi-Tech SOHO Execs......@$85/M

Home Office Entrepreneurs
1,448,050 Total File ....@$80/M

Homeworkers Plus
37,413 Total Buyers........................@$90/M

Home Workers Success Manual
1,379,294 Total Buyers/Inquirires ..@$80/M

IMEX Inc. Home Mailers Program
512,238 Masterfile ....@$80/M

King Media Satellite Distributors
32,434 Total File ....@$85/M

Learning Strategies Corp. Paraliminal Tape Buyers
202,597 Total Buyers......................@$80/M

Money Making Opportunities Active Subscribers
1,100,438 Masterfile........................$85/M

New Career Center
219,181 Total File ....@$80/M

Opportunity World Magazine Start-Up Business Entrepreneurs
49,473 Active Subscribers ....@$90/M

Spare Time Magazine Active Subs
1,651,976 Active Subs....................@$85/M

Spare Time Magazine Enhanced Masterfile
1,488,743 Total Masterfile ....@$85/M

Specialty Merchandise Corp. Opportunity Wholesalers
1,440,424 Total Respondents..........@$85/M

Specialty Merchandise Corp. Enhanced Masterfile
420,420 Masterfile ....@$90/M

Success Now Business Opportunity Buyers
362,986 Active Buyers....................@$85/M

Sundance Distributors Business Opportunity Book Buyers
181,310 Masterfile ....@$90/M

Supermoney Opportunity Seekers
1,004,500 Masterfile ....@$75/M

The Money Machine Commerce Web System
61,891 Buyers...............................@$90/M

EMAIL LISTS

Business Opportunity Seekers Selex
2,700,000 Opt-in Email Subscribers
Highly educated, high income, professional business entrepreneurs interested in a wide variety of b-to-b offers and opportunities.

VNU Business Media Masterfile
100,151 Opt-In Email Entrants ....$300 CPM
VNU Business Media is the leading list of advertising, marketing and media professionals. These executives have subscribed to one of their premier publications: MediaWeek, MediaWeek Directory, BrandWeek, BrandWeek Directory, AdWeek, AdWeek Directory, IQ, IQ Directory, E & P, MC, and Shoot.

Avid Trading Company
18,000 Opt-in Email Entrants........@$225/M

B2B FreeNet
200,000 Opt-in Email Entrants.......@$225/M

BizLand
560,000 Opt-in Email Entrants......@$250/M

BizTalk
925,000 Opt-in Email Entrants......@$250/M

Business.com
100,000 Opt-in Email Entrants......@$250/M

Datastream Group
600,000 Opt-in Email Entrants......@$225/M

FreeForum.com
550,000 Opt-in Email Entrants......@$225/M

FreeForum Sweepstakes
160,000 Opt-in Email Entrants......@$225/M

My Free
300,000 Opt-in Email Entrants......@$225/M

For a full data card on any of these postal lists, please contact David Brill at 212.655.5153, email dbrill@ven.com or visit us at www.venturedirect.com and click on List Management.

For a full data card on any of these email lists, please contact an XactMail Specialist at 212.655.5231, email xactmail@ven.com or visit our website at www.xactmail.com

Reference Code: BO1001

Chapter Ten

Although I Live in California
I Buy My Grapefruit from Florida!

I get stacks of direct mail every day and love to go through it seeing what is being offered and enjoying the creativity that has gone into it. When I first see a display ad or infomercial, I try to guess which will be the winners. I recommend that you do the same. It will be a wonderful learning experience for you. After awhile you will find, as I do, that you know almost instinctively which offers will make it and which won't. It's a great way to learn about mail order.

I have a fun story to tell you. I received a four-page circular one morning that raved about succulent, naturally sweet, fully-tree ripened, orchard-fresh, ruby-red grapefruit. I was intrigued by the writer's enthusiasm. He sounded completely sincere as he extolled the taste delights of his grapefruit.

The more I read, the more I became intrigued with his offer. He stated that he would send 15 out-of-this-world grapefruits and that no money need be sent up front. Four of them could be eaten and if they weren't the best, the tastiest grapefruit ever, the rest could be returned at his expense.

I sent back the order card that came with the letter. One morning soon thereafter, the grapefruit arrived at my office. I put them in the refrigerator to chill as per the enclosed instructions. My office staff and I had fun tasting and evaluating them during our afternoon break. Everyone unanimously agreed that they were absolutely delicious, in fact the best grapefruit we had ever eaten. We all became devotees of Harry's Crestview Groves grapefruit from Florida.

I am now a steady customer and have ordered dozens of boxes of fruit for family, friends, and customers, who have all been delighted with both the surprise and the terrific fruit.

See pages 171 through 174 for the sales letter that first intrigued me to order. The taste-for-free offer clinched the deal for me. I have since had fun becoming a grapefruit connoisseur. I've done taste tests comparing Harry's grapefruit with the ones in the markets. The store-bought versions seem tasteless compared to Harry's. Don't I sound like a salesman for the company? Interestingly, before I started buying grapefruit through the mail, I doubt if I ate more than one a year. I preferred oranges.

Reminders Bring in Extra Orders

During the month of November, I received a special, two-page Christmas sales letter and order form from Harry's, shown on pages 175 through 176. It was a good reminder. Once again I ordered grapefruit. I sent out ten gift packages as suggested by the order form. The company puts out a beautiful full-color catalog with all kinds of other fruits, cakes, pies, candy, nuts, relishes, hams, and smoked salmon. They are running a perfect mail order operation, and would you believe it, they never even read my book!

The Florida Gift Fruit Shippers Association reports that they send out three million boxes of fruit a year. That doesn't surprise me. When I used to vacation in Florida during the winter season, it was traditional to send baskets of fruit to people back home, especially if they lived in the northern part of the country or in Canada. One of the ways we determined how good a time we were having was to find out the daily weather report for up north. The colder it was, the happier we were that we weren't there, and the better time we had! Funny, isn't it?

Better than Good Is Best

Let's get back to the initial sales letter on pages 171 through 174. Can you relate to the headline? I think it's weak. Can you come up with a stronger one? A few subheads? What do you think of the one subhead on page 173 that reads: BUT A WORD OF WARNING! Do you believe it? I wish the writer had left it out. It left me cold. It's the first time the offer falls down. See page 174. If this had been my offer, I would have filled the half-blank page with testimonials and used the subhead: Read what satisfied customers have to say about our ruby red grapefruit. Testimonials are powerfully convincing. They add greatly to the credibility of the offer. Notice the use of the P.S. It provided the opportunity of delivering the message again.

I would have used a lift letter that reads on the outside: Read this only if you have decided not to order. Inside I would have written: Frankly, I can't understand your not taking advantage of our free taste offer and giving yourself the pleasure of experiencing our scrumptious grapefruit. (And so on.)

Here's the point: Even though the sales letter is successful, it could be stronger. With a much improved letter, I know the results could at least double! That would make a big difference in the company's profitability. As a result, they could test new mailing lists and do bigger mailings. Can you think of categories of people who would respond to this letter? Look in the yellow pages of your phone book if you need ideas. I am curious which lists are proving successful and which have flopped. If you are also intrigued by this thought, it means you are getting into the challenging, creative aspect of the mail order business, which to me is always fascinating.

Foods are Big Business

Another very famous mail order fruit company is Harry & David, 2518 South Pacific Highway, Medford, Oregon 97501. They put out a beautiful full-color catalog. And their cheese cake is delicious.

There's a mail order dried fruit/nut company with a retail outlet on the main road just outside of Palm Springs, California called Hadley's. Lots of people pass it on their way home and stop to buy some of the famous goodies. It's an experience to go there. Products are displayed prominently and samples are everywhere. Can anyone eat a few cashew nuts and stop? They're so good, people end up buying some to take home. They are famous for their date milk shakes, too. Who can resist?

Have you heard of Omaha Steaks International? They are at 4400 So. 96th Street, Omaha, Nebraska 68103. Would you ever think someone could run a multi-million dollar operation selling steaks and other meat products through the mail? It still sounds incredible to me but the company has been in business a long time and they have a loyal following. The meat is packed in dry ice, sent out by overnight delivery, and arrives the next day. I asked some of my mail order students who are customers of the company, why they buy steaks by mail instead of at their local supermarket. The answer was invariably that you can't beat the taste and quality of Omaha's meats.

See pages 177 through 183 for part of the Omaha Steaks International mailing package. What you think of their four-page sales letter. On a scale of 1 to 10 how would you rate it? I would rate it A-1. The first two paragraphs on page 177 immediately grab attention because of the free gift. Their first mistake is asking for the order too soon. It appears on page one before reader has been sufficiently motivated to buy. The copy on pages two and three build that motivation. The order should be solicited after those pages, not before. I like that there are subheads, but I would make them bolder to set them off from the rest of the copy.

I love the guarantee on page 179, and the added enticement of the reusable container and cookbook "loaded with tips most cooks don't know about." To top it all off, the steaks are registered by a serial number and the customer gets a numbered certificate verifying the Gold Seal of Approval. Don't the steaks sound like something special? That's clever advertising.

The guarantee is out of this world. If you don't like the steaks, you don't have to pay for them— and there's nothing to return. How can you beat that? You also get six fabulous Ground Gourmet Burgers FREE. If you order the second package at the regular price, you get six more FREE burgers. Notice in the first P.S. you must order by the expiration date on the accompanying certificate to take advantage of this offer, and there's an 800 number for easy ordering.

Note the P.P.S. It's a reminder of the free 4-piece "Scissors 'N Shears" set. And if you order by the cut-off date (no pun intended), you also receive a terrific table top calculator. Those are a lot of add-ons for buying the steaks. They supply a business reply envelope, but it is not prepaid. Note that they are also members of the Direct Marketing Association, a professional trade association.

Crawford Lobster Company, 62 Badgers Island, Kittery, Maine 03904, Graffam Bros. PO Box 340, Rockport, Maine 04856, and Legal Sea Foods, 33 Everett Street, Allston, Massachusetts 02134 are three companies that sell live lobsters via direct mail order. They are shipped by overnight delivery. Legal Sea Foods also operates several fine restaurants in the Boston area. Their seafood is delicious. Boston is my home town and whenever I go back to visit, I make sure to dine at Legal's.

As you are well aware by now, you can have the greatest product in the world and have it still be a dud if your ads and direct mail pieces don't sizzle. Good ad copy is the catalyst that drives a business. I've seen plenty of otherwise ordinary products come to life and be gigantic winners when someone had the vision to promote them imaginatively. Many products make it this way. And numerous companies have staggering sales figures. They all started with one item they believed in and marketed it properly.

How to Make Your Direct Mail a Winner

The average direct mail package contains

1. An outside envelope.

2. A personal letter.

3. A brochure and/or pertinent literature.

4. An order form.

5. A return envelope.

Generally, direct mail literature contains the same elements as good display advertisements. However, with direct mail you have the advantage of not being confined to a limited amount of space. You can use as long a sales letter as you want to convince your customers that they will improve their lives by ordering your product. You have the option of a black-and-white or full-color brochure and choices of paper to run it on. The same applies to your outgoing and return envelopes. You can use special guarantee literature and a separate sheet containing the names and photographs of satisfied customers. You have your choice of sending the mailing piece first class or third class. You might want to use hand-written envelopes for special mailings, perhaps even calligraphied. There is no end to the variety of options. Now let's discuss each of the five elements of a good direct-mail package.

How to Save Your Offer from a Terrible Fate

OUTSIDE ENVELOPE

The wastebaskets of the nation are loaded with unopened envelopes that contain valuable ideas that could save recipients money, make them a lot of money, or give news about products and services that could change their lives. The first hurdle to surmount is getting the recipient to open the envelope containing your literature. Advertisers use a variety of means to accomplish this. Although there are no sure-fire, guaranteed-to-work-every-time answers, there are things you can do that will help keep your literature out of the "round file."

One possibility is to print something on the outside of the envelope. There is some controversy as to the wisdom of doing this however, because it immediately tips off the recipient that the package is a direct mail offer. You'll have to use your own judgement on this one. Perhaps you'll want to do a test and see if the envelope text helps or hurts your response rate.

If you have been placing your name on various mailing lists as I have suggested throughout this book, you will begin receiving increasing amounts of direct mail. Notice which envelopes tempt you to open them. What distinguishing marks or messages do they have on them? Are there any envelopes you would throw away if you weren't interested in analyzing the materials inside as part of your mail order education? Be sure to pay attention to any envelope markings or messages that show up again and again on pieces from different companies. They are probably working. This is all valuable information that will help dictate how you will structure your own offers.

Here are a few ideas that are known to be effective. You have probably seen them often on mailings you have received.

POSTMASTER: PLEASE DELIVER IMMEDIATELY. DATED MATERIAL. Creating a sense of urgency is the key here.

HERE'S THE INFORMATION YOU REQUESTED. Can be used if the individuals sent away for the literature. (And even it they didn't, they might think they did.)

MAKE $1,000 IN 30 DAYS! Such statements (called teasers) are used in hopes of making the recipient curious about the offer contained in the envelope.

The Power of a Personal Touch

PERSONAL LETTER

This is the most important of the five elements of a direct mail package. Even the most elaborate, expensive brochure can't do the job as well as a personal letter. Neither, for that matter, can a full-page ad unless the ad reads like a letter, as many of the most successful full-page ads do.

It must capture the prospect's interest immediately. And it is critical that the tone be very personal. It must seem as though the letter were written especially for the recipient, even if his name isn't on it—which brings up the subject of personalization. At first blush, it seems that a personalized letter would be more effective than a non-personalized one in achieving an intimate tone, which is precisely the opinion of some large mail order companies. But I'm not entirely convinced it does a better job. Sophisticated consumers of today know that a form letter with their name on it is computer generated. They have received many such letters and may be turned off by the attempt at familiarity. In addition, the process of personalization is too expensive for most mail order beginners. If you decide to test the concept, wait until the money is rolling in and you can easily afford it.

The letter should be written from the *you* standpoint, rather than from the *we* standpoint. "I can help you succeed," rather than "Our program has been unusually successful." A useful device is to pretend you are writing to one person who is your prime prospect. Never write to a "crowd." Tell the person how your product or service can help make life easier. Write as though you were writing to a friend.

Keep your language simple, as you would in a personal letter. You are not trying to impress the recipient with your knowledge, rather you are trying to encourage him to buy your product for his own good.

Here's how to create good personal letters:

1. State or imply a problem
   OR: Make a believable promise that will appeal to the reader's self-interest.

2. Promise that the product will alleviate or solve the problem. Create an emotional appeal that the product will improve the reader's life.

3. Back up this benefit with proof—testimonials, scientific evidence, and/or recommendations of experts. Use interesting subheads and illustrations.

4. Promise additional benefits that will help motivate the recipient to respond. Paint strong visual images with words.

5. Support statements with proof whenever possible.

6. Tell the reader exactly what he is going to get. For example: A 352-page workbook plus 11 audio tapes and a bonus tape.

7. Reiterate what he'll gain and suggest what he might lose if he doesn't buy your product.

8. Give the price and tell why it's a bargain, even if your product is a high-ticket item. (The offer is the most important part of any direct-mail campaign. It often includes not only a special price, but also premiums, gift bonuses, or other things that help to reduce sales resistance and make the offer seem like a terrific value.)

9. Urge the reader to act now and explain how he would benefit by doing so. Perhaps to get extra bonus gifts offered only until a specific date, to save money by purchasing at a temporarily reduced price, to guarantee delivery by a certain date (such as before a gift-giving holiday), or so he can start immediately to make money, feel better, accomplish his goals, etc.

10. Use a P.S.

The More You Tell, the More You Sell

BROCHURE

The brochure is a piece of printed material. It can be a single sheet, a catalog, or anything in between. What you use depends upon your product and your resources. The same rules for writing good display ads apply to brochure writing. That's why you can often convert a successful brochure into a powerful display ad. Remember to tell as complete a story as space permits about your product and how it can benefit the reader.

Make it Easy to Order
And Easy to Get the Product to the Customer

ORDER FORM

People are more likely to respond to an order if it's effortless. That's why payment by credit card and 800 numbers are commonly used in mail order offerings. If the customer has to choose a size, color, etc. be sure that the choices are clear and the selection can be made quickly and easily. And repeat the guarantee.

The order form has another important function. It provides the advertiser with credit card information and the name and address of the customer, none of which will be of any value if they cannot be read. You might be surprised by the number of illegible coupons that come in if the order form doesn't specifically ask the customer to print or type the requested information.

Can You Tip the Scales in Your Favor?

RETURN ENVELOPE

You must decide if you want to supply a return envelope. In theory you should, but I don't always use one because I have found that it isn't always cost effective.

If you do use a return envelope, should it be postpaid? Ideally it should, since a major requirement of direct mail offers is that they be as easy as possible to respond to. However, with the postage rates being as high as they are, you may want to test a stamped versus unstamped return envelope. When I use a return envelope, I do not pay for the postage. No one yet has ever complained about it and we have our share of mailings that do exceedingly well.

If a mailing doesn't do well, I wouldn't blame the lack of a business reply stamped envelope. I've convinced myself that it doesn't matter whether or not the postage is paid—or for that matter, whether there is a return envelope altogether. I've proved to my own satisfaction that it doesn't much matter by mailing out 20,000 direct mail packages—10,000 with a stamped business reply envelope and 10,000 unstamped. There was no appreciable difference in the responses. I've run the same test many times and gotten the same results.

Your Free Education

If you put yourself on various mailing lists as I have suggested, you will have all kinds of direct mail coming to your home and/or office. As you receive it, examine each offer carefully and notice how every element in the mailing package is executed. For example:

Is there attention-getting copy on the envelope? Would it get you to look inside if you weren't using the package as a learning tool?

How many pieces does the package contain?

What is each piece and what is its function?

How many pages is the covering letter? Does it look professional? Are there grammatical and spelling errors? What is the tone of the letter? Does it accomplish what it is supposed to? Do you like the headline? Is there an incentive to buy immediately? Is there a guarantee? What is it? Is it strong enough?

What kinds of merchandise are being offered?

Is the brochure effective?

Is the return envelope postage paid?

Are you motivated to buy the product?

Could you improve any parts of the offer?

Is there a possibility of copycatting the offer?

On a scale of 1 to 10, how would you rate the mailing package?

When your direct mail is successful, you might want to consider running a two-minute spot or a 30-minute infomercial. You would begin by taping shows and becoming knowledgeable about the business. There's a fortune to be made once you have a product suitable for television. It can be like hitting the jackpot—and I know many people who have done just that.

Because television time has become very expensive, you need a big winner to use this media. Once you are on television, you must watch your sales, costs, and expenditures every day and make weekly decisions about staying on, expanding your base, or pulling back. You need to become an expert. Once you understand the business, your judgement will be as good as anyone else's. One successful show will make you an authority overnight.

I had published 50 books before I published *Psycho-Cybernetics*. When the book got onto the *New York Times* Bestseller List and I had sold one million copies, I became an "instant book publishing expert."

Interestingly, the accolades I received from family, friends, and colleagues had a profound effect on my psyche. It gave me a psychological boost that was reflected in my publishing decisions. In a relatively short period of time, I had several other million sellers and achieved the reputation of being a "hot publisher."

I realize that becoming successful in mail order may seem overwhelming to you. But if you follow my suggestions for finding products, writing advertising copy, and running ads, you'll finally succeed. Financial independence, personal freedom, and making money doing something you love are all by-products of your endeavor. You can feel as I do. Work to me is never work. I love going to office to see what the mail will bring and who will call. Every day is exciting.

HARRY'S CRESTVIEW GROVES

PHONE: 1-800-285-8488

9030 17th PLACE ● VERO BEACH, FL 32966-6601

```
* * * * * * * * * * * * * * * *
*                              *
*    ANNOUNCING A GRAPEFRUIT   *
*                              *
*      GUARANTEED SO SWEET     *
*                              *
*  YOU'LL NEVER PUT SUGAR ON IT *
*                              *
* * * * * * * * * * * * * * * *
```

Dear Friend,

   With your permission I'm going to send you one of the most unusual packages you'll ever receive. When it arrives you'll find a treat that's sure to make the cold winter months healthier and happier for you and your family.

   In this package you'll find 15, of the most unusual grapefruit you'll ever see. This grapefruit is unusual because it's so sweet you'll never need to add sugar. This I guarantee!

   Let me tell you how this grapefruit was developed:

   As you know, the Indian River area of Florida has been famous for a hundred years as a great <u>orange</u> producing region. There are good reasons for this. You see the Indian River is not really a river at all - but a tidal lagoon. The nearby fields are actually the remnants of land that was under the sea millions of years ago. You take soil like this - add a perfect climate, and you have all the factors to make Indian River Oranges world famous. (And they are world famous simply because Indian River Oranges are larger, juicier and sweeter).

   I reasoned if we could grow oranges this sweet here in Florida, we ought to be able to grow grapefruit <u>just as sweet</u> and juicy as our oranges. But how can a grapefruit ever be as sweet as an orange?

   Well, it has taken years of trial and error with setbacks and disappointments. Our Florida nurserymen experimented crossing a grapefruit with an orange, but failed. They tried grafting a grapefruit onto an orange tree and failed again. Finally a break through: By taking a young orange tree and "budding" it, we can successfully change the top of the tree from oranges to grapefruit.

(over please)

171

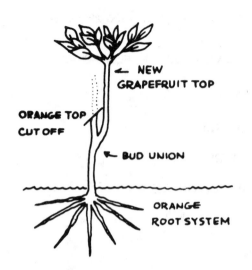

NEW GRAPEFRUIT TOP

ORANGE TOP CUT OFF

BUD UNION

ORANGE ROOT SYSTEM

I've crawled on my hands and knees down the rows of young orange trees setting in the delicate grapefruit buds right at ground level. I've cared for the trees for months getting this new bud to take hold and grow ... then I've gone back and cut off the tops of the orange trees to make room for the tender new grapefruit tops to grow.

It has taken years of backbreaking work nuturing these trees, getting them to bear fruit. This is why Harry's Orchard Fresh Ruby Red Grapefruit never need sugar.

When finally our own trees set on their first fruit ... two or three fruit to a tree, we ate them all ourselves. Since then we've had enough of these luscious grapefruit to send a few packages to friends and relatives up north. How they did rave with the first taste of our grapefruit! Nothing would do but they had to have a box sent up every month. They shared the fruit with neighbors who wrote back placing standing orders for my Orchard Fresh Ruby Red Grapefruit.

This year the trees have set on enough fruit to where we'll have a limited supply ripening each month ... but since I'm fussy about my grapefruit (I think they're too good to sell through ordinary supermarkets) I've decided to ship them direct - and this is why I'm writing you this letter.

Just how good are Harry's Orchard Fresh Ruby Red Grapefruit? What are they really like?

They are naturally sweet - sweeter than you thought a grapefruit could ever be.

They are seedless. They are flowing with luscious juice.

Instead of being an orange color as you'd expect, they have a red blush.

They are large, each weighing a full pound or more.

They have the ability to keep perfectly for weeks.

I could write more, but you just have to taste them yourself to know what my Orchard Fresh Ruby Red Grapefruit are like. You have to taste them to know how really sweet and good a grapefruit can be.

So let me send you the pack containing 15 of these choice grapefruit. When your shipment arrives, place four of these big beauties in your refrigerator until thoroughly cool. Then cut them in half, and have your family sample them.

"This Treat Is On Me!" You decide whether these grapefruit are really as sweet as I say - and whether you and your family want to be one of the first to enjoy this vitamin-rich fruit during the cold winter days ahead.

Each month this winter, I'll ship you a box containing 15 of my Orchard Fresh Ruby Red Grapefruit from Florida. Each fruit will weigh a full pound or more, with perfect delivery guaranteed. You pay nothing in advance. Merely remit after receiving each shipment. I'll pick, pack and ship each month through April ... but you may skip or cancel a shipment at anytime simply by telling me your wishes.

Let me prove to you how great Harry's Orchard Fresh Ruby Red Grapefruit really are. Sign and mail the enclosed card today.

Then, you'll receive a package containing your 15 red grapefruit for you and your family to try. After eating four of the fruit, decide whether my Ruby Reds are so wonderful they cause your family to sing with praise and clamor for more.

If your answer is "Yes" keep the remaining grapefruit, and send a check for the modest invoice. You will automatically receive a similar shipment each month through April. Otherwise, return the unused fruit in the first shipment, at my expense, and you won't owe me a single penny.

BUT A WORD OF WARNING!

Only by acting quickly -- and mailing the order card now -- will you be in time to share in this year's limited crop of Harry's Orchard Fresh Ruby Red Grapefruit. As you can imagine, there are only a limited number of these "top-worked" trees now in production. It's strictly first come, first served!

So rush the order card ... and accept my offer to send you this first shipment for a taste-test in your own home. See first-hand the quality of Harry's Orchard Fresh Ruby Red Grapefruit, shipped directly to you from the groves of the famous Indian River region here in sunny Florida. Enjoy this orchard-fresh fruit, and protect yourself so you can have regularly scheduled shipments this winter. Be one of the first to taste Harry's Orchard Fresh Ruby Red Grapefruit.

Sincerely,

Harry King

HK/CAA

P.S.   Until you've tasted my Orchard Fresh Ruby Red Grapefruit, you're never going to know how truly delicious and sweet a grapefruit can be. Don't delay, mail the enclosed order card today for your taste-test.

HARRY'S CRESTVIEW GROVES

PHONE: 1-800-285-8488

9030 17th PLACE ● VERO BEACH, FL 32966-6601

Dear Friend,

    Before you know it, you will be seeing the familiar signs "only
10-more, 7-more, 3-more shopping days until Christmas!"

    You're probably busy now with last minute gift shopping for
friends and relatives. Seems there's always another name that comes
to mind - just as the crowds are thickest in the stores.

    But, there is an easier way to do your late shopping!
Just make your selections from my new Holiday Gift Book
enclosed and mail your order today - or call me direct
- **TOLL FREE 1-800-285-8488, AND I'LL DO ALL THE REST!**

    Orchard Fresh Ruby Red Grapefruit and Big, Juicy Oranges are
always a real favorite during the Holiday Season. For each gift I
will select only large ... fully tree-ripened ... orchard fresh fruit.
My Ruby Reds are seedless ... a lovely red color and so sweet no sugar
is ever needed ... and my Oranges are the top-of-the-crop.

    Take a few moments to browse through my new catalog enclosed and
see how easy it is to select a gift that will please anyone on your
gift list! There are beautiful fruit laden Baskets ... delicious and
unusual combinations of fresh fruits and other treats. For an extra-
special gift choose a membership in my Winter Fruit Club or, for that
unique gift, The Parade of Gifts! The thanks you'll receive will be
warm and sincere.

    No money is needed now! Your credit is good. Each gift will be
handsomely prepared and guaranteed to please in every way. And, you
may remit after all the packages have been received in good condition.

    But remember, time flies ...

(Turn to back, please)

Last minute shopping can be easy and fun this Holiday Season. Choose your selections ... fill out your order and mail it today ... or, call me direct ... **TOLL FREE** ... **1-800-285-8488**.

Your gifts will be carefully prepared and shipped in sturdy travel-safe cartons to withstand the handling of the Holidays, with your special greetings included. I guarantee each package will arrive perfectly.

But hurry ...

Sincerely,

Harry King

HK/GC

P.S. Remember, Christmas is swiftly approaching! Make your gift selections and mail your order today ... or call me ... **TOLL FREE** ... **1-800-285-8488!**

Omaha Steaks ® ®
International ®

Your Reply Will Really Be Appreciated!

A Private Message To a Very Special Person

Dear Friend,

This private invitation is going out to just a handful of people, yourself included. I hope you'll accept my invitation. But even if you decide not to, I want to send you a gift... ABSOLUTELY FREE.

Yes. A 4-piece "Scissors 'N Shears" set, with extra-sharp, stainless steel blades and lightweight plastic grip handles will be delivered right to your door. This versatile, must-have set can be yours... without any obligation...simply by saying you'd like to have it!

Why I'm Writing to You

I believe you're someone who travels well, eats in fine restaurants --- and appreciates the difference between dinner at a four-star restaurant and a sandwich on the run.

You know, of course, it isn't unusual to pay a day's wages for a steak dinner. Fine, cornfed beef is impossible to find in many areas. We at Omaha Steaks International® know this well, because many of the most famous restaurants in the nation buy their gourmet steaks from us.

I'm writing to invite you to have those same gourmet steaks --- steaks you never on earth could get at any supermarket, steaks most restaurants can't even buy because there just aren't enough of them to go around. I want you to try some of our Special Filet Mignons, and I'm prepared to do what I have to do to convince you they're the gourmet treat of your lifetime.

Four (6 oz.) Omaha Steaks® Filets, flash frozen, packed with dry ice, and shipped to you in our marvelous reusable container, are regularly $49.95. I've enclosed a discount certificate, good as cash for $20.00, which means the steaks are yours for an introductory offer price of $29.95, plus $6.50 for shipping and handling. And with your purchase you'll receive FREE six of our 4 oz. Gourmet Burgers.

Great News! Your Introductory Order will be rushed to you, delivered by Federal Express®. You'll have it within 3 business days from the day we receive your order.

Back in 1917, my family began selling cornfed Midwestern Beef to a couple of the swanky restaurants in Omaha.

Soon word got around about the tenderness, juiciness and flavor of Omaha Steaks®. Before long we expanded to serve some of the great restaurants in America. We still do.

Naturally, individuals began asking for our steaks by name. That's how we began sending steaks direct, and I can tell you that our list of customers is a real Who's Who.

What Can You Expect?

First of all, our steaks look marvelous, as well they should. Line one up alongside an ordinary filet and you'll instantly see the difference in beautiful marbling, close, hand trimming and sturdy, vacuum packaging. It's like putting an elegant limousine alongside a stripped-down economy car.

But the real test "is in the eatin'." If you're serving to guests, surprise them: for the first time in their lives, they'll be able to slice steaks with their forks, because that's just how tender an Omaha Steaks® Filet Mignon is.

That tenderness comes from slow, natural aging. It requires 21 days. And during the process, the beef must be maintained at a very exact temperature. Most beef suppliers are in too big a hurry to bother with aging. That's why the melt-in-your-mouth tenderness of these Filets will amaze you.

Ah, but now the ultimate way of judging a steak...taste...

It's the corn feeding, along with the natural aging, that sets these steaks apart from the beef available for mass consumption through supermarkets and most butcher shops. Corn feeding beef gives the meat a wonderful interior marbling. The marbling dissolves during cooking.

It makes the meat sensationally juicy...with a flavor you'll crave once you've tasted it!

This cornfed beef is chosen with the care you'd give to a lifetime treasure. (That's what it is, to us, because our reputation is right on the line with every single Omaha Steaks® Filet Mignon.)

When I tell folks we guarantee our steaks, I often hear, "How in the world can you do that? Your customers can't return any steaks because they eat them."

Well, I certainly hope you eat them, but that doesn't affect our Guarantee.

Just about every guarantee you've ever seen includes the word "return." You have to return the merchandise, or the unused portion, or whatever, in order to get your money back. Not ours! You can keep the remaining steaks and still get your money back.

So order your steaks today. You'll get them in perfect condition, shipped in a container you can reuse for years, when you go on picnics or take an automobile trip or spend a day at the beach or decide to visit someone and take the steaks with you (they'll be talking about it for weeks). I'll include a copy of our Cookbook, yours to keep. It's loaded with tips most cooks don't know about. Your steaks will be registered by actual serial number; in fact, you'll get a numbered Certificate verifying the Gold Seal of Approval.

When you order, you'll have our promise...

IF YOU'RE NOT ABSOLUTELY THRILLED WITH YOUR ORDER FROM OMAHA STEAKS® - FOR ANY REASON AT ALL - WE'LL CHEERFULLY REPLACE YOUR ORDER OR REFUND YOUR MONEY, WHICHEVER YOU PREFER.

I think you deserve this wonderful treat. I think I've proved, by sending you this exclusive private invitation, that we at Omaha Steaks® believe you should have the same fantastic steak the rich and famous enjoy.

Do you agree you should sample Omaha Steaks®, especially since you can have them at more than 40% off the usual price? Do you agree you should give me the opportunity to prove my point: that you deserve the best, and this is it? Do you agree you can't lose, since I'm taking all the risk as proof that we do want you in the select group we regard as "family" -- those who have tasted the royalty of fine steaks?

I hope you do. I want you to taste our steaks and test my Guarantee.

I'm counting on your experiencing one of the great gourmet events of your lifetime (and the lifetimes of your fortunate guests, as well). You'll never have a better opportunity.

Sincerely,

Frederick J. Simon

Frederick J. Simon
President, Gourmet Division

P.S.   Act now and enjoy 4 (6 oz.) Filet Mignons for the special introductory price of $29.95. Plus you'll also receive 6 of our fabulous Ground Gourmet Burgers FREE. (Sorry, only one package of Filets at this special price. But you may order a second package of 4 (6 oz.) Filet Mignons for just $39.95, and we'll send you 6 more FREE burgers, still a bargain.) Don't wait until the expiration date on your certificate is on top of you. We guarantee your satisfaction. What can you lose? Call now TOLL FREE 1-800-228-9055.

        PLEASE...THIS SPECIAL OFFER IS FOR YOU AND YOU ALONE.
                IF YOU ARE NOT INTERESTED, DO NOT PASS IT ON.

P.P.S. Remember, a versatile, 4-piece "Scissors 'N Shears" set will also be delivered right to your door FREE. Even if you decide not to place your order for luscious, fork-tender Omaha Steaks® right away, the set is yours FREE. If you place your order by the date shown on the enclosed insert, you will also receive a terrific table top calculator. Read about both of these great gifts on the insert included in this mailing.

F·I·L·E·T   M·I·G·N·O·N·S

from
Omaha Steaks® International®

Unlike Any Steak You've Ever Tasted

No "supermarket" steak, regardless of cut, can begin to equal the perfect taste and tenderness of a genuine Filet Mignon from Omaha Steaks.

No, these superb filets aren't everyday fare! They're for the person you want to impress. They're for you when you want to serve the best filets money can buy. They're elegant gifts for the person who "has everything" — and who, enjoying the filets' good taste, will appreciate your good taste.

Omaha Steaks Filet Mignons are flash-frozen at just the right moment of aging. They're shipped in a reusable insulated chest, protected by dry ice so that wherever in the world they go, they're absolutely perfect when they arrive.

Each filet is a genuine "Gold Seal" filet; your shipment is registered and numbered, and the Registration certificate is your assurance that each filet is Omaha Steaks-inspected for perfection.

Your shipment of genuine Omaha Steaks Filet Mignons is numbered and registered. A certificate is awarded only to these flawless filets. They'll arrive in a sturdy, reusable cooler.

TURN OVER FOR MORE INFORMATION

***Included FREE**

The Omaha Steaks Cookbook . . . full of tips for preparing steaks and other delicacies the way the great chefs do, including exclusive recipes by the great gourmet expert James Beard.

G5536-0194

For that special occasion...
Filet Mignons from
Omaha Steaks®

Questions and Answers About Omaha Steaks®

Q. Is there really a difference between these Filet Mignons and the very best steaks I can buy in a supermarket?

A. You bet there is. You'll not only taste the difference, you actually can see it. It's the difference between good commercial-grade steaks and filets the very rich or world-famous gourmets usually can enjoy whenever they wish.

Q. Do people buy Omaha Steaks® Filet Mignons as a gift?

A. They're a much-wanted gift, because throughout the world Omaha Steaks® Filet Mignons are known as the very best.

Q. What makes them the best?

A. Every Omaha Steaks® Filet is USDA inspected and cut from the finest cornfed beef, selected before any commercial market even sees it. Omaha Steaks International® offers this unconditional guarantee:

⊙⊙⊙⊙⊙ **YOU MUST BE THRILLED** ⊙⊙⊙⊙⊙

Guarantee...
If you are not absolutely thrilled with your order
from Omaha Steaks® — for any reason at all —
we'll cheerfully replace your order or refund
your money, whichever you prefer.

Unbelievable? Not for the finest filets in the world.

REGISTERED
Nº 877370

THE ULTIMATE SYMBOL OF GOOD TASTE...

Omaha Steaks® 🔲 *International®*

4400 South 96th Street • P.O. Box 3300 • Omaha, NE 68103

CALL TOLL FREE 1-800-228-9055

Omaha Steaks® are awarded a unique
Registered Gold Seal of approval after
passing a series of rigid quality tests.

©1993 Omaha Steaks International, Inc.

182

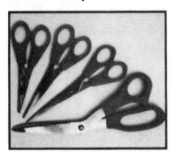

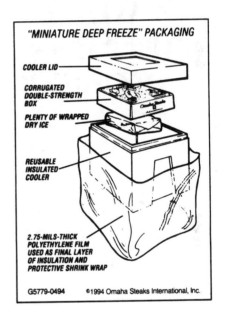
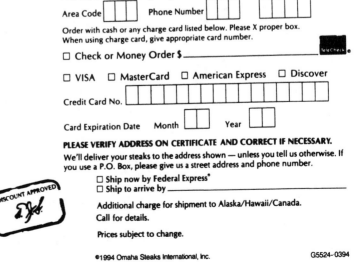

YOU ARE NOT ONLY
WHAT YOU ARE TODAY,
BUT ALSO WHAT YOU CHOOSE
TO BECOME TOMORROW

Chapter Eleven

Nuts and Bolts of Mail Order Success

The major complaint against most mail order companies is that the delivery is too slow. That's a complaint I have never received. We send out all of our orders within one week and we are frequently complimented on our prompt and efficient service.

We also follow up on inquiries quickly. Our advertising package goes out within a few days. It's important to get back to the prospective customer while he's still hot about your offer, otherwise he may lose interest or respond to the competition before he's received your literature.

Keeping Track of Your Profits

You must keep accurate records to determine whether or not you are making money. That means keeping track of the number of daily sales and the income generated for each product you are selling. You need to determine in the shortest time possible if you have a winner that should be run again or if you have a loser that should be rethought before spending more money on it. Although this probably sounds very basic, you might be surprised by the number of people who don't do it.

Predicting Your Winners

Part of the excitement of being a mail order entrepreneur is calculating results as they come in and predicting your winners. How can you accurately predict your sales? Here are two ways I use with my own ad campaigns.

RULES-OF-THUMB

When you run a newspaper display ad, you'll have a good indication the next day of what your total response will be. And you'll be able to project the total number of responses very accurately by the third day because the bulk of them will already have come in. You can expect to receive all the responses within one week, as most of the papers will have been thrown out by then.

Although it usually takes 30 days to receive most of the responses generated by a classified or display ad in a monthly publication, you will receive 25% of them seven days after you receive your first order. After two weeks, you will have received about 50%.

When you run on television, you will call your 800 answering service 30 minutes after your commercial has run to find out how many sales it generated. Hopefully the numbers will be substantial. If you are running multiple times at night, you will call early the next morning. It's a glorious feeling when you have a hit. Then it all seems so easy.

PAST PERFORMANCE

You can determine what your total responses will be for any ad by comparing your daily receipts with the daily receipts of previous ads that you have run. If your first week's total, for example, is more than the first week's total on a previous successful campaign, you can bet you have another winner. If on the other hand, the total on the new campaign is the same or less than the total on a previous losing campaign, beware. You know that you'll lose money if you continue the present campaign.

Monthly Record of Ad Receipts

It is imperative that you keep track of all pertinent data on your ads and mailings. It's easy to do when you use my Monthly Record of Ad Receipts. I provided the form for you on page 191. I suggest that you make photocopies and use a separate form for each ad and direct mailing. (You may want to expand on this form and tailor it specifically to your needs.) I've also included some other helpful forms at the end of this chapter.

The Monthly Record of Ad Receipts helps to compare one publication with another, making test results easy to evaluate. It shows which advertisements pull the most orders per dollar of advertising cost. It's easy to use, and properly interpreted, the collected data will help you to expand sales, change advertisements, and alert you to any problems before they become significant. Of course, these records are only of value if you gather the information carefully and take prompt action to make necessary improvements.

Concrete test data ensures your objectivity. It will tell you the truth about your ad. That can be invaluable when your emotions tell you to press on because of all you already have invested in the campaign. The decision as to whether or not to continue a campaign must be based on the numbers. There is no way around it. The ad makes it or it doesn't.

Don't let your enthusiasm or ego or wishful thinking get in the way of making the decision to stop an ad when it clearly isn't making money.

The more data you collect, the better will be your decisions about what, when, and where to advertise, and the more accurate your sales projections will be.

Now I'll explain what information should go into each part of the Monthly Record of Ad Receipts:

Product: Item being advertised.

Selling price: Retail selling price.

Key: The department number or code you place in the order form to track the number of orders from the publication or mailing piece.

Publication: Name of publication the ad is running in or name of mailing list used.

Circulation: Circulation figure of the magazine or total number of names mailed to.

Issue: Exact date of the issue. Magazines, tabloids, and newspapers publish monthly, bi-monthly, weekly, and daily. Be specific.

On sale: Date publication actually goes on sale. (The March issue is on sale in February and so on.)

Cost: Cost of the advertisement or mailing.

Size of ad: Exact size, such as 7" x 10"; or a list of the mailing pieces used in the package, such as personal letter, brochure, return envelope.

Monthly Profit/Loss: Compute these figures at the end of the month.

Projected number of orders: The number of orders you anticipate receiving.

Projection of cash: Set realistic goals.

Month: Month the ad is running.

Daily number of orders: Number of orders received that day.

Total number of orders: Adding each day's total to the preceding day's total gives you the cumulative number of orders to date.

Daily receipts: Daily orders multiplied by the selling price of the product.

Total receipts: Adding each day's receipts to the preceding total gives you total receipts to date.

Total: End of the month total. (You may need to use a second form for the month after the new issue of the publication comes out, as orders will still trickle in from those who held onto your literature for awhile before sending in their money.)

The Order Incentive That Isn't Worth Using

I have stopped sending anything C.O.D. because half to three quarters of the time, the orders come back. Either the customer wasn't home at the time of delivery or he changed his mind. When this happens it costs you money for delivery, labor for processing the order, packaging, etc. I suggest you stay away from this method of payment.

Drop Shipping Makes It Easy to Fulfill Orders

Drop shipping is a great way for fledgling mail order businesses to fulfill orders. It is the method used in the beginning by many large successful mail order businesses. As was briefly discussed earlier, drop shipping means that the manufacturer of the product you are selling takes the responsibility of fulfilling your company's orders by sending products directly to your customers. All you do is open the mail, prepare shipping labels, write a check to the manufacturer for the wholesale cost of the products you have sold, and send the letter off to your drop shipper. This method is by far the safest. It is one you should seriously consider before committing capital to inventory. It gives you the chance to see if the product (or which products) are going to sell before you stock anything.

Not all companies are set up to handle drop shipments. Try to work with those that will until you can judge how much inventory you might want to carry.

Here are the advantages of a drop-shipment arrangement:

1. No investment in product inventory.

2. No investment in shipping supplies

3. No overhead for a warehouse.

4. No labor charges.

5. No merchandise to handle.

6. Promotional material is offered by manufacturer.

7. Your customers pay you first. You deposit your profit as you order the products.

8. It takes a small capital investment to get started in the business. All you need are stationery, shipping labels, a typewriter or computer, and your kitchen table.

9. Operating expenses are covered by the orders.

When you receive an order for products that will be shipped by more than one drop shipper, advise your customer that items will arrive separately by including a note to that effect or by typing on each label "Balance of Order to Follow. "

If You Stock Inventory

How do you know the right amount of stock to keep on hand if you decide to do all the shipping? Inventory is a tricky part of any sales business. My advice, which I've always taken myself, is to order minimum quantities until your Monthly Record of Ad Receipts data tells you loud and clear that it's safe to purchase more. Don't be bashful about this. You don't want to get stuck because you felt uneasy about ordering a small quantity.

The size of your inventory will vary upon how fast the merchandise is selling. Your products may have a fast turnover or they may not. As your business grows, you'll see how much product you usually sell over a particular period of time. That is what dictates the quantities you should order. You want enough on hand to not run out, but not so much that if the sales slow down, you are stuck with product.

Follow the Rule

What happens if in spite of your best efforts, you run out of product? You are legally bound to follow Federal Trade Commission rules governing late or undelivered merchandise. It's inevitable that some of your customers will complain about not receiving merchandise that was ordered. When you get complaints handle them as quickly and courteously as possible.

The Federal Trade Commission (FTC) has issued the Mail Order Rule to correct non-receipt problems. It states that you must ship merchandise on time. When you cannot, you must notify your customers of the delay and provide them with the option of either cancelling and getting a refund, or agreeing to wait for the merchandise. "On time" means within 30 days of your receipt of their order unless you have specified a longer period in the advertisement or made other provisions in the offer.

As soon as you know that the shipment is going to be delayed, you are required to send an "Option notice." See page 192. This advises the customer that there is a delay in shipment and gives him a new shipping date, which must be within 30 days after the original date.

If there is a further delay, you are required to send an additional notice called a "Renewed Option." See page 193. This form must be sent to customers stating their right to cancel the order and receive an immediate refund, or once again to consent to wait until the new estimated delivery date.

You are required to send these notices by first-class mail and provide a return card for your customer's response. If you must cancel the order entirely, you are required to inform him as soon as possible and to refund his money promptly.

In the appendix of this book I have reproduced the free pamphlet published by the FTC, *A Business Guide to the Federal Trade Commission's Mail Order Rule*. See pages 217 to 235. The commission prepared this guide for mail order sellers. It will answer any questions you have about filling orders and will help prevent problems with your customers.

It is important that you read the guide, understand it, and run your mail order business according to the rule. It isn't hard to do. I have never had a single problem with it in my many years of being in business. It makes good business sense and keeps your customers happy.

From time to time, update your information by writing to the Federal Trade Commission, Washington, D.C. 20580.

MONTHLY RECORD OF AD RECEIPTS

Product		Selling Price		Key	
Publication		Circulation		Issue	On Sale
Cost		Size of Ad		Monthly Profit	Monthly Loss

Projection: Total Number of Orders   Total Cash

Month_____ Day of Month	Daily Number of Orders	Total Number of Orders	Daily Receipts	Total Receipts	
1					
2					
3					
4					
5					
6					
7					
8					
9					
10					
11					
12					
13					
14					
15					
16					
17					
18					
19					
20					
21					
22					
23					
24					
25					
26					
27					
28					
29					
30					
31					
Total					

Comments _____

4 Sample Notices

Sample Option Notice

[Rule Section 435.l(b)(1)(ii)]

When you are unable to ship on time and wish to provide a **revised shipping date which is 30 days or less** after the original date, use a form such as this to notify your customers. This form must be sent out by first class mail within a reasonable time after you become aware that there will be a shipping delay. It must be sent before the promised date, or if no date was promised, within 30 days after you receive a properly completed order.

Dear Customer:

Thank you for your order. We are sorry to inform you that there will be a delay in shipping the merchandise you ordered. We shall make shipment by the revised shipping date of (   ). It is quite possible we could ship earlier.

You have the right to consent to this delay or to cancel your order and receive a prompt refund. Please return this letter in the enclosed postpaid envelope with your instructions indicated by checking the appropriate block below.

Unless we hear from you prior to shipment or prior to *the revised shipping date*, it will be assumed that you have consented to a delayed shipment on or before the definite revised shipping date stated above.

Sincerely yours,

Name & Title of Signer
Company Name
Address

Enclosure: Envelope

☐ Yes, I will accept a delay in shipment of my order for this item until
_____
(Insert date which is 30 days or less.)

☐ I cannot wait. Please cancel my order for this item and promptly refund my money.
_____
Please Sign Here

Sample Renewed Option Notice

[Rule Section 435.1(b)(2)(i)-(ii)]

When you are unable to ship merchandise on or before the promised definite revised shipping date, and wish to provide **a new definite revised shipping date,** use a form such as this to notify your customers.

Dear Customer:

We are sorry to inform you that there will be a further delay in shipping the merchandise you ordered. We shall make shipment by *(new definite revised shipping date)*. It is quite possible we could ship earlier.

You have the right to consent to a further delay or to cancel your order and receive a prompt refund. Please return this letter in the enclosed postpaid envelope with your instructions indicated by checking the appropriate block below.

Unless we hear from you prior to the old shipping date to which you previously agreed, it will be assumed that you have rejected any further shipping delay and your order will be canceled and a prompt refund made.

Sincerely yours,

Name & Title of Signer
Company Name
Address

Enclosure: Envelope

☐ Yes, I will accept a further delay in shipment of my order for this item until _____
(Insert date which is 30 days or less.)

☐ I cannot wait. Please cancel my order for this item and promptly refund my money.

_____
Please Sign Here

INQUIRY FLOW CHART

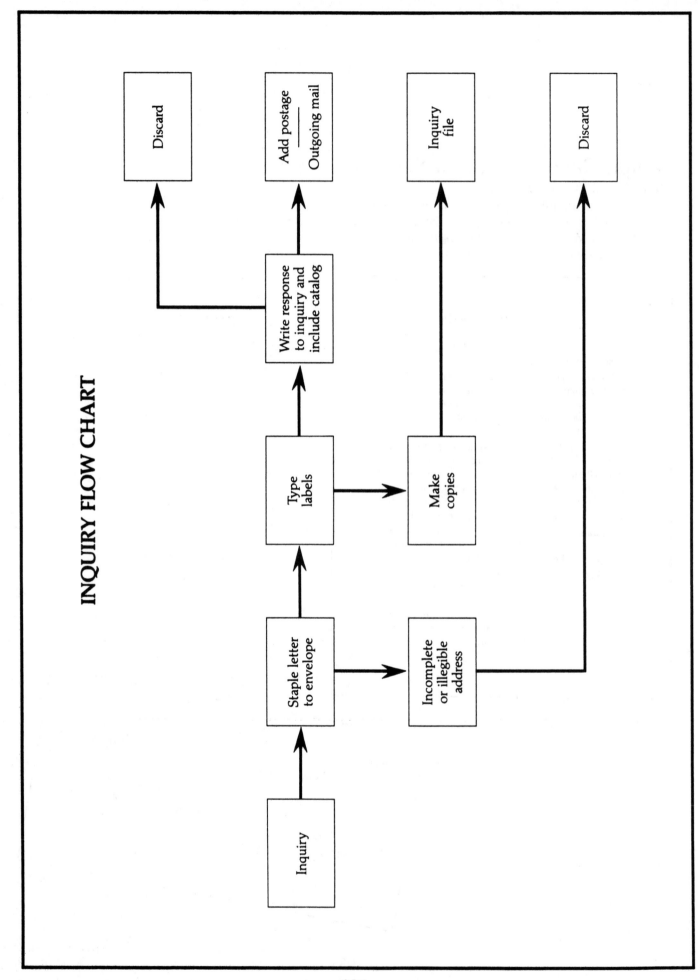

ORDER PROCESSING FLOW CHART

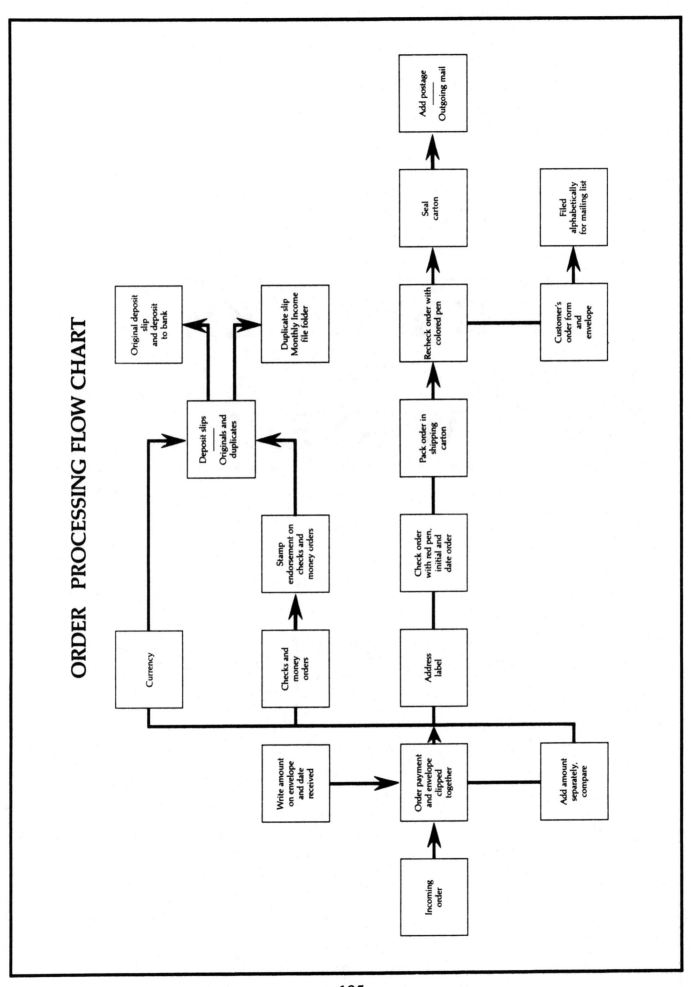

THINK LIKE A WINNER!

Chapter Twelve

What If You Can't Get Your Business Running Successfully? What's Wrong? How to Correct It

Let's assume you've read my book, found a product or products, ran some ads and/or did some direct mail and you are not making a profit. What's wrong? Obviously, the answer is that there's a problem with one or more of the following: the ads you are running, your follow-up sales material, the selling price of the product, the particular publication or mailing list you are using, or the product, itself. Remember, there's always a reason for a campaign not working.

Become a Mail Order Detective

Suppose you were running an ad and received dozens of requests for product information. You sent out your sales literature package within a few days but didn't receive enough orders to even cover your costs. In this case, you know the ad was working. The prospects who answered were interested in your offer at the time they sent away for your literature. They invested time and effort in requesting more information because they thought you had something they may want. It was your sales literature's job to convince them that you did indeed have exactly what they wanted and needed—but it failed to do that. The fault then is with your follow-up literature which fails to convert inquiries to sales. So it's back to the drawing board. But be happy. Your ad is good and there's interest in your offer. Once your literature measures up, your business can fly!

Good Advertising Copy is the Lifeline of Your Business

Review the elements essential to good ad copy and analyze your literature to see where it may be falling down on the job. What about a change of headline? Are you using subheads? If so, are they interesting? Do you start off your body copy in an interesting, provocative, or intriguing way? Are the benefits clearly defined? Is the tone of your offer friendly? Do you have a personal letter going out with your brochure? Would it help to make the offer more personal by using your own name instead of a company name? (For the most part, I've used Melvin Powers in my advertising.) Is your guarantee clear and inviting? Ask yourself these and the many other questions that need to be answered in order to find a solution to your problem.

Ask yourself if anyone else is successful selling a product or products like yours. If so, that's a good sign. They are making money. That means you can too. Analyze the differences between their campaign and yours. Is your selling price in line with theirs? Are you using the same initial product to capture the attention of interested buyers and then sending them a literature package? Perhaps the back-end catalog items are where they are making their money. Go over their campaign from stem to stern and see where yours may not be as effective. Make the necessary changes and try again.

If You Still Haven't a Clue and You're Considering Throwing Away Your Detective's Badge

If your ads aren't pulling inquiries, it may or may not be the fault of the ad, itself. Is it running in the right publications under the right category? Are you running ads for seasonal items at the wrong time of year? If your response is marginal, could it have anything to do with the months of the year or days of the week you are advertising?

And even if your product isn't seasonal, the timing for it can be bad if it is the type of product that sells according to public interest cycles.

Interest Cycles Can Drive Sales Up . . . and Down

If there has recently been a flurry of interest in your type of product it could be that public interest in the product has peaked and you are at the tail end of its popularity. That happens. Public interest runs in cycles.

I have often seen cycles of public interest impact sales, driving them way up and forcing them way down. Some years ago when the CB radio craze was hot, every publisher in the world rushed to get out a book on the subject. Only two or three books were successful. It's not surprising when you think about it. How many could the market support? The bookstore buyers weren't interested in purchasing more than a couple of titles in this category.

A similar thing happened in the summer of 1976, when Viking space probes 1 and 2 ventured out and became man's first attempts at locating extraterrestrial life. Suddenly there was a resurgence of interest in the possibility of extraterrestrial intelligence. I sold thousands of copies of a book called *Extraterrestrial Intelligence: The First Encounter* using classified ads, display ads, and direct mail. It was easy. Everything worked like a charm. See pages 203 and 204 for the direct mail piece that I used. When the interest slowed down, the sales slowed down, too.

Some years ago it happened again when Bobby Fisher met Boris Spasky for the world chess championship. I first heard about it a year before it was scheduled to occur. I had an intuitive feeling that I could sell a tremendous number of chess books because of it. I rushed to publish a dozen chess books, which I added to the three I already had. As the championship approached, worldwide interest became intense.

Sure enough, every classified ad I ran for chess books made money. Every display ad made money. When fulfilling orders for the chess books I had advertised, I enclosed a listing of my other chess books. The result: All 15 titles flew out of the warehouse! It was the busiest time of my mail order career. Nothing else ever came close to it. The phones were ringing all day. I couldn't keep up with the demand. My printer couldn't print them fast enough. I was even restricting the number of books I was selling to bookstores. After the tournament, the sales gradually diminished.

In normal times, you need to peak the interest of the customer or advertise in those publications that logic would dictate. That means specialized publications devoted to subject matter of the book or product category that you want to sell.

If You Can't Figure Out What Ails Your Campaign
It May Be Time to Call a Doctor

When a new television show isn't making it, the call goes out to a "script doctor" who analyzes the show and makes suggestions on how to improve it. Sometimes even with the suggested changes, the prognosis isn't too favorable. Other times, when the ailment isn't too extensive, great improvement can be obtained and the show saved.

Mail order print campaigns and television sales campaigns have much in common. Both require careful analysis when they aren't working. Sometimes it is difficult for those involved in the creation of a campaign to clearly see what's wrong with it.

My background and experience in mail order consulting led me naturally into consulting on television infomercials. I've been called in on many two-minute spots and 30-minute infomercials that were having problems. I found that not all shows can be saved, just as all print campaigns cannot. Sometimes it's smarter, easier, and less expensive to shoot an entirely new show than to invest major time, energy, and money into restructuring a weak one. Other times, the show isn't at fault. The entire concept is abandoned because the product just doesn't make it. Celebrity-driven products can pose their own set of problems—poor chemistry between the star and the host, a product that is better presented by a non-celebrity, etc. The problems can be varied and challenging, yet there is always an answer.

When you can't figure out what is wrong, consider showing your material to someone who can offer a fresh perspective on your offer and literature package. An impartial opinion can be invaluable.

I'm pleased to recommend a prolific, freelance copywriter and mail order consultant who does excellent work and speaks fluent Spanish and French. He's creative, diligent, and completes his assignments on schedule. His clients include beginners as well as major mail order companies. Do yourself a favor and contact him for help with your ads, mail order program, and Web site development. Talk to him about advertising your product on the Internet and possibly getting a PI deal. Write, call, or fax: Charles Prosper, P.O. Box 29699, Los Angeles, CA 90029-0699. Phone: (323) 662-7841. Fax: (323) 644-8221. E-mail: cprosper@prosperballoons.com. Web site: www.prosperballoons.com.

Free Help from Uncle Sam

The United States government Small Business Administration will help you get started in your mail order business. You'll find it listed in your local or nearest big city phone book. Call and explain what type of help you need. They offer free workshops and seminars, and individual counseling is available through an organization within the SBA called SCORE (Service Corps of Retired Executives). Volunteers have knowledge and experience in many different fields. There may be an advertising or mail order executive available. There is absolutely no charge for this service and the executives are pleased to donate their time for as long as it takes to do the job. It's their opportunity to use their creative ability and to feel good by helping others get into businesses and run them profitably.

For a list of free publications and services, write to: U.S. Small Business Administration, National Office, 1129 20th Street, N.W., Suite 410, Washington, DC 20416. Telephone: (202) 653-6279.

When Your Best Shot Isn't Good Enough

If all your efforts to find and correct the problems with your advertising campaign have been unsuccessful and you are still not making money, I suggest that you change the product or product category.

Start fresh by sending away for *The Best Catalogs in the World* published by Publisher Inquiry Services, 951 Broken Sound Parkway NW, Building 190, PO Box 5057, Boca Raton, Florida 33431-0857. The cost is $3.00 postpaid. This beautifully illustrated catalog of catalogs will give you hundreds of ideas for successful mail order operations. Send away for the catalogs described that are of interest to you, and get started again.

Two other very good sources for catalogs are *The Directory of Mail Order Catalogs* published by Grey House Publishing, Inc., Pocket Knife Square, Lakeville, Connecticut 06039 and *The National Directory of Catalogs* published by Oxbridge Communications, Inc., 150 Fifth Avenue, New York, New York 10011. Similar mail order directories are available at the library. Look through all these sources with fresh eyes. Take a new approach.

The Directory of Mail Order Catalogs has the names and addresses of 7,500 mail order catalog dealers in 33 different categories. *The National Directory of Catalogs* has the names and addresses 8,000 U.S. and Canadian mail order catalog dealers in 40 different categories. Keep in mind that most of these companies were started and nourished by individuals like you. Every one of them at some time started with nothing more than a dream of mail order success. They kept their eyes on their goal and kept trying and testing and building, and they never gave up. Generally success doesn't come overnight. It's a continuous learning process. That's why I keep stressing the importance of continuing your education indefinitely by reading, taking seminars, listening to audio tapes, watching business-related business video tapes, and attending as many trade conventions as you can.

If you are interested in selling gadgets, send away for *The Sharper Image Catalog*, 650 Davis Street, San Francisco, CA 94111. This multi-million dollar company started with the owner, Richard Thalheimer, selling a runner's watch. He's running a perfect operation—one that you can emulate. Remember, there are no secrets in the mail order business. You can repeat any company's success by searching for their product sources in trade publications listed in *Standard Rate and Data/Trade Publications*.

You can call and ask if a company's mailing list is available for rent. You will find out how many orders they get each year and the average price of each mail order sale. By doing a little bit of mathematics, you can approximate their yearly sales. Usually there's a hot name list for those who have purchased merchandise in the last three months. Again, that's valuable information. If the numbers sound good and you are enthusiastic about the category of products, develop your own variation of their business and go for it!

The Key to Mail Order Success

Your attitude should be that if someone else is doing it, so can you. Take it one step at a time and gradually build up the business. Become knowledgeable by reading mail order books, trade publications, going to trade shows, meeting other people in the business, and thinking and acting like a winner.

Whatever else you do, don't give up! No matter how frustrated with your initial efforts you may be, no matter how many times the little voice within says that you aren't meant to be a mail order mogul after all, don't quit! You haven't failed until you quit. Don't listen to when it says mail order is not for you or that it's just too difficult. Instead, think about the thousands of individuals who are making it in mail order. Remind yourself that they all started out like you—with an idea, then a few products and one ad that may or may not have worked. They made it because they kept trying to make it, no matter what difficulties stood in their way. They did whatever it took. If you adopt the same attitude, eventually, you too will succeed. That commitment is the key to mail order success.

Many sincere people with lofty mail order goals give lip service to wanting to be successful, but for some inexplicable reason, never take the necessary steps to make it happen. Hopefully, you won't be one of them. Keep your long-range goal in mind while doing your homework. Before long you'll smell the sweet scent of success and have the daily, exhilarating feeling of shaking checks, cash, and money orders from stacks of mail sent to you!

Scientists Find Statistical Cues
For the Possibility of
Extraterrestrial Intelligence

Dear Friend:

I'm excited by a new book that I think will excite you too. For centuries, from the earliest legends of the man on the moon, mankind has fantasized and speculated about other life in the universe. With the discovery of biochemical evolution which showed how life could evolve out of simple compounds, those speculations took on a new dimension. Most scientist now believe that it is possible there is other intelligent life in the universe.

What are the possibilities of our making contact with ETI's in the profound vastness of space? What will be the consequences to our images of ourselves and our world of the first proven contact with beings from another planet, since they are likely to be of superior intelligence? Could we still believe in the value of life as we live it? How would it affect mankind's religions, both Western and Eastern? Would it in fact mean, as Arthur C. Clarke has said, an end to mankind's childhood?

These and other questions are explored in *Extraterrestrial Intelligence: The First Encounter*—from the most practical issues, such as how the news of contact should be handled, to the most exciting and troubling questions of philosophy, religion, and science. *Extraterrestrial Intelligence* begins the search for a cosmic context for mankind. It leads the way in reflecting on the next stage in our gradual self-discovery.

Summer 1976 coincided with summertime on Mars. That's when Viking space probes 1 and 2 ventured out and became man's first attempts to locate extraterrestrial life. As we continue to explore the universe, the idea of life in space moves increasingly from the realm of science fiction into the domain of scientific possibility.

Scientific breakthroughs are often based on interdisciplinary research unfamiliar to the layman. Scientists, writers, and publishers need to supply the public with this important background information, so that new frontiers in science are made understandable. *Extraterrestrial Intelligence* is a book that does just that. It presents the views of fourteen men qualified to speculate on the vast implications of the subject. Contributors include well-known writers Bradbury, Frazier, Azimov, and Tennessen; distinguished scientists and academics Abell, R. Smith, and Desan; philosophers Royce, Christian, Tooley, and Angeles; and theologians Huntington, Hamilton, and Doss; and Leonard Lemoy, who was America's most popular extraterrestrial on the highly successful television series Star Trek. James Christian, editor, has selected his articles to cove a broad and provocative range of possible ETI phenomena, which (according to astronomer Carl Sagan) could confront mankind within the next fifty years.

That intelligent life is natural and inherent on a cosmic scale can be understood through a combined study of astronomical and biological discoveries of the last five decades. Authors Christian and Abell clearly summarize these findings: that advanced radio-telescope research estimates our galaxy to contain some 400 thousand million suns; that our universe contains some 200 billion galaxies; that it is common and natural for non-binary suns to produce planets; and that these planets are built of the same basic elements as our own. The experiments of Stanley Miller in 1953 gave the first indications that living organisms evolved form inorganic constituents. His theory (chemical biogenesis) would indicate that life can evolve anywhere that the basic chemicals and radiation exist. Since we have encountered no evidence of chemicals other than those found on earth in our telescopic exploration of deep space, we may assume that "the elemental constituents of living organisms are cosmic."

Extraterrestrial life exists: but does extra terrestrial intelligence? Can such intelligence cross the light years between even the closest neighboring stars? What are the implications of such an advanced technology? What is the lifespan of technological civilizations? And, should we encounter ETIs, would we be able to recognize them as intelligences? Smith and Tooley focus their articles on these scientific and philosophical questions.

Presuming that technology can advance far enough without destroying itself in the process, allowing ETIs to contact us, theologian Hamilton questions whether mankind could withstand the psychological impact. The implications may be devastating: mankind will have to re-philosophize and re-theologize. Contact with alien intelligence may totally alter our own concept of cognition, as psychologist Joseph Royce suggests in his article on the new dimensions of cosmic man.

Questions and possibilities raised by mere statistical inevitability of ETIs are endless and fascinating. As Azimov says:
> If we ever establish contact with extraterrestrial life, it will reveal to us our true place in the universe, and with that comes the beginnings of wisdom.

Send today for your copy of the exciting *Extraterrestrial Intelligence*.

NO-RISK COUPON

Please send me a copy of *Extraterrestrial Intelligence*.
Enclosed is my ( ) check ( ) cash ( ) money order for $8.00 postpaid (CA res. $8.66).

Name_____

Address_____

City_____ State_____ Zip_____

Mail to:
    Melvin Powers, 12015 Sherman Road, No. Hollywood, CA 91605

Chapter Thirteen

The Melvin Powers Strategy for Mail Order Success

Having read this far, most likely you already have some idea of what my attitude is toward business, life, myself, and other people. I credit this attitude not only with my own success, but with making my life a full, satisfying, exciting one in which every day is an adventure. That's what I wish for you. So here are a few words of parting wisdom to start you on your way to the life you really want. First we'll talk about your business, then about you.

Keep Your Customers Happy

The success of your mail order business depends upon repeat customers. How do you develop them? By remembering that every customer is important and making sure that each has a positive experience with your company. That means doing everything possible to ensure customer satisfaction with your product and service. Let them know they are valuable to you by treating them as you would want to be treated. Your reward will be loyal customers who buy again and again, and who refer new customers to you by telling others about your products and service.

Before long you'll begin receiving complimentary letters, thanking you for everything from fast, efficient service, to good products that live up to promises made in your advertising. File these for possible use as testimonials. These unsolicited testimonials are the best because they are genuine. The people's sincerity comes across, making them particularly believable. (Before you can use a customer's comments or name in a testimonial, you must have his written permission.)

On the other hand, some letters may include valid complaints. These can be very useful as they alert you to something that needs to be improved. Look into any such problem immediately and make any necessary changes so the problem will not recur with other customers. And be sure to answer all such letters promptly and courteously. Your concern about your customer's complete satisfaction should be made obvious to him. Do whatever is necessary to make him happy. A valid complaint can serve as a vehicle for winning the long-term loyalty of a customer if it is handled properly. Unanswered letters cause friction and can flare into refund requests and loss of customers. Often a response to a customer's letter is all that is needed for him to feel he has been heard and his comments appreciated.

Whenever I get a complaint, I invariably get on the phone and resolve it immediately. The customer is usually surprised and delighted that I took the time to call. The problem is always resolved to the customer's satisfaction, I have kept a customer, and we are both happy.

Be Accessible and Listen

I thoroughly enjoy the contacts with my customers. Many visit my office just to say hello. They keep me current on which offers are working and which are not. They give me new ideas on how to present my products, and they challenge me to think in creative, new directions. I view such visits as opportunities to get important feedback on my operation. I ask whether they were pleased with their last purchase, and I find out if they received good service. Be sure to ask for this valuable information whenever the opportunity arises—and listen to the answers. It will help you prosper.

Because I want to make sure that my offers more than fulfill the expectations of my customers, and because no one is better able to tell me how to achieve that than the customers themselves, I always ask for feedback on what I'm doing. When I was teaching mail order and motivational seminars, I handed out evaluation sheets at the end and had my students give me their opinion of my presentation. I told them they need not sign their name, and that I would appreciate the feedback because I was interested in improving the seminar. The information helped me become a better instructor.

Information provided by readers has helped me become a better publisher, too. I'm the only one I know of who asks for feedback on every book he publishes. This research has helped me to stay in touch with my customers and to follow the ever-changing cycles of public interest. Find out what your customers think, what they want, and what their experience has been with your company. Listen and act on what they tell you. See page 216.

There's an annual reference book for aspiring authors called *Writer's Market*. It lists several thousand book publishers. I'm the only one who welcomes phone calls to discuss proposed books. Other companies want the writer to submit a detailed chapter outline and/or synopsis, and three sample chapters. Although we have the same requirement for formal submissions, I am happy to encourage writers when they have a marketable idea and just as happy to save them the trouble of developing and submitting a manuscript to us that we would have no interest in publishing.

Whether the writers get my name from *Writer's Market* or are customers who have purchased numerous Wilshire books and were inspired to write a similar work, the conversation with me establishes a positive personal link to the company and builds good will with the public.

I always feel wonderful when I receive letters thanking me for taking the time to talk to people, encouraging them, and sharing my opinion about the viability of their proposed book. By being accessible I've acquired excellent books and have made a great deal of money in the process.

My door was open even when I was in the music publishing business. I had, and still have, an upright piano and guitar in my office. Songwriters were welcome to come and play three of their best songs, and I gave them the same kind of feedback I offer to aspiring writers who call about their manuscript or manuscript concept.

Make Your Education Continuous

There are many publications pertaining to the mail order business that I read every month, and I strongly suggest that you read some of them as well. They will be a constant source of information and inspiration that will help you build your mail order business.

I highly recommend that you send for sample copies of the four magazines listed on the next page. Every month you'll read about successful mail order operations. If you haven't yet chosen an area of interest, perhaps you'll be inspired by one of them to start a similar operation. In any event, the stories are uplifting, and full of great ideas that may work in your own business.

You'll learn about forthcoming conventions, seminars, and meetings, some of which you should try to attend. Becoming involved in your chosen industry helps you to feel a part of it. And traveling in professional circles can help you establish valuable contacts, find new products and resources, learn more about the industry, and keep current with new developments.

Remember, the more information you accumulate, the better you will be able to make good decisions that will affect your business positively. As Benjamin Franklin said, "An investment in knowledge pays the best dividends."

On your business stationery, request a sample copy of the following publications: (You need only one letter for the top two magazines.)

Catalog Age
911 Hope Street,
Six River Bend Center, PO Box 4949,
Stamford, Connecticut 06907-0949.

Direct - The Magazine of Direct Marketing Management
911 Hope Street,
Six River Bend Center, PO Box 4949,
Stamford, Connecticut 06907-0949

DM News - The Weekly Newspaper of Record for Direct Marketers
100 Avenue of the Americas
New York, New York 10013

Target Marketing
401 N. Broad Street
Philadelphia, Pennsylvania 19108

The Moment of Truth

We have come to the moment of truth. Will you follow the course of action I have set out for you or will you let this wonderful opportunity pass you by? Perhaps you are still wondering about your potential for success and asking yourself if you really can make money in mail order. The answer is that it depends upon your time investment, levels of enthusiasm and dedication, business common sense, and mental attitude.

It doesn't depend upon investing large sums of money in your mail order operation. Again and again I have advised you to start in a small way with a minimum investment of money and a maximum investment in research. The question is, will you do it? I certainly hope so.

Once you wholeheartedly decide to go for it, it's only a matter of time until you find products of interest to sell, produce winning advertisements and catalogs, and achieve financial security. As you begin to think creatively, the ideas will flow, and some of them will be winners. Be patient and keep going—trying, testing, learning—no matter what, knowing that eventually the rewards will come. I suggest that in the meantime you view the developing and building of your business as a learning process that will ultimately culminate in success.

Take Responsibility for Your Success

The media and books are full of stories about successful people who started with little money or formal education, yet managed to amass great wealth in all kinds of businesses. I personally know many. The common denominator they share is a powerful motivation to succeed and a positive attitude about life. They are dreamers first, then doers. For such people, every challenge becomes an opportunity. Guided by logic, these determined, motivated individuals methodically take one step at a time until they reach their goals.

My experience in songwriting is a perfect example of putting one's creative talent into a new endeavor and achieving a goal. I had never written songs before, but I loved country western music and decided one day that I wanted to write some songs and see if I could get them on the charts. I took songwriting classes at UCLA, read everything on the subject I could find and analyzed current hit songs to see what made them hits and then tried to duplicate their winning elements in my own songs. Within six months, I had two songs on the country music charts, and I was invited to Nashville to accept an award for one of them, entitled "Who Wants a Slightly Used Woman?" See page 213.

That's when I decided to produce my first album of music. Some people I know said, "What do you know about producing an album?" My answer was, "Absolutely nothing, but I have a great concept and I really think I'll be able to sell it to a major record company." I knew the concept was a winner, just as I have known that certain books and products were winners. My belief in the value of what I had to offer carried me through.

I picked the songs to be recorded, including several of my own (of course), hired the best musical arranger I could find and told him the exact sound I had in mind. I went first class with my presentation, and guess what. I sold the album to MGM Records, Inc. for an advance of $15,000 against royalties. To me that $15,000 was worth a million! See pages 214 and 215. Do you recognize Linda Carter?

This story is an example of how dedication, enthusiasm, and perseverance can help you reach your goals, even if you have no previous experience in a particular endeavor. Do you think it sounds too simplistic and Pollyannaish? I don't think so. I have always believed this to be true. It has encouraged me to explore my talents in many areas. I also know numerous successful people who are living proof that I am right.

Your Creative Challenge

Your creative challenge is to come up with a product or product line that will sell as a result of your enthusiasm and promotion, to seek whatever knowledge you need to make it work, and to stay with it until it does.

Take the Long-Range View

Successful people take a long-range view of whatever they are doing. Every day becomes a learning experience. They don't allow themselves to become discouraged. When they become successful, they often talk about "having paid their dues." Generally, this philosophy is necessary to carry you through the early learning stages of the business. Although it's quite possible to become extremely successful almost overnight once the proper elements come together, you cannot count on it and then give up if it doesn't happen that way. Hoping for immediate success and quitting when it doesn't occur is one of the single most destructive, self-defeating ways to approach any new endeavor—yet it's precisely the way many people do it.

Get the Midas Touch

Over the years, I have developed a winning attitude about everything I do. I know that once I put my creative energies into any venture, it will succeed. I've proved it many times in unrelated business endeavors in everything from raising champion Arabian horses to being a motivational speaker. It has been said that I have the Midas touch.

How can you develop the Midas touch? Begin by thinking of yourself as an entrepreneur and developing a winning attitude. Assume the mind set of an entrepreneur. Seek opportunity rather than waiting for it to happen. Go after your goals. Be determined to make it. Learn from those who have done it. See yourself as filled with untapped potential and the world as openly waiting to receive and reward it. Can you do it? Of course you can! No one is born an entrepreneur. You gradually become one by assimilating knowledge, developing skills, and assuming the attitude of entrepreneurs.

Develop a Winning Attitude

Success begins with a proper mental attitude. It's the all-important starting point for all areas of successful living. In time you'll learn the mechanics of whatever you are pursuing, and the combination of proper attitude, know-how, and action will ultimately lead to the attainment of your goals. Then you'll experience firsthand how success breeds success.

Even in athletics, a proper attitude often makes the difference between a winner and a loser. Magic Johnson made the decision not to continue coaching the Los Angeles Lakers. Why? Apparently the attitude of the players was a key factor. Larry Drew, the Laker's assistant coach said, "I won't say the players drove him away. But what he wanted to accomplish and try to do just wasn't happening. He wanted to change their attitudes about approaching the games. He wanted to change their attitudes during the games. Being focused. If we lost, he wanted them to understand why we lost. That didn't happen, and those are all the factors that snowballed."

Unfortunately, there's a lot of negativity around from other people and sometimes even from one's own psyche. Again and again, you'll hear, "You can't. You can't. You can't." Don't listen when you are told you can't do what you want to do, regardless of the source. Instead, listen to this from one who has repeatedly proven that people can make their fondest dreams come true, You absolutely, positively can attain the goals you set out for yourself. (In a testimonial given for one of my television infomercials, a student of mine said, "Melvin Powers is like a beacon flashing on and off saying, "You can. You can. You can." It delighted me when viewers later told me that the vision of that beacon has frequently popped into their heads when they most needed encouragement. Perhaps it will be of help to you, too.)

Most successful entrepreneurs continuously nourish their attitude with a steady diet of uplifting, positive thoughts. I still go to bookstores to buy new inspirational books. You should do the same. Read positive-thinking books such as *Think Like a Winner!* by Dr. Walter Staples, *The Magic of Thinking Success* by Dr. David Schwartz, *Psycho-Cybernetics* by Dr. Maxwell Maltz, *Think & Grow Rich* by Napoleon Hill, and *Your Thoughts Can Change Your Life* by Dr. Donald Curtis.

And listen to motivational tapes. I still do that, too, on the way to and from my office. Programming your mind with thoughts of accomplishment works subconsciously and automatically. You'll be surprised at what happens to you as you fill your mind with constructive thinking.

For more than 10 years, I taught mail order seminars to help people get the information and develop the attitude they need to become successful entrepreneurs. Now you can hear the same material and get the same help by listening to my audio tape program.

Melvin Powers Mail Order Millionaire Course

If you are serious about making money in mail order, you may want to take your next educational step by "attending one of my seminars" in the privacy and comfort of your own home or automobile. You'll hear me discussing various aspects of the mail order business in depth, just as if you were sitting in my classroom. In addition, there's a very informative tape which includes a fascinating interview with an entrepreneur who is running a highly successful mail order book business using classified ads. He's following the exact techniques I have outlined in this book. Maybe in the future, I'll be interviewing you as you share your success story. Why not? The person on this tape started exactly where you are.

The *Mail Order Millionaire Course* consists of my 352-page book *How to Get Rich in Mail Order*, 11 audio tapes, and the special bonus tape, 50 Proven Mail Order Products. It usually sells for $107, but I'm offering it to readers of *Making Money with Classified Ads* at the special price of $82.00 postpaid—a saving of $25.00. If you already have *How to Get Rich in Mail Order*, you can order the tapes only for $62.00 postpaid. Naturally, both the course and tapes come with a 30-day, money-back guarantee.

Also consider learning how to write effective advertising copy from the world's leading authority by sending for Victor O. Schwab's *How to Write a Good Advertisement*, $22.00 postpaid. You'll be glad you did.

These purchases are tax deductible, as are all purchases of educational material that relates to starting and operating a mail order business.

To charge by phone, call (818) 765-8579. Or send payment to: Melvin Powers, 12015 Sherman Road, North Hollywood, California 91605-3781.

Read This Only If You Have Decided Not to Order

Frankly, I'm surprised you've decided not to take advantage of this outstanding offer. You have nothing to lose and everything to gain. (Get the idea? You know the rest.) I'm taking my own advice and using a lift letter . . . I mean paragraph. We'll see if it works!)

Tap the Powerful Positive Forces Within You

Being an entrepreneur is an exciting way of life. The world seems full of potential. Challenging goals are an adventure. There are no limits on what you can accomplish. I hope you choose to give yourself the gift of starting on the entrepreneurial path.

I wish you good luck and much success as you start your mail order business. "May the road rise to meet you and the wind be always at your back. . . ." I look forward to toasting you and welcoming you into the Mail Order Millionaires' Club!

THE AMERICAN SOCIETY OF
COMPOSERS, AUTHORS AND PUBLISHERS

PROUDLY PRESENTS THIS
AWARD OF MERIT

TO

MELVIN POWERS.

WRITER OF THE OUTSTANDING
COUNTRY SONG

"WHO WANTS A SLIGHTLY USED WOMAN"

SECRETARY
SOUTHERN REGIONAL DIRECTOR
PRESIDENT

NASHVILLE. TENNESSEE. OCTOBER 13. 1976

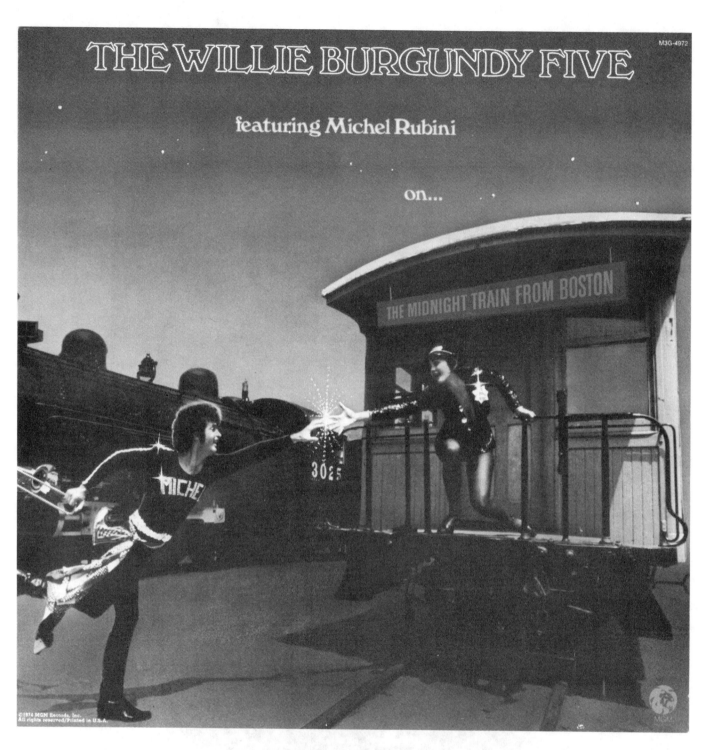

This is the front cover of the album, THE WILLIE BURGUNDY FIVE — ON THE MIDNIGHT TRAIN FROM BOSTON. From left to right . . . Michel running to catch The Midnight Train, and beautiful Linda Carter, better known as Wonder Woman, the female conductor, giving him a helping hand.

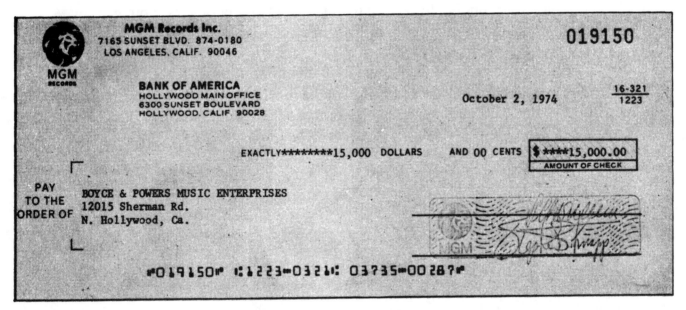

Here's a $15,000 check from MGM Records to Tommy Boyce & Melvin Powers Music Enterprises representing an advance against royalties for the album WILLIE BURGUNDY FIVE—ON THE MIDNIGHT TRAIN FROM BOSTON.

Melvin Powers
Wilshire Book Company

12015 Sherman Road
No. Hollywood, CA 91605-3781

Phone: (818) 765-8579
Fax: (818) 765-2922
E-mail: mpowers@mpowers.com
Web site: www.mpowers.com

Dear Friend:

I hope that *Making Money with Classified Ads* will enable you to start a successful mail order business in your spare time, as have many other readers of this book. Much success has been achieved on the Internet. I suggest that you become knowledgeable about this relatively new medium for making money in mail order.

Go to your public library and read as many books as you can on marketing on the Internet. Then put the information to work for you.

Because the success of my readers is important to me, I want this book to be as clear and useful as possible. If you have any comments or suggestions for improvement, I would appreciate receiving them.

Melvin Powers

A Business Guide to the Federal Trade Commission's Mail Order Rule

The Federal Trade Commission prepared this business guide to the FTC Mail Order Rule for your use as a mail order seller. It should answer questions you may have about the Rule's requirements and reduce customer problems in this area.

Contents

 Introduction

 How to Comply With the Rule

 Questions and Answers About the Rule

 Sample Notices

1 Introduction

What is the Mail Order Rule

The Mail Order Rule was issued by the Federal Trade Commission (FTC) to correct growing problems with late or undelivered mail order merchandise. Under this Rule, you have a duty to ship merchandise on time. You also must follow procedures that the Rule requires if you cannot ship ordered merchandise on time.

When there is a shipping delay, the Rule requires that you notify your customers of the delay and provide them with an option either to agree to the delay or to cancel the order and receive a prompt refund. For each additional delay, your customers must be notified that they must send you a signed consent to a further delay or a refund will be given.

Why Was the Rule Issued

The Rule was issued after federal, state, and local consumer protection authorities received thousands of consumer complaints about mail order problems. The major complaints were: failure to deliver merchandise, late delivery of merchandise, failure to make prompt refunds, and failure to answer customer inquiries about delayed or lost orders. For example:

- One consumer wrote about Christmas decorations she ordered in early October that were finally shipped the day before Christmas. This consumer wrote twice to the company about her order, the second time requesting a refund. Both inquiries were ignored.
- Another consumer complained about a company that failed to send a stereo component he ordered with payment in July. By late October, the only communication he received from the company was his canceled check.

Title 16 — Commercial Practices
CHAPTER I — FEDERAL TRADE COMMISSION
PART 435 — MAIL ORDER MERCHANDISE
Promulgation of Trade Regulation Rule

THE FEDERAL TRADE COMMISSION, pursuant to the Federal Trade Commission Act, as amended, 15 U.S.C. 41, et seq., and the provisions of Subpart B, Part I of the Commission's Procedures and Rules of Practice, 16 CFR 1.11, et seq., has conducted a proceeding for the promulgation of a Trade Regulation Rule concerning Undelivered Mail Order Merchandise and Services. Notice of this proceeding, including a proposed Rule, was published in the FEDERAL REGISTER on September 28, 1971 (36 FR 19092 (1971)). Interested parties were thereafter afforded opportunity to participate in the proceeding through the submission of written data, views and arguments, and to appear and express their views orally and to suggest amendments, revisions, and additions to the proposed Rule.

The FTC received 3,200 similar consumer complaints prior to beginning its rulemaking process. In addition, the President's Office of Consumer Affairs (OCA) received over 1,000 complaints concerning mail order practices, 60% of which concerned non-delivery. OCA complaint statistics for mail order were second only to complaints about autos and auto services.

The rulemaking record contains more than 10,000 pages of complaints regarding mail order sales. State and local agencies urged the Commission to take action to correct these problems. Industry members provided valuable input as to the feasibility and practicality of a mail order rule.

On October 22, 1975, the FTC promulgated the Mail Order Rule, and it went into effect on February 2, 1976.

 ## Why You Should Comply with the Rule

When you comply with the Rule, you are being responsive to your customers. This is beneficial to you and to your customers because it promotes a positive industry image. Compliance creates consumer trust in buying by mail and fosters repeat mail order business. Of course if you ship on time, the requirements of the Rule pertaining to "option notices" do not apply.

Although most members of the mail order industry adhere to the Rule's requirements, there are some who do not. The FTC's Bureau of Consumer Protection monitors consumer complaints to ensure that businesses comply with the Rule. The FTC also provides compliance information, such as this manual, and assistance to all industry members.

AFTER IT HAD CONSIDERED THE SUGGESTIONS, CRITICISMS, objections, and other pertinent information in the Record, the Commission on March 8, 1974, published a revised proposed rule in a notice in the FEDERAL REGISTER (39 FR 9201 (1974)) extending an opportunity to interested parties to submit data, views or arguments regarding the revised proposed Rule. A period of over 90 days was allowed for the submission of written comments on the revised proposal. Written comments of the Direct Mail/Marketing Association (DM/MA) were admitted into the Record at a subsequent date and the public was given 30 days to submit written views and comments related to the DM/MA submission (39 FR 40515 (1974)).

The Commission has now considered all matters of fact, law, policy and discretion, including the data, views and arguments presented on the Record by interested parties in response to the Notices, as prescribed by law, and has determined that the adoption of the Trade Regulation Rule set forth herein and its Statement of Basis and Purpose[1] is in the public interest.

Accordingly, the Commission hereby amends Subchapter D, Trade Regulation Rules, Chapter I of 16 CFR by adding a new Part 435 as follows:

Sec.
435.1   The Rule.
435.2   Definitions.

AUTHORITY: The provisions of this Part 435 issued under 38 Stat. 717, as amended, 15 U.S.C. 41, et seq.

---

[1]Statement of Basis and Purpose filed as part of the original document.

2 How to Comply with the Rule

This section of the manual provides **THE TEXT OF THE RULE, WITH EXPLANATIONS OPPOSITE** of how to comply with the Rule.

§ 435.1 The Rule.

IN CONNECTION WITH MAIL ORDER SALES in commerce, as "commerce" is defined in the Federal Trade Commission Act, it constitutes an unfair method of competition, and an unfair or deceptive act and practice for a seller:

(a)(1) To solicit any order for the sale of merchandise to be ordered by the buyer through the mails unless, at the time of the solicitation, the seller has a reasonable basis to expect that he will be able to ship any ordered merchandise to the buyer: (i) within that time clearly and conspicuously stated in any such solicitation, or (ii) if no time is clearly and conspicuously stated, within thirty (30) days after receipt of a properly completed order from the buyer.

(2) To provide any buyer with any revised shipping date, as provided in paragraph (b), unless, at the time any such revised shipping date is provided, the seller has a reasonable basis for making such representation regarding a definite revised shipping date.

(3) To inform any buyer that he is unable to make any representation regarding the length of any delay unless (i) the seller has a reasonable basis for so informing the buyer and (ii) the seller informs the buyer of the reason or reasons for the delay.

(b)(1) Where a seller is unable to ship merchandise within the applicable time set forth in paragraph (a)(1), above, to fail to offer to the buyer, clearly and conspicuously and without prior demand, an option either to consent to a delay in shipping or to cancel his order and receive a prompt refund. Said offer shall be made within a reasonable time after the seller first becomes aware of his inability to ship within the applicable time set forth in paragraph (a)(1), but in no event later than said applicable time.

What to Know When You Make an Offer

When you offer to sell merchandise by mail, the Rule requires you to have a "reasonable basis" for expecting to ship within the time stated in your solicitation.

For example, if you know before advertising your products that your suppliers are on strike and are likely to remain on strike for several months, you do not have a "reasonable basis" for expecting to ship within a month.

The shipping date, when provided in your offer, must be clearly and conspicuously stated:

ADVERTISEMENT
Cardigan Sweaters
S, M, L—Beige or Blue
$29.95 plus tax
Allow 5 weeks for shipment.

If you do not provide a shipping date, you must ship the merchandise within 30 days of receiving a "properly completed" order. An order is properly completed when you receive payment accompanied by all information you need to fill the order. Payment may be made by cash, money order, check, or credit card, according to your company policy. If a credit card is used for a purchase, the order is properly completed when you charge your customer's account.

When you cannot ship on time, you must provide your customer with an "option" notice. The notice must provide an option to cancel the order and receive a prompt refund, or to agree to a delay in shipping. And, as with the original date, you must have a reasonable basis for setting that shipping date.

You must also have a reasonable basis for telling your customers that you do not know when you can ship merchandise. In that case, you must provide the specific reasons for the shipping problem. For example, you could state that a fire destroyed the warehouse holding the goods and you are unable to provide a revised shipping date because you

221

do not know how long it will take to replace the merchandise.

When You Should Send a First Notice

If a shipment is delayed, the Rule requires that you give your customers an option:
- to consent to a delay; or
- to cancel the order and receive a prompt refund.

People in the trade often refer to the notice as a "delay" notice. More accurately, it should be called an "option" notice. You violate the Rule if you only provide a notice of delay without also providing an option to cancel the order.

Remember, you must send the notice after you first become aware that there will be a shipping delay. The notice must be sent:
- before the promised shipping date; or
- within 30 days after you receive the order (if no date was provided in your solicitation).

What a First Notice Must Say

If you provide a revised shipping date of 30 days or less, you must have a reasonable basis for making the change. The notice must inform your customers that non-response is considered consent to be a delay of 30 days or less.

If you are unable to provide a revised shipping date, your notice must state that you cannot determine when the merchandise will be shipped. It must also state that the order will be automatically canceled unless:
- you ship the merchandise within 30 days of the original shipping date and you have not received your customer's cancellation before shipment; or

(b)(i) **ANY OFFER TO THE BUYER** of such an option shall fully inform the buyer regarding his right to cancel the order and to obtain a prompt refund and shall provide a definite revised shipping date, but where the seller lacks a reasonable basis for providing a definite revised shipping date the notice shall inform the buyer that the seller is unable to make any representation regarding the length of the delay.

(ii) **WHERE THE SELLER HAS PROVIDED** a definite revised shipping date which is thirty (30) days or less later than the applicable time set forth in paragraph (a)(1), the offer of said option shall expressly inform the buyer that, unless the seller receives, prior to shipment and prior to the expiration of the definite revised shipping date, a response from the buyer rejecting the delay and canceling the order, the buyer will be deemed to have consented to a delayed shipment on or before the definite revised shipping date.

(iii) Where the seller has provided a definite revised shipping date which is more than thirty (30) days later than the applicable time set forth in paragraph (a)(1) or where the seller is unable to provide a definite revised shipping date and therefore informs the buyer that he is unable to make any representation regarding the length of the delay, the offer of said option shall also expressly inform the buyer that his order will automatically be deemed to have been canceled unless (A) the seller has shipped the merchandise within thirty (30) days of the applicable time set forth in paragraph (a)(1), and has received no cancellation prior to shipment, or (B) the seller has received from the buyer within thirty (30) days of said applicable time, a response specifically consenting to said shipping delay. Where the seller informs the buyer that he is unable to make any representation regarding the length of the delay, the buyer shall be expressly informed that, should he consent to an indefinite delay, he will have a continuing right to cancel his order at any time after the applicable time set forth in paragraph (a)(1) by so notifying the seller prior to actual shipment.

(iv) Nothing in this paragraph shall prohibit a seller who furnishes a definite revised shipping date pursuant to paragraph (b)(1)(i), from requesting, simultaneously with or at any time subsequent to the offer of an option pursuant to paragraph (b)(1), the buyer's express consent to a further unanticipated delay beyond the definite revised shipping date in the form of a response from the buyer specifically consenting to said further delay. *Provided, however,* that where the seller solicits consent to an unanticipated indefinite delay the solicitation shall expressly inform the buyer that, should he so consent to an indefinite delay, he shall have a continuing right to cancel his order at any time after the definite revised shipping date by so notifying the seller prior to actual shipment.

(b)(2) Where a seller is unable to ship merchandise on or before the definite revised shipping date provided under paragraph (b)(1)(i) and consented to by the buyer pursuant to paragraph (b)(1)(ii) or (iii), to fail to offer to the buyer, clearly and conspicuously and without prior demand, a renewed option either to consent to a further delay or to cancel the order and to receive a prompt refund. Said offer shall be made within a reasonable time after the seller first becomes aware of his inability to ship before the said definite revised date, but in no event later than the expiration of the definite revised shipping date. Provided, however, that where the seller previously has obtained the buyer's express consent to an unanticipated delay until a specific date beyond the definite revised shipping date, pursuant to paragraph (b)(1)(iv) or to a further delay until a specific date beyond the definite revised shipping date pursuant to this paragraph (b)(2), that date to which the buyer has expressly consented shall supersede the definite revised shipping date for purposes of this paragraph (b)(2).

(i) **ANY OFFER TO THE BUYER** of said renewed option shall provide the buyer with a new definite revised shipping date, but where the seller lacks a reasonable basis for providing a new definite revised shipping date, the notice shall inform the buyer that the seller is unable to make any representation regarding the length of the further delay.

(ii) The offer of a renewed option shall expressly inform the buyer that, unless the seller receives, prior to the expiration of the old definite revised shipping date or any date superseding the old definite revised shipping date, notification from the buyer specifically consenting to the further delay, the buyer will be deemed to have rejected any further delay, and to have canceled the order if the seller is in fact unable to ship prior to the expiration of the old definite revised shipping date or any date superseding the old definite revised shipping date.

- you receive within 30 days of the original date your customer's consent to the delay.

Your notice must provide this information if the definite revised shipping date is more than 30 days after the original date.

When you are unable to provide a revised shipping date, you must inform your customers of their continuing right to cancel the order by notifying you prior to actual shipment.

What Later Notices Must Say

If you are unable to ship the merchandise on or before your revised shipping date, you must notify your customers again. This is called a "renewed option" notice. This notice must inform your customers of their right to consent to a further delay, or to cancel the order and receive a prompt refund.

The renewed option notice must inform customers that if they do not agree in writing to this delay, their order will be canceled. Unless you receive your customer's express written consent to the second delay before the first delay period ends, you must cancel the order and provide a full refund.

Keep in mind that you do not have to offer a "renewed option" to customers who consent to an indefinite delay in response to the first option notice. But any customer who agrees to an indefinite delay has the continuing right to cancel the order at any time before the merchandise is shipped.

How You Should Send Notices

You should send any option notice by first class mail, and your notice should provide a written means for your customers to respond. A prepaid business mail reply or prepaid postage card meets this requirement.

The notice is most advantageous for you if at some point you have to prove that you complied with the Rule. If the FTC takes action against a company, the firm must be able to show that any other form of notice it used was equal to or better than the written form described in the Rule. For example, an "800" telephone number for customers' use in canceling orders is an adequate substitute, if you can prove that the system met the Rule's requirements. This would include being able to show that the 800 number could readily and consistently be used to cancel an order because you provided adequate and competent staff to take cancellations. You should keep records of all cancellations.

When You *May* Cancel an Order

In some cases you can have an option to cancel an order or to send out another notice. You may make this decision when you are unable to ship merchandise on time or within the delay period to which your customer agreed. But if you decide to cancel the order,

Provided, however, that where the seller offers the buyer the option to consent to an indefinite delay the offer shall expressly inform the buyer that, should he so consent to an indefinite delay, he shall have a continuing right to cancel his order at any time after the old definite revised shipping date or any date superseding the old definite revised shipping date.

(iii) This paragraph (b)(2) shall not apply to any situation where a seller, pursuant to the provisions of paragraph (b)(1)(iv), has previously obtained consent from the buyer to an indefinite extension beyond the first revised shipping date.

[i]t constitutes an unfair method of competition, and an unfair or deceptive act and practice for a seller:...

(b)(3) WHEREVER A BUYER HAS THE RIGHT to exercise any option under this part or to cancel an order by so notifying the seller prior to shipment, to fail to furnish the buyer with adequate means, at the seller's expense, to exercise such option or to notify the seller regarding cancellation. In any action brought by the Federal Trade Commission alleging a violation of this part, the failure of a respondent-seller:

(i) To provide any offer, notice or option required by this part in writing and by first class mail will create a rebuttable presumption that the respondent-seller failed to offer a clear and conspicuous offer, notice or option;

(ii) To provide the buyer with the means in writing (by business reply mail or with postage prepaid by the seller) to exercise any option or to notify the seller regarding a decision to cancel, will create a rebuttable presumption that the respondent-seller did not provide the buyer with adequate means pursuant to this subparagraph (3).

NOTHING IN PARAGRAPH (B) of this part shall prevent a seller, where he is unable to make shipment within the time set forth in paragraph (a)(1) or within a delay period consented to by the buyer, from deciding to consider the order canceled and providing the buyer with notice of said decision within a reasonable time after he becomes aware of said inability to ship, together with a prompt refund.

[i]t constitutes an unfair method of competition, and an unfair or deceptive act and practice for a seller:...

(c) To FAIL TO DEEM AN ORDER CANCELED and to make a prompt refund to the buyer whenever:

(1) The seller receives, prior to the time of shipment, notification from the buyer canceling the order pursuant to any option, renewed option or continuing option under this part;

(2) The seller has, pursuant to paragraph (b)(1)(iii), provided the buyer with a definite revised shipping date which is more than thirty (30) days later than the applicable time set forth in paragraph (a)(1) or has notified the buyer that he is unable to make any representation regarding the length of the delay and the seller (i) has not shipped the merchandise within thirty (30) days of the applicable time set forth in paragraph (a)(1), and (ii) has not received the buyer's express consent to said shipping delay within said thirty (30) days;

(3) The seller is unable to ship within the applicable time set forth in paragraph (b)(2), and has not received, within the said applicable time, the buyer's consent to any further delay;

(4) The seller has notified the buyer of his inability to make shipment and has indicated his decision not to ship the merchandise;

(5) The seller fails to offer the option prescribed in paragraph (b)(1) and has not shipped the merchandise within the applicable time set forth in paragraph (a)(1).

you must inform your customer of this decision and provide a prompt refund.

Whether you cancel or send another notice, you must inform your customer about it within a reasonable time after you know you cannot ship the merchandise.

When You *Must* Cancel an Order

You must cancel an order and provide a prompt refund:

- when your customer does not agree to a delay and exercises the option to cancel an order before it has been shipped;
- when you notify your customer of your inability to ship the merchandise and of your decision to cancel the order;
- when you are unable to ship merchandise before the revised shipping date and you have not received your customer's consent to a further delay;
- when the delay is indefinite and you have not shipped the merchandise or received your customer's consent to an indefinite delay;
- when the definite revised shipping date in the first option notice is more than 30 days after the original shipping date, and you have not shipped the merchandise, nor received your customer's consent to the delay within 30 days of the original shipping date; or
- when you cannot ship on time and do not notify your customers of their options.

All refunds must be sent to the buyer by first class mail. If the buyer paid by cash, check, or money order, you must refund payment within seven (7) days after the order is canceled. For credit card sales, you must make refunds within one billing cycle after the order is canceled. Under no circumstances are you to substitute credit vouchers or script for a refund.

Why You Should Keep Records

If for some reason your company has problems in shipping on time, your customers may begin to file complaints with you, and with local, state, or federal law enforcement agencies. Because the Federal Trade Commission has enforcement jurisdiction under the Mail Order Rule, many complaints are forwarded to the FTC from other agencies.

When the FTC takes action against a company and alleges that it violated the Rule, the company must have records or other documentary proof that will show the steps it took to comply. Systems and procedures for complying with the Rule are carefully reviewed. Lack of such proof creates a rebuttable presumption that the company failed to comply. This means that the seller must be able to show that it used reasonable systems and procedures to comply with the Rule. Consequently, it is in your best interest to establish an accurate, up-to-date record-keeping system.

(a)(4) IN ANY ACTION BROUGHT BY THE FEDERAL TRADE COMMISSION, alleging a violation of this part, the failure of a respondent-seller to have records or other documentary proof establishing his use of systems and procedures which assure the shipment of merchandise in the ordinary course of business within any applicable time set forth in this part will create a rebuttable presumption that the seller lacked a reasonable basis for any expectation of shipment within said applicable time.

(d) In any action brought by the Federal Trade Commission, alleging a violation of this part, the failure of a respondent-seller to have records or other documentary proof establishing his use of systems and procedures which assure compliance, in the ordinary course of business, with any requirement of paragraphs (b) or (c) of this part will create a rebuttable presumption that the seller failed to comply with said requirements.

What the Rule Does Not Cover

The following mail order sales are exempt from the Rule:
- magazine subscriptions (and similar serial deliveries), except for the first shipment;
- sales of seeds and growing plants;
- orders made on a collect-on-delivery basis (C.O.D.);
- transactions covered by the FTC's Negative Option Rule (such as book and record clubs);
- mail order photo-finishing; or
- orders made by telephone and charged to a credit card account.

NOTE 1: This part shall not apply to subscriptions, such as magazine sales, ordered for serial delivery, after the initial shipment is made in compliance with this part.

NOTE 2: This part shall not apply to orders of seeds and growing plants.

NOTE 3: This part shall not apply to orders made on a collect-on-delivery (C.O.D.) basis.

NOTE 4: This part shall not apply to transactions governed by the Federal Trade Commission's Trade Regulation Rule entitled "Use of Negative Option Plans by Sellers in Commerce," 16 CFR 425.

Where to Go for Help

For more information, contact:
- the Federal Trade Commission, Enforcement Division, B.C.P., Washington, D.C. 20580,
- the Direct Marketing Association, 1730 K Street, N.W., Washington, D.C. 20006;
- your local United States Postal Service; and
- your local consumer protection office.

State and local governments also may have requirements with which you must comply. You should consult each agency for information about laws that affect your operations.

NOTE 5: By taking action in this area, the Federal Trade Commission does not intend to preempt action in the same area, which is not inconsistent with this part, by any State, municipal, or other local government. This part does not annul or diminish any rights or remedies provided to consumers by any State law, municipal ordinance, or other local regulation, insofar as those rights or remedies are equal to or greater than those provided by this part. In addition, this part does not supersede those provisions of any State law, municipal ordinance, or other local regulation which impose obligations or liabilities upon sellers, when sellers subject to this part are not in compliance therewith. This part does supersede those provisions of any State law, municipal ordinance, or other local regulation which are inconsistent with this part to the extent that those provisions do not provide a buyer with rights which are equal to or greater than those rights granted a buyer by this part. This part also supersedes those provisions of any State law, municipal ordinance, or other local regulation requiring that a buyer be notified of a right which is the same as a right provided by this part but requiring that a buyer be given notice of this right in a language, form, or manner which is different in any way from that required by this part.

In those instances where any State law, municipal ordinance, or other local regulation contains provisions, some but not all of which are partially or completely superseded by this part, the provisions or portions of those provisions which have not been superseded retain their full force and effect.

NOTE 6: If any provision of this part or its application to any person, partnership, corporation, act or practice is held invalid, the remainder of this part or the application of the provision to any other person, partnership, corporation, act or practice shall not be affected thereby.

NOTE 7: Section 435.1(a)(1) of this part governs all solicitations where the time of solicitation is more than 100 days after promulgation of this part. The remainder of this part governs all transactions where receipt of a properly completed order occurs more than 100 days after promulgation of this part.

Definitions

§ 435.2 Definitions.

For purposes of this part:

(a) "Shipment" shall mean the act by which the merchandise is physically placed in the possession of the carrier.

(b) "Receipt of a properly completed order" shall mean:

(1) Where there is a credit sale and the buyer has not previously tendered partial payment, the time at which the seller charges the buyer's account;

(2) Where the buyer tenders full or partial payment in the proper amount in the form of cash, check or money order, the time at which the seller has received both said payment and an order from the buyer containing all the information needed by the seller to process and ship the order.

Provided, however, that where the seller receives notice that the check or money order tendered by the buyer has been dishonored or that the buyer does not qualify for a credit sale, "receipt of a properly completed order" shall mean the time at which (i) the seller receives notice that a check or money order for the proper amount tendered by the buyer has been honored, (ii) the buyer tenders cash in the proper amount or (iii) the seller receives notice that the buyer qualifies for a credit sale.

(c) "Refund" shall mean:

(1) Where the buyer tendered full payment for the unshipped merchandise in the form of cash, check, or money order, a return of the amount tendered in the form of cash, check, or money order;

(2) Where there is a credit sale:

(i) And the seller is a creditor, a copy of a credit memorandum or the like or an account statement reflecting the removal or absence of any remaining charge incurred as a result of the sale from the buyer's account;

(ii) And a third party is the creditor, a copy of an appropriate credit memorandum or the like to the third party creditor which will remove the charge from the buyer's account or a statement from the seller acknowledging the cancellation of the order and representing that he has not taken any action regarding the order which will result in a charge to the buyer's account with the third party;

(iii) And the buyer tendered partial payment for the unshipped merchandise in the form of cash, check, or money order, a return of the amount tendered in the form of cash, check, or money order.

(d) "Prompt refund" shall mean:

(1) Where a refund is made pursuant to Definition (c) (1) or (2) (iii), a refund sent to the buyer by first class mail within seven (7) working days of the date on which the buyer's right to refund vests under the provisions of this part;

(2) Where a refund is made pursuant to Definition (c) (2) (i) or (ii), a refund sent to the buyer by first class mail within one (1) billing cycle from the date on which the buyer's right to refund vests under the provisions of this part.

(e) The "time of solicitation" of an order shall mean that time when the seller has:

(1) Mailed or otherwise disseminated the solicitation to a prospective purchaser;

(2) Made arrangements for an advertisement containing the solicitation to appear in a newspaper, magazine, or the like, or on radio or television, which cannot be changed or canceled without incurring substantial expense; or

(3) Made arrangements for the printing of a catalog, brochure or the like which cannot be changed without incurring substantial expense, in which the solicitation in question forms an insubstantial part.

Effective: February 2, 1976.

Promulgated October 22, 1975, by the Federal Trade Commission.

CHARLES A. TOBIN,
Secretary.

[FH Doc. 75-28203 Filed 70-21-75; 3:45 am]

3 Questions and Answers About the Rule

The FTC receives questions from mail order sellers who want to know how to comply with the Rule. The following questions are those that are asked most frequently.

What to Do When You Start a Mail Order Business

Q: *What advice do you give someone who is planning to start a mail order business?*

A: The FTC suggests that you do the following:
- Learn the requirements of the Mail Order Rule.
- Familiarize yourself with state laws in areas where you plan to do business. For example, some states, such as Wisconsin, have additional mail order requirements that should be followed.
- Ask experienced mail order sellers for practical hints to help you avoid the pitfalls in mail order business.

Q: *How important is it to set up a customer service procedure?*

A: An efficient customer service procedure is beneficial to you and your customers. Customers often complain that they have been treated badly by the companies they have contacted. But the number of complaints should drop significantly if your customer service personnel communicate responsively with your customers when they have problems.

Q: *Our company has read the Mail Order Rule, but we still have questions about what we can and cannot do. Who should we contact?*

A: It depends on whether you need a formal or an informal response.
- You should feel free to write the FTC Enforcement Division to ask questions about the Rule and how your operations are affected. Staff advice is not binding on the Commission, but this advice can be helpful.
- You may obtain a binding advisory opinion from the Commission if you send a specific, written inquiry about the legality of certain conduct. Advisory opinions apply only to proposed conduct, not to conduct that is in practice. The opinions are usually restricted to questions that are not clearly answered by the terms of the Rule. Ask the FTC staff about the procedure for obtaining an advisory opinion.

When You Must Ship an Order

Q: We advertise a shipment date of six weeks. What happens if there is a workers' strike or some other unanticipated event and shipment is delayed? Have we violated the Rule?

A: If you calculated the shipping date correctly in the first place, you have complied with the Rule. But if you discover that a delay cannot be avoided, you must notify your customers and provide the option notice. If you fail to do this, you have unilaterally changed the sales contract and have violated the Rule.

Q: We advertise several products but do not indicate a shipping date in our ads. When must we ship?

A: If your solicitation does not state when you plan to ship the merchandise, the Rule requires that you ship it within 30 days after you receive a properly completed order (that is, when you have received payment and sufficient information to fill the order).

Q: How can we protect our company accounts from customers who bounce checks or do not qualify for credit?

A: Be prompt in depositing checks and checking your customers' credit-worthiness. Remember, the order is properly completed, triggering the 30-day period, when you receive payment and all information needed to process the order. For example, if the buyer does not send enough cash to cover the cost of an order, the order is not properly completed. You may wait for the check to clear before mailing, as long as you ship within the 30-day period.

Q: What about a credit sale?

A: When you receive a properly completed order with a charge account number, the clock starts when you charge your customer's account.

Q: If a customer orders an item which is not in stock when the order is received, can we substitute an item of similar or better quality without the customer's consent?

A: No. The FTC has established that you must obtain your customer's authorization to substitute merchandise different from that ordered.

What Items Are Covered

Q: Are mail order sales between businesses covered by the Rule?

A: Yes. Mail order transactions between businesses are covered. This would include specialty items, such as calendars, pens, and ashtrays which bear advertising messages and are not sold to the general public.

Q: Does the Rule cover orders placed by telephone?

A: The Rule covers those situations in which you solicit orders by telephone and require your customers to mail the order accompanied by payment. If the mail is used to finalize the sale, the Rule applies. If mail is not used, the Rule does not apply.

Q: Does the Rule cover orders placed over the telephone involving credit card payment?

A: No. The Rule does not cover charges to a credit card account when the order is placed over the telephone.

What Rule Applies to Unordered Merchandise

Q: Is it legal to send unordered merchandise through the U. S. Mail?

A: No. The unordered merchandise statute provides that only two kinds of merchandise can be sent legally through the U.S. Mail without a consumer's prior consent:
- free samples that are clearly and conspicuously marked as such; and
- merchandise mailed by a charitable organization asking for contributions.

Consumers may consider unordered merchandise sent through the U.S. Mail as a free gift. They are not obligated to return it or to pay for it. Also, it is illegal for a company to send any bill or dunning communication seeking payment or return of unordered merchandise.

Q: Does the Rule require us to keep records?

Why Record-Keeping is Important

A: No. The Mail Order Rule does not impose record-keeping requirements on mail order sellers. But if you are ever involved in an action with the FTC, you must have records that prove you complied with the Rule. Therefore, it is advisable to establish a record-keeping method that best suits your situation and demonstrates compliance with the Rule.

Q: How long do we have to keep customer complaint letters?

A: The Rule does not specifically indicate whether or how long you must keep complaint letters. Complaint letters, when adequately answered, may be used as proof that you complied with the Rule if you are ever questioned. It is probably advisable to keep such correspondence and other records for a period of three to five years.

When the FTC Takes Action

Q: What actually happens when the FTC receives a complaint against a company?

A: The staff checks to see whether the company has been advised of the Rule's requirements. If not, then a copy of the Rule with an explanation letter is usually sent to the firm. The FTC evaluates consumer complaints to see whether a pattern of violations is developing. The FTC then contacts the company to determine whether further action is necessary.

Q: Under what circumstances will the Commission sue a mail order firm for violating the Rule?

A: If a company is violating the Rule, it runs the risk of being sued. The Commission evaluates many criteria to determine whether an action is in the public interest.

Q: What are the penalties for violating the Rule?

A: The FTC Act provides that a person, partnership, or corporation may be liable for civil penalties of up to $10,000 per

Q: *What can industry members expect from the FTC in the future?*

violation. In addition, the FTC can sue for consumer redress.

A: Because the industry is steadily growing, an increased enforcement presence can be expected. This may mean actions for civil penalties against firms who fail to comply with the Rule. At the same time, the FTC is part of a government-wide effort to encourage industry members to effectively regulate themselves. The FTC is working to assist businesses as they undertake voluntary compliance with the Rule. This manual is part of that effort.

4 Sample Notices

Sample Option Notice

[Rule Section 435.1(b)(1)(ii)]

When you are unable to ship on time and wish to provide a **revised shipping date which is 30 days or less** after the original date, use a form such as this to notify your customers. This form must be sent out by first class mail within a reasonable time after you become aware that there will be a shipping delay. It must be sent before the promised date, or if no date was promised, within 30 days after you receive a properly completed order.

Dear Customer:

Thank you for your order. We are sorry to inform you that there will be a delay in shipping the merchandise you ordered. We shall make shipment by the revised shipping date of (   ). It is quite possible we could ship earlier.

You have the right to consent to this delay or to cancel your order and receive a prompt refund. Please return this letter in the enclosed postpaid envelope with your instructions indicated by checking the appropriate block below.

Unless we hear from you prior to shipment or prior to *the revised shipping date*, it will be assumed that you have consented to a delayed shipment on or before the definite revised shipping date stated above.

Sincerely yours,

Name & Title of Signer
Company Name
Address

Enclosure: Envelope

☐ Yes, I will accept a further delay in shipment of my order for this item until _____
(Insert date which is 30 days or less.)

☐ I cannot wait. Please cancel my order for this item and promptly refund my money.

_____
Please Sign Here

Sample Renewed Option Notice

[Rule Section 435.1(b)(2)(i)-(ii)]

When you are unable to ship merchandise on or before the promised definite revised shipping date, and wish to provide **a new definite revised shipping date,** use a form such as this to notify your customers.

Dear Customer:

We are sorry to inform you that there will be a further delay in shipping the merchandise you ordered. We shall make shipment by *(new definite revised shipping date)*. It is quite possible we could ship earlier.

You have the right to consent to a further delay or to cancel your order and receive a prompt refund. Please return this letter in the enclosed postpaid envelope with your instructions indicated by checking the appropriate block below.

Unless we hear from you prior to the old shipping date to which you previously agreed, it will be assumed that you have rejected any further shipping delay and your order will be canceled and a prompt refund made.

Sincerely yours,

Name & Title of Signer
Company Name
Address

Enclosure: Envelope

☐ Yes, I will accept a delay in shipment of my order for this item until

_____
(Insert date which is 30 days or less.)

☐ I cannot wait. Please cancel my order for this item and promptly refund my money.

_____
Please Sign Here

A Fun Assignment

This is an exercise in creativity. I hope you find the challenge exciting. Your assignment is to come up with a campaign to sell the University of Hard Knocks ring that appears on page 237.

Who do you think would buy this ring? Why would they spend $429 or $599 for a gold ring, or even $149 for one in sterling? Would women buy the ring if one were offered with a more delicate design? Would they buy it if it were offered as a pendant? Do you think this ad can make money? What products would be appropriate for the back end?

Where would you place full-page magazine ads? Would you run in newspapers? If so, which ones and in what section? Could the ring be sold off a classified ad? A small display ad? What about direct mail? What mailing lists would you try? What do you think are the chances of selling it with two-minute television spots? Could it be sold on radio? On what type of stations would you run it? Do you think the product lends itself well to free publicity? To which publications would you send publicity releases?

What about having an annual "alumni" meeting in Las Vegas for all those who purchased rings? Do you think it would go over? What characteristics would these people have in common and what topics do you think would be discussed? Do you think the alumni meeting would generate media interest? What other ways can you think of to promote this product? What about having "the university" award scholarships to bona fide schools.

If you would like to share your ideas for a campaign, I would be pleased to hear them.

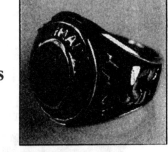
237

Sales and Marketing

Self-Publishing Success Story:
Melvin Powers

by **Marty Foley**

Here I interview long-time direct marketing (mail order) and self-publishing expert, Melvin Powers.

[Marty]: Melvin, can you give us a little background on your business record for readers that aren't already familiar with you?

[Melvin]: I've been publishing books for 50 years and selling half of them by mail order, on the Internet and through book stores. My multi-million bestsellers include: THINK AND GROW RICH by Napoleon Hill, PSYCHO-CYBERNETICS by Maxwell Maltz, M.D., and THE MAGIC OF

THINKING BIG by David Schwartz, Ph.D.

[Marty]: I've read a couple of those books myself, Melvin. What would you say are some keys to making money with info-products?

[Melvin]: Pick subjects that have wide appeal. My latest book, MAKING MONEY WITH CLASSIFIED ADS, written by yours truly, is doing extremely well by direct mail, the Internet and in book stores. It's currently my number one book in sales.

[Marty]: Which avenues are paying

off the best for you?

[Melvin]: Running two-step classified ads and one-inch ads are still the workhorses. We then send out our literature if they haven't gone to our web site. I'm still sending out thousands of pieces of direct mail and always trying various mailing lists.

Over the years, I've sent out millions of pieces of mail. Some lists make money - and others don't. The point is, you need to keep going. All of my classified and display ads run on a till-forbid basis. We check the amount of

Over the years, I've sent out millions of pieces of mail. Some lists make money - and others don't. The point is, you need to keep going.

238

inquiries and results from each ad. Be sure to key every ad.

I produced an infomercial for my Mail Order Millionaire Course that sold thousands. I was on the air for several years. When my infomercial slowed down, someone else went on the air with a similar product and did well.

I also made an infomercial for Slick 50, an engine treatment, and sold thousands of bottles. Fifty percent of the people bought two bottles. I hadn't expected that; it was a pleasant surprise. Again after a year, the pulling power slowed down and I went off the air. Someone else started selling a similar product. So it goes.

Maintain the attitude that if others have done it, so can you. Think like a winner and you'll be one! Don't expect success overnight. Keep reading books and trade publications to find out what's going on in the mail order business. Attend trade shows to find new products and learn what's going on in your particular field. Subscribe to the free Internet newsletters, which contain a wealth of information.

[Marty]: Well thanks, Melvin. I consider that a compliment, since you've been subscribed to ProfitInfo Newsletter for several issues now.

What mistakes have you made in business that others could learn from?

[Melvin]: I haven't made too many. I never go for the hype. I take one step at a time.

[Marty]: What major mistakes do you see other entrepreneurs make?

[Melvin]: Expecting success overnight. I published 50 books before I hit it big with PSYCHO-CYBERNETICS. I've sold over 5,000,000. The same is true with THINK AND GROW RICH, of which I've sold over 7,000,000 copies.

[Marty]: A side point I'd like to make for ProfitInfo's readers is that more than a few of the most successful Internet marketers "got their feet wet" in the mail order field. Successful direct marketing (mail order) principles are usually quite applicable toward online marketing, as well.

Melvin, now that you're doing business online, would you agree with that statement?

[Melvin]: They are the same principles. What is working extremely well for me is including my Internet address in all of my ads, stationery, and literature that I send out. Potential customers see my Internet address and buy my mail order course and books right from the web site.

This saves postage, literature, labor, and you catch the individual when his/her interest is high. These orders can amount to over $100.00. We are getting orders from around the world. The follow-up works the same. Answer your e-mail promptly. You'll often get the sale.

[Marty]: Thanks for allowing me to interview you, Melvin.

[Melvin]: It's been my pleasure.

Melvin Powers - Book Publisher - Author of How to Get Rich in Mail Order, Making Money with Classified Ads, and others. Visit his web site to see why Melvin has been called "The Man with the Midas Touch." http://www.mpowers.com. E-mail: mailto:mpowers@mpowers.com. Tel:(818) 765-8579 Fax:(818) 765-2922. To jump start your Internet sales, see Marty Foley's brand new handbook, "Internet Marketing Goldmine," which also includes interviews with nine other successful Internet marketers: http://profitinfo.com/resources/1064. **OW**

How to Self-Publish Your Book & Have the Fun & Excitement of Being a Best-Selling Author

An expert's step-by-step guide to marketing your book successfully

Table of Contents

240 Pages . . . $22.00 postpaid